Becoming a Critically Reflective Teacher

Second Edition

Stephen D. Brookfield

JB JOSSEY-BASS™
A Wiley Brand

Published by Jossey-Bass
A Wiley Brand
One Montgomery Street, Suite 1000, San Francisco, CA 94104-4594—www.josseybass.com

Jossey-Bass books and products are available through most bookstores. To contact Jossey-Bass directly
call our Customer Care Department within the U.S. at 800-956-7739, outside the U.S. at 317-572-
3986, or fax 317-572-4002.

Wiley publishes in a variety of print and electronic formats and by print-on-demand. Some material
included with standard print versions of this book may not be included in e-books or in print-on-
demand. If this book refers to media such as a CD or DVD that is not included in the version you
purchased, you may download this material at http://booksupport.wiley.com. For more information
about Wiley products, visit www.wiley.com.

Library of Congress Cataloging-in-Publication Data

Names: Brookfield, Stephen, author.
Title: Becoming a critically reflective teacher / Stephen D. Brookfield.
Description: Second edition. | San Francisco, CA : Jossey-Bass, [2017] |
   Includes bibliographical references and index.
Identifiers: LCCN 2016043328 | ISBN 9781119049708 (cloth) | ISBN 9781119050650 (ePDF) |
ISBN 9781119050711 (epub)
Subjects: LCSH: College teaching. | Critical thinking.
Classification: LCC LB2331 .B677 2017 | DDC 378.1/25—dc23 LC record available at
https://lccn.loc.gov/2016043328

Cover design: Wiley
Cover image: © Jeff Foott/ Minden Pictures/Getty Images, Inc.

Printed in the United States of America

SECOND EDITION
HB Printing 10 9 8 7 6 5 4 3 2 1

Contents

Preface

The first edition of this book was written in the last part of the last century. It was initially published in 1995 before the explosion of the Internet and before social media changed how people communicate at the most basic level. But although the first edition could be considered technologically antediluvian, its basic project of exploring how we might build the critically reflective habit into our teaching seems to have endured. Today I get just as many people coming up to me and talking about the influence this book has had on them as I did in the immediate years after its publication. The four lenses of critical reflection—students' eyes, colleagues' perceptions, theory, and personal experience—are just as relevant now as they were twenty-five years ago, and the desire to make sure our practice is based on accurate assumptions regarding how to help students learn is central for any teacher who wants to do good work.

In the decades since the first edition appeared I've been asked to do multiple presentations, speeches, and workshops on the topic of critical reflection in all kinds of contexts. So I've got a lot more experience of what this process looks like in practice and the kinds of problems and questions people have about it. I've come to a better understanding of its culturally and racially variable nature and the ways social media can be incorporated. I've had three more decades dealing with power and trying to judge what an ethical

and responsible use of power looks like. And I've come to understand that critical reflection is just as central to leadership as it is
to teaching. Anyone who wants to lead well wants to be sure the
assumptions they hold about what constitutes a justifiable exercise
of authority are accurate and valid.

I've also had the chance to experiment with the process in my
own work. When the first edition came out I'd used the Critical
Incident Questionnaire (CIQ) described in chapter 6 only for a
few years. Now I have a quarter of a century of experience with
this instrument, and I've learned a lot about my own assumptions as a result. I've come to a deeper appreciation of the importance of modeling and the fact that communication—the how of
leadership—is so crucial. I've realized that the use of autobiographical narrative is a powerful tool to draw people into learning and
that small-group work—properly structured—is consistently the
most appreciated classroom activity. The CIQ has also shown me
that students regard team teaching as the most effective pedagogic
model. And, I'm more aware of the presence of racial dynamics and
have completely revised the assumption that I was a good white
person (Sullivan, 2014).

The core thesis of this second edition is the same as that of the
first. Critically reflective teaching happens when we identify and
scrutinize the assumptions that shape our practice. The way we
become aware of these is by seeing our actions through four complementary lenses. The first of these lenses is the lens of *students'
eyes*, most often represented by classroom research and classroom-
assessment activities that give us reliable information on how
students experience our classrooms. The second is *colleagues'
perceptions*, most commonly present when we team teach but also
available in support and reflection groups. Third is the lens of *theory*, comprising research, philosophy, and narrative descriptions of
teaching in higher education. This literature can open up entirely
new ways of thinking about familiar problems and dilemmas. And
finally the lens of *personal experience* provides a rich vein of material for us to probe. Reflecting on good and bad experiences as

learners gives us a very different perspective on power dynamics and the responsible exercise of authority.

The theoretical tradition that informs this understanding of critical reflection is that of critical social theory. Critical theory seeks to understand how people come to accept blatantly unjust systems as a normal and natural state of affairs. It's particularly interested in the process of ideological manipulation: of getting people to internalize ways of thinking and acting that ensure their continued marginalization and disempowerment. Situating critical reflection in a critical theory tradition leads us to a focus on two kinds of assumptions: (1) assumptions about power dynamics and what constitutes a justifiable exercise or abuse of power and (2) assumptions that seem commonsense and serve us well but that actually work against our best interests (what are called *hegemonic assumptions*).

Although many of the ideas from the first edition have made their way into this version, I have completely rewritten the whole book from the opening sentence to the last. Some chapters have retained their old titles but all have been completely rewritten. Six new chapters—almost half the book—have been written specifically for this edition. Based on feedback from readers of the first edition I have described more deeply what constitute assumptions of power (chapter 2) and hegemony (chapter 3). The lens of colleagues' perceptions has had its analysis extended to include the process of team teaching (chapter 8). Today's social media landscape was entirely absent in the early 1990s so chapter 11 examines how to incorporate social media into critical reflection. The need to address race and racism has become glaringly obvious on twenty-first-century college campuses, and chapter 12 deals with how to create these conversations. And the way that critical reflection is endemic to effective leadership is considered in a new chapter 14.

Audience

This book is for all teachers who think about their practice. The primary audience is likely college and university teachers in two- and

four-year institutions, vocational and technical institutes, and pro-
prietary schools. But practitioners in staff development and training in a wide range of organizations should also find it helpful. The
ideas and practices in the book have been field-tested with everyone from the Occupy movement to the Marine Corps; the World
Bank to mining schools; art, fashion, and theater institutes to oil
corporations; hospitals to seminaries; and prisons to parent groups.
I've written it for instructors across the disciplines; whether you
teach biology or aeronautics, art history or engineering, theology
or accounting, the analyses and practical examples are intended to
be relevant for you.

I've tried to write this second edition using the accessible and
personal style of the original. Far too many books on teaching are
written in a bloodless, disembodied fashion. I want this book to
connect viscerally as well as emotionally. So I write in the first person throughout, use lots of contractions, and try to include autobiographical experiences when these seem to fit. People used to a
more distanced, third-person style will probably find this distract-
ing, at least at first. But I've persisted with this style specifically
because so many people who'd read the first edition said they liked
its informal tone and personal voice.

Overview of the Contents

The book opens with a description of the critically reflective
teaching process. I clarify its purpose and distinguish among three
different kinds of assumptions that are typically uncovered: paradigmatic, prescriptive, and causal. I introduce the four lenses of
critically reflective practice and then explore in depth the specific
project that makes reflection critical: uncovering assumptions
about power and power dynamics and recognizing when hegemony
is in place.

Unearthing assumptions of power is the focus of chapter 2.
I start by discussing some commonplace assumptions about
teaching and then look specifically at assumptions concerning

power dynamics. To illustrate power's complexity I provide two scenarios common in higher education classrooms: arranging the chairs into a circle for classroom discussion and trying to remove yourself from discussions to be a fly on the wall. Chapter 3 explains the concept of hegemony—the process of actively embracing ideas and actions that serve the dominant order and are harmful to you—and gives some examples of this in action. I look at seven common hegemonic assumptions: the assumption that teachers use their charismatic singularity to motivate students, the idea that good teachers always have things under control, the belief that resistance to learning can be removed, the need to achieve perfect evaluation scores from students, the faith that someone somewhere has the answer to your problems, and the certainty of feeling you can fix racism, sexism, and the other ills you see around you.

Chapters 4 and 5 provide the first in-depth look at the four complementary lenses of critical reflection. Chapter 4 summarizes the contribution each lens makes and chapter 5 justifies why using these lenses is so important. I argue that critical reflection helps us to take informed actions, develop a rationale for practice, survive the emotional roller coaster ride of teaching, prevent self-laceration, enliven our classrooms, keep us fully engaged in work, model the democratic impulse, and increase trust.

The next group of chapters elaborates each of the critically reflective lenses in turn. In chapter 6 I present some techniques for seeing ourselves through students' eyes such as the one-minute paper, the muddiest point, the learning audit, clickers, social media, the Critical Incident Questionnaire and the letter to successors. Chapter 7 examines how to benefit from colleagues' perceptions and offers suggestions for setting up collegial reflection groups. Directions are given for using start-up sentences, beginning with critical incidents, the Chalk Talk exercise, the Circular Response method, Bohmian Dialogue, and the Critical Conversation Protocol. The analysis of the collegial lens is extended to team teaching in chapter 8. Team teaching enables you to model critical reflection for students and helps you manage the emotional aspects of your work.

The way that personal experience provides a lens on teaching is explored in chapter 9. I show how we can gain insight by examining personal experiences of learning, such as participation in graduate study, professional development workshops, academic conferences, and recreational learning. My story of learning how to swim as an adult is retained from the first edition because so many readers picked that out as a highlight. Chapter 10 considers the final lens of theory. I discuss how different kinds of literature (particularly narrative theorizing) shake us up, open new perspectives, help us recognize ourselves, and combat groupthink.

Chapters 11 and 12 are new to this edition of the book. Chapter 11 considers how social media can be incorporated into critical reflection, particularly back channels of communication. I discuss how social media allow for anonymous feedback and their contribution toward inclusivity. Chapter 12 examines the reasons why critical reflection on race and racism is so difficult and how narrative disclosure can be employed to set a tone for examining race. I focus particularly on what students tell us about how to set up and negotiate racial discussions.

Negotiating the risks of engaging in the critically reflective process is the subject of chapter 13. I look at how to deal with impostorship (feeling as if you're a fraud), cultural suicide (unwittingly threatening colleagues when you confront accepted assumptions), lost innocence (realizing that no one perfect response to difficult problems exists), and marginalization (finding yourself pushed to the fringes because you're challenging the system). The final chapter 14 is also a new chapter and turns to the ways in which critical reflection is applied to leadership. In particular I provide an analysis of how the most common institutional activity—meetings—can be turned into a critically reflective opportunity. The book ends with a comment on how to model critically reflective leadership.

Acknowledgments

A big thank-you to all the people who have come up to me in the years since this book first appeared to tell me how much it meant to them. I wish I'd been smart enough to keep a record of who you are. Your enthusiasm for the first edition and your endorsements of its worth convinced me to revisit the book and produce an entirely new edition. Writing is such a solitary process and without external reaction it's easy to believe that your words are just disappearing into the ether. But hearing from you at conferences or via e-mail that this book had some meaning for you was the soul fuel I needed to spend a year revising it.

Stephen D. Brookfield
St. Paul, Minnesota

About the Author

The father of Molly and Colin and the husband of Kim, Stephen D. Brookfield has written, coauthored, and edited eighteen books on adult learning, teaching, discussion methods, critical theory, and critical thinking, six of which have won the Cyril O. Houle World Award for Literature in Adult Education (in 1986, 1989, 1996, 2005, 2011, and 2012). He also won the 1986 Imogene Okes Award for Outstanding Research in Adult Education and the 2013 Phillip E. Frandson Award for Outstanding Literature in Continuing Education. His work has been translated into German, Finnish, Korean, Japanese, Polish, and Chinese. He has been awarded three honorary doctor of letters degrees from the University System of New Hampshire (1991), Concordia University (2003), and Muhlenberg College (2010) for his contributions to understanding adult learning and shaping adult education. In 2001 he received the Leadership Award from the Association for Continuing Higher Education (ACHE) for "extraordinary contributions to the general field of continuing education on a national and international level." He currently serves on the editorial boards of educational journals in Britain, Canada, Italy, and Australia, as well as in the United States. During 2002 he was a visiting professor at Harvard University. After a decade as professor of higher and adult education at Columbia University in New York, he has spent the last twenty-five years at the University of St. Thomas in Minneapolis, Minnesota, where he holds the title of the John Ireland Endowed Chair. In 2008 he won the university's Diversity in Teaching and Research Award and the John Ireland Teaching and Scholarship Award. In 2008 he was also awarded the Morris T. Keeton Award from the Council on Adult and Experiential Learning. In 2009 he was inducted into the International Adult Education Hall of Fame. In his other life he leads a pop punk band— The 99ers—which has released five albums on Spinout Records (Nashville, Tennessee).

Becoming a Critically Reflective Teacher

1

What Is Critically Reflective Teaching?

Every good teacher wants to change the world for the better. At a minimum we want to leave students more curious, smarter, more knowledgeable, and more skillful than before we taught them. I would also want my best teaching to help students act toward each other, and to their environment, with compassion, understanding, and fairness. When teaching works as I want it to, it creates the conditions for learning to happen. Students increase their knowledge, deepen their understanding, build new skills, broaden their perspectives, and enhance their self-confidence. They see the world in new ways and are more likely to feel ready to shape some part of it in whatever direction they desire.

Teaching can also work in the opposite way by confirming students' belief that education is a pointless and boring waste of time in which nothing of interest, relevance, or value happens. Here teaching confirms people's adherence to the status quo by strengthening whatever mechanisms of social control are in place and deepening students' apathy and conformism. So for good or ill the world is never the same after teaching.

Of course this neatly bifurcated way of presenting teaching as inherently liberating or conforming is actually far more complex in reality. I may design an exercise that I believe engages students and promotes participation, but they may experience it as a manipulative exercise of power. For example, in my first-ever course I taught in the United States I announced at the first class that students had control over deciding what should be the course curriculum. I assumed this announcement would produce an intoxicating and welcome sense of freedom, but I was told only that they'd paid a lot of money to learn from me, the expert. As unconfident novices in a new subject area they said I was setting them up for failure by not providing sufficient guidance for their learning.

One of the hardest lessons to learn as a teacher is that the sincerity of your actions has little or no correlation with students' perceptions of your effectiveness. The cultural, psychological, cognitive, and political complexities of learning mean that teaching is never innocent. By that I mean that you can never be sure of the effect you're having on students or the meanings people take from your words and actions. Things are always more complicated than they at first appear.

For example, in my own practice I place a strong emphasis on narrative disclosure. I like to provide examples from my life that illustrate points I'm making. I do this because students across the years have told me that this captures their attention and helps them understand a new concept. But there is another side to using personal examples and that's being seen as self-obsessed. Sometimes students' evaluations of a particular class have called me *arrogant*, a term that bothers me greatly because I hate self-importance so much. When I describe a situation or incident in my own experience that I think clarifies a complicated idea or shows how a new piece of information might be applied, I assume I'm being helpful. Yet some interpret this as an unhealthy fascination with the minutiae of my own life, as borderline self-indulgence. Investigating and clarifying these kinds of complexities is what critically reflective teaching is all about.

Critically Reflective Teaching

Our actions as teachers are based on assumptions we have about how best to help students learn. These assumptions come from a number of sources: our own experiences as learners and the way we interpret these, advice from trusted sources (usually colleagues), what generally accepted research and theory say should be happening, and how we see students responding. Sometimes these assumptions are justified and accurate, sometimes they need reframing to fit particular situations, and sometimes they're just plain wrong.

Critical reflection is, quite simply, the sustained and intentional process of identifying and checking the accuracy and validity of our teaching assumptions. We all work from a set of orienting, stock assumptions that we trust to guide us through new situations. Some of these are explicit and at the forefront of our consciousness. For example, I hold two strong explicit assumptions. The first is that whenever possible teachers should initially model for students whatever it is they wish those students to do. The second is that the best teaching happens in teams. That's because team teaching enables teachers to bring different knowledge and perspectives to bear on topics and to model intellectual inquiry by asking questions, seeking to understand differences, and disagreeing respectfully.

Other assumptions are much more implicit. Implicit assumptions soak into consciousness from the professional and cultural air around you. Consequently they're often harder to identify. For example, for many years I assumed that discussion was the best teaching method to use with adults. This implicit assumption came from three sources. First, my personal experience of schooling was characterized by lectures, dictation, and top-down approaches, something I found really boring. When I became a teacher I was determined not to replicate that approach and so moved instinctively to using discussion. Second, the theory I was reading in my professional preparation drew from English and American traditions that explored education for social justice and community development. This theory, particularly that of Freire (Freire and Bergman, 2000), emphasized the importance of dialogic processes, and this deepened the commitment to discussion that arose from my bad memories of school.

Third, pretty much every one of my colleagues at the adult education center where I worked advocated discussion as the most appropriate teaching method for working with adults. Over time the assumption that discussion-based approaches were inherently superior and the most "adult" just became part of who I was. It ceased to be something I thought consciously about and just embedded itself into my habitual practice. Planning a new course? Use discussion! Setting up a staff development effort? Start with small groups!

I still argue strongly for the relevance of this approach (Brookfield and Preskill, 2016). But since I started deliberately and regularly examining my assumptions I've realized that sometimes it doesn't make sense to begin a new course or professional development with a discussion. When students are complete novices, being asked to discuss new content is intimidating and often counterproductive. It's also unfair. How can people discuss something they know nothing about? When there's a history of institutional mistrust on the part of students, or when they've been burned by participating in discussions in the past, holding a discussion as the first thing you do is probably going to backfire.

Assumptions become tweaked over time, deepened in complexity. You realize that for a particular assumption to work, certain conditions need to be in place. For example, in my habitual, knee-jerk turn to discussion I've come to realize that discussions set up to explore contentious issues usually benefit if certain ground rules are stated early. In addition, I need to use protocols to secure everyone's participation and to give silent processing as much prominence as verbal exchange. I also know that discussion leaders need to be open to critique and willing to reconsider their own assumptions. So my implicit assumption that discussion should be used in all situations has been refined and contextually finessed through conscious examination.

To recap, critically reflective teaching happens when we build into our practice the habit of constantly trying to identify, and check, the assumptions that inform our actions as teachers. The chief reason for doing this is to help us take more informed actions so that when we do something that's intended to help students learn it actually has that effect.

Types of Assumptions

Assumptions are the taken-for-granted beliefs about the world and our place within it that guide our actions. In many ways we *are* our assumptions. They give meaning and purpose to who we are and what we do. Becoming aware of our assumptions is one of the most puzzling intellectual challenges we face. It's also something we instinctively resist for fear of what we might discover. Who wants to clarify and question assumptions they've lived by for a substantial period of time, only to find out that they don't make sense?

Of course assumptions are not all of the same kind. Some are broad in scope, some specific to a particular situation. Some are explicit, some implicit. I find it useful to distinguish among three broad categories of assumptions—paradigmatic, prescriptive, and causal.

Paradigmatic Assumptions

These are the structuring assumptions we use to order the world into fundamental categories. Usually we don't even recognize them as assumptions, even after they've been pointed out to us. Instead we insist that they're objectively valid renderings of reality, the facts as we know them to be true. Some paradigmatic assumptions I've held at different stages of my life as a teacher are the following:

- Adults are naturally self-directed learners.
- Critical thinking is the intellectual function most characteristic of adult life.
- Good classrooms are inherently democratic.
- Education always has a political dimension.

Paradigmatic assumptions are examined critically only after a great deal of resistance, and it takes a considerable amount of contrary evidence and disconfirming experiences to change them. But when they are challenged the consequences for our lives are explosive.

Prescriptive Assumptions

These are assumptions about what we *think* ought to be happening in a particular situation. They're the assumptions that are surfaced as we examine how we think teachers should behave, what good educational processes should look like, and what obligations students and teachers should owe to each other. Note the word *should*. A prescriptive assumption is usually stated with that word smack in the middle. Organizational mission statements and professional codes of practice are good sources for revealing prescriptive assumptions.

Some prescriptive assumptions I've held or hold are the following:

- All education should promote critical thinking.
- Classrooms should be analogs of democracy.
- Teachers should clarify expectations, objectives, and criteria of assessment as early as possible in an educational episode.

Prescriptive assumptions are often grounded in, and extensions of, our paradigmatic assumptions. For example, if you believe that adults are self-directed learners then you'll probably assume that good teachers encourage students to take control over designing, conducting, and evaluating their own learning. And, of course, you shape your teaching to accomplish this, which leads us to the third kind of assumptions—causal.

Causal Assumptions

These are assumptions about how different parts of the world work and about the conditions under which these can be changed. They are usually stated in predictive terms. Examples of causal assumptions I've held or hold are the following:

- Using learning contracts increases students' self-directedness.
- Making mistakes in front of students creates a trustful environment for learning in which students feel free to make errors with less fear of censure or embarrassment.
- Rearranging rows of chairs into circles creates a welcome environment for learning that students appreciate.
- Teaching in teams opens students to a greater breadth of perspectives than is possible in solo teaching.

Causal assumptions are the easiest to uncover. But discovering and investigating these is only the start of the reflective process. We must then try to find a way to work back to the more deeply embedded prescriptive and paradigmatic assumptions we hold.

How Do We Examine Assumptions?

The best way to unearth and scrutinize our teaching assumptions is to use four specific lenses available to us: students' eyes, colleagues' perceptions, personal experiences, and theory and research. Viewing what we do through these different lenses helps us uncover when and how certain assumptions work and when distorted or incomplete assumptions need further investigation. This can't be a one-time scrutiny; it must be consistent and regular—daily, weekly, monthly. That's the discipline of critical reflection.

Students' Eyes

Seeing ourselves through students' eyes makes us more aware of the effects of our words and actions on students. This helps us clarify our assumptions and decide when they make sense and when they need to be changed or discarded. A common meta-assumption is that the meanings we ascribe to our actions are the same ones students take from them. But when we collect data from students we see the different ways they interpret what we say and do.

Colleagues' Perceptions

Inviting colleagues to watch what we do or engaging in critical conversations with them helps us to notice aspects of our practice that are usually hidden from us. As they describe their readings of, and responses to, situations that we face, we often see our practice in new ways. Colleagues can suggest perspectives we might have missed and responses to situations in which we feel clueless.

Personal Experience

Our own experiences as learners provide important clues to the kinds of classroom dynamics that hinder or further the ability to learn. This is why I feel the best use of professional development money is to fund teachers to take a course release so they can enroll as learners in courses in which they are truly novices. Becoming a student enables you to study your experiences and transfer the insights about what does, or doesn't, work to your own teaching.

Theory and Research

Theoretical and research literature can provide unexpected and illuminating interpretations of familiar as well as newly complex situations. For example, reading Michel Foucault's (1980) analysis of power shed an unexpected but very illuminating light on my work as a teacher. Practices that I thought were transparent and empowering (for example, using learning contracts or rearranging classroom furniture by putting chairs into circles) were experienced by some as invasive and aggressive or as trying to wish away my power in a wholly unconvincing way.

So What Makes Reflection Critical?

Most reflection remains within the technical realm. We reflect about the timing of coffee breaks; how to use blackboards, flip charts, or screens; whether to ban hand-held devices from class; or the advisability of sticking rigidly to deadlines for the submission of students' assignments. We can't get through the day without making numerous technical decisions concerning timing and process. These technical decisions become critical when we start to see them in their social or political context, influenced by the structures and workings of power that exist outside the classroom.

What is it, then, that makes reflection critical? Is it just a deeper and more intense form of reflection? Not necessarily. Informed by the critical theory tradition, reflection becomes critical when it's focused on teachers understanding power and hegemony. As such, critical reflection has two distinct purposes:

Illuminating Power

Critical reflection happens when teachers uncover how educational processes and interactions are framed by wider structures of power and dominant ideology. It involves teachers questioning the assumptions they hold about the way power dynamics operate in classrooms, programs, and schools and about the justifiable exercise of teacher power.

Uncovering Hegemony

Critical reflection happens when teachers try to uncover assumptions and practices that seem to make their teaching lives easier but that actually end up working against their own best long-term interests—in other words, assumptions and practices that are hegemonic. It involves examining how to push back against this exploitation by changing structures and alerting others to its presence.

Critical Reflection as the Illumination of Power

Structures and forces present in the wider society always intrude into the classroom. Classrooms are not limpid, tranquil, reflective eddies cut off from the river of social, cultural, and political life. They are contested arenas—whirlpools containing the contradictory crosscurrents of the struggles for material advantage and ideological legitimacy that exist in the world outside.

One of my flawed assumptions as a beginning adjunct technical college teacher was that what happened in my classrooms was largely of my own making. I assumed that what I did and the way that I did it were largely under my own control. Certainly I knew there were examinations I had to prepare students for and that these would test students' knowledge and understanding of the content outlined in the syllabus. But I viewed my classroom as my own domain. I believed I could make pretty much all the decisions about the timing and flow of how we covered the required content and that the teaching methods and approaches were chosen by me.

In fact, as I moved through my first few years of adjunct work it became increasingly evident that structures and forces completely out of my control substantially shaped my supposedly independent classroom universe. First, the syllabus reigned supreme in my kingdom. Classroom discussions would start to ignite as students brought in personal experiences but I'd constantly have to cut these short in order to get back to the "official" business of covering the designated content. Sometimes when students seemed the most engaged I had to act as the enforcer of dullness, dragging them back to the study of disembodied content. I couldn't contact examiners or syllabus designers to ask them to change the tests to reflect the new areas we were exploring in class. Because exam questions and curriculum were predetermined they existed in a universe to which I had no access. The timing of examinations was set years in advance so there was no opportunity to let discussions run on. If I did that we wouldn't have the time to cover the next chunk of curriculum properly. And that could, after all, be a chunk that was stressed in this year's examination questions.

I also became aware of wider social norms of what constituted appropriate behavior. In my first weeks of teaching I tried to get as much classroom discussion going as possible. Sometimes my students became volatile, shouting and moving around the room. I encouraged them to change groups and to get up out of their seats if they needed a break. Full-time colleagues passing by my adjunct classroom must have thought chaos or anarchy had broken out! My class was loud, looked disorganized, and definitely did not fit the norm of students sitting quietly in orderly rows while the teacher talked.

I don't want to suggest that any of my exercises or activities actually worked. I'm sure students took advantage of my inexperience and saw me as a soft touch, someone they could take liberties with. And I'm convinced there was a high degree of chaotic disorganization evident. Not surprisingly I received not-so-subtle indications from colleagues that the noise my students created was interfering with what was going on in adjoining classrooms and that I needed to have better control of what was happening in mine.

Now there was no stated policy on student behavior, no set of college guidelines on what a "proper" classroom should look like. But clearly something was in the air—a number of paradigmatic and prescriptive assumptions—that was pressuring me to make sure my classroom appeared and sounded a certain way. This "something" was dominant ideology.

Dominant Ideology

Dominant ideology is a central idea in critical theory (Brookfield, 2004), which is the chief intellectual tradition informing my own understanding of critical reflection. It refers to the set of beliefs and assumptions that are accepted as normal and commonsense ways of explaining the world. Some dominant ideologies in the

United States are those of capitalism, positivism, democracy, militarism, white supremacy, and patriarchy, and each of them contains a core premise:

Capitalism

assumes that the free manufacture and exchange of goods and services secures freedom of speech and protects individual liberty. Under capitalism entrepreneurial creativity is unleashed in ways that nurture the human spirit.

Positivism

assumes that the world and its constituent elements can be measured, assessed, and graded in quantifiable ways. The most reliable knowledge is produced through the application of the scientific method, so education should focus first and foremost on the STEM (science, technology, engineering, mathematics) disciplines. Students educated in these disciplines will help the US economy remain the most dominant.

Democracy

assumes that the most reliable and morally appropriate way to make decisions is through a majority vote. A majority of people thinking the same way about something represents the uncommon wisdom of the common people.

Militarism

assumes that, as the world's foremost superpower, the United States must maintain the strongest arsenal of weapons and personnel on the planet. Only by maintaining its superiority in armaments will the country's security be assured. Funding military, paramilitary, and other security agencies is the best way to keep America safe because the exercise of force is something that enemy states understand and respond to.

White Supremacy

assumes that because of their superior intellect and capacity to think logically and rationally, white people should naturally assume positions of power and authority. People of color are governed by emotions rather than logic and do not have the impulse control that effective leaders require. Furthermore, because whites consistently perform better in tests and examinations, their greater intelligence means we're safer if they're in control.

Patriarchy

assumes that men's superior intellect and capacity to think logically and rationally means they should naturally occupy positions of authority. Women are governed by emotions rather than logic and do not have the impulse control that effective leaders require. Feeling sways them when it comes to decision making so they can't be trusted to think rationally about the common good. Consequently men should be entrusted with decision-making power.

Ideologies such as capitalism, majority-vote democracy, and militarism are very public, praised in the media, and commonly accepted as morally desirable. Some ideologies, such as white supremacy and patriarchy, are less overtly expressed because they contradict tenets of other ideologies, such as democracy. They are expressed in jokes and whispers privately among groups of "friends," that is, people who can be trusted to think in the same way.

Critical theory views all these ideologies as mechanisms of control, designed to keep a fundamental unequal system safe from challenge. If the majority of people could see that they live in a world designed to keep a small minority in a position of overwhelming material superiority, then revolution would break out. But if you can keep people thinking that this is the natural, commonsense way the world works, then you secure their consent to this state of affairs. When dominant ideology works most effectively people react to stock market crashes, widespread layoffs, budget cuts, and hospital and public service closures in the same way they react to weather changes. Hurricanes, ice storms, and heat waves are out of our control and to be shrugged off as best we can. Similarly, dominant ideology causes us to interpret economic and social disasters as equally unpredictable and beyond our sphere of influence.

Critically reflective teachers are on high alert for the presence of dominant ideology in educational processes and decisions. They see its influence as particularly evident in battles over curriculum where white supremacy and patriarchy come into play. Changes to tuition levels, differential funding for schools and departments, or the widespread adoption of rubrics in student assessment are analyzed in terms of the workings of capitalism and positivism.

Unearthing Power Dynamics

Critical reflection as the examination of power is not just concerned with how educational processes function as systems of social control or the way common institutional practices reflect elements of dominant ideology. Uncovering how power dynamics operate in the microcosm of classroom and staff room interactions is just as important.

Many teachers who work in a critically reflective way identify themselves as progressives interested in democratizing classrooms and empowering students. I'm one of these self-identified "progressives." Most of my approaches and activities are dictated by my desire to increase student participation and create an inclusive environment. In my own mind my actions are transparent and innocent. I assume that the sincerity with which I invest them is clear and that it produces the desired positive effects in students. I also assume that my actions designed to democratize the classroom, engage students, and convey authenticity are experienced in the way I intend. But because I built the critically reflective habit into my practice, the lenses of students' eyes, colleagues' perceptions, my own experiences, and theory have called these assumptions into question.

As an illustration let me briefly examine some assumptions regarding teacher power. As someone committed to working democratically I believe in my "at-one-ness" with students. Believing my students to be moral equals I like to think I'm really no different from them. I want them to treat me as an equal, a friend not an authority figure. The fact that there's an institutionally mandated imbalance of power between us, and that I usually know a lot more about the content, is in my mind a temporary imbalance. I view us as co-learners and co-teachers.

This belief exerts a strong influence on me. But by using the four reflective lenses of students, colleagues, experience, and theory I know that my assumption that declaring my at-one-ness with students causes them to see me as one of them is way too naive. In fact the strongly hierarchical culture of higher education, with its structures of authority and its clear demarcation of roles and boundaries, means that I can't simply wish my influence away. No matter how much I might want it to be otherwise and no matter how informal, friendly, and sincere I might be in my declarations of at-one-ness, I *am* viewed as fundamentally different.

Culturally learned habits of reliance on, or hostility toward, authority figures (especially those from the dominant culture) can't be broken easily. This is particularly evident when the teacher's identity is clearly different from students; for example, a man teaching a mostly female class, an upper-class teacher working with working-class students, a person of color teaching white students, or vice versa. In these instances declarations of at-one-ness will come across at worst as lies and at best as inauthentic attempts to curry favor.

Critically aware teachers reject the naive assumption that by saying you're the students' friend and equal you thereby magically become so. Instead, they research how students perceive their actions and try to understand the meaning and symbolic significance students assign to them. They come to understand that authentic collaborations will happen only if teachers spend considerable time earning students' trust by acting democratically, fairly, and respectfully toward them.

Critical Reflection as Uncovering Hegemony

Hegemony (hedge-a-moh-knee) and hegemonic (hedge-a-monic) are hard words to get your tongue around let alone to understand. But they are crucial to understanding the critical part of critical reflection. As developed by a founder of the Italian communist party (Gramsci, 1971), the term *hegemony* describes the process whereby ideas, structures, and actions that benefit a small minority in power are viewed by the majority of people as wholly natural, preordained, and working for their own good. In contrast to earlier notions of ideology that stressed its imposition from above as a mechanism of control, hegemony stresses learning from below. Gramsci maintained that people proactively learn their own oppression by internalizing the commonsense ideas swirling in the air around them in families, friendships, communities, culture, and social institutions.

Not only are the practices of hegemony actively learned but also people take pride in enacting them. They get pleasure from having perfect attendance records at school, being the first to show up for work and the last to leave, earning extra credit or merit pay for taking on more work, amassing the symbols of a successful life (car, house, consumer goods), and so on. But these ideas and practices that seem so obvious and commonsense are constructed and transmitted by powerful minority interests to protect the status quo that serves these interests so well.

The subtle cruelty of hegemony is that over time it becomes deeply embedded, part of the cultural air we breathe. We can't peel back the layers of oppression and point the finger at an identifiable group of people whom we accuse as the instigators of a conscious conspiracy to keep people silent and disenfranchised. Instead, the ideas and practices of hegemony—the stock opinions, conventional wisdoms, or commonsense ways of seeing and ordering the world that people take for granted—become part and parcel of everyday life. If there's a conspiracy here, it's the conspiracy of the normal.

A crucial purpose of critical reflection is to uncover and challenge hegemonic assumptions. These are assumptions that we think are in our own best interests but that actually work against us in the long term. With teachers, hegemonic assumptions about what makes them good or what represents best practice serve the interests of groups that have little concern for teachers' mental or physical health. The dark irony of hegemony is that teachers take pride in acting on the very assumptions that work to enslave them. In working diligently to implement these assumptions, teachers become willing prisoners who lock their own cell doors behind them.

As an example, think of the way so many teachers construct their work as fulfilling a vocation. Teaching as vocation implies that we are selfless servants of our calling, our students, and our institutions. Teachers who take this idea as the organizing principle for their professional lives may start to think of any day in which they don't come home exhausted as a day wasted. Or, if not a day wasted, then at least a day when they haven't been all that they can be (to adapt a slogan that first appeared in commercials for army recruitment).

When service to a vocational calling becomes the metaphor you choose to construct your teaching career, then you open the door to hegemony. This is because institutional notions of what it means to be in vocational service subtly co-opt what fulfilling one's vocation looks like. Without you realizing what's happening, your notion of service becomes fused with institutional priorities such as increasing student test scores, securing grants, recruiting more students, spending more time building community relationships, giving prestigious conference presentations, or engaging in scholarly publishing.

This diligent devotion to institutional ends comes to be seen as the mark of a good teacher. A sense of calling becomes distorted to mean that faculty members should deal with larger and larger numbers of students; regularly teach overload courses; serve on search, alumni, and library committees; generate external funding by winning grant monies; and make regular forays into scholarly publishing. What started out as a desire to be in service to students' learning becomes converted into a slavish adherence to promoting institutional priorities.

So what seems on the surface to be a politically neutral idea on which all could agree—that teaching is a vocation calling for dedication and hard work—becomes distorted into the idea that teachers should squeeze the work of two or three jobs into the space where one can sit comfortably. *Vocation* thus becomes a hegemonic concept—an idea that seems neutral, consensual, and obvious and that teachers gladly embrace, but one that ends up working against their own best interests. The concept of vocation ends up serving the interests of those who want to run colleges efficiently and profitably while spending the least amount of money and employing the smallest number of staff members that they can get away with.

The ingenious cunning of hegemony is that it is embraced, not resisted. Teachers actively look to serve on committees, take on summer school, travel to professional conferences, and increase their advisee roster all to show what good institutional citizens they are. They interpret requests to do more as a welcome sign of their indispensability to the institution. Extra sections, extra committees, extra publishing commitments are accepted with a sense of pleasure. The fact that they're exhausted is taken as a sign of devotion, of superlative commitment, of going the extra mile. The more tired they get, the prouder they feel about their vocational performance.

Of course sooner or later the center cannot hold and they get ill, collapse in exhaustion, or just go on automatic pilot. I know this from personal experience. In the last fifteen years I've had three work-related collapses. One in my office on campus, one at an airport getting ready to board a plane to give a speech, and one driving back from a meeting (I did manage to pull over before passing out!). Each time I was taken to the emergency room for a battery of tests, only to find out that I was physically fine.

If hegemony were a concept of medical pathology my doctors would have been correct to diagnose me as suffering from it. I don't know what prescription they would have written for me: a week of political detoxification maybe? Now bear in mind these three collapses all happened as I was teaching about hegemony, writing books on critical theory examining the idea, and warning people about it. In fact they all occurred well after the first edition of this book, with its attendant analysis of hegemony, was published! So don't think that just knowing about hegemony intellectually means you're always able to recognize when you're caught in its grip.

Conclusion

In this chapter I've tried to set out the fundamentals of critical reflection. To recap, it's a process of intentional and continual scrutiny of the assumptions that inform your teaching practice. These assumptions are scrutinized by viewing them through the four lenses available to any teacher: students' eyes, colleagues' perceptions, personal experience, and theory. What makes this reflection critical is its focus on power and hegemony. Informed by the critical theory tradition, critically reflective teachers try to understand the power dynamics of their classrooms and what counts as a justifiable exercise of teacher power. They also attempt to uncover and challenge hegemonic assumptions—those they embrace as being in their best interests that actually cause them harm.

2

Uncovering Assumptions of Power

Critical reflection is all about hunting the assumptions that frame our judgments and actions as teachers. This chapter provides examples of some general pedagogic assumptions about how best to support learning and then narrows the focus to assumptions concerning the power dynamics of classrooms.

Commonsense Assumptions about Good Teaching

Common sense is another term for dominant ideology. I don't mean that common sense is always wrong, the result of ideological manipulation. But commonsense understandings are usually shaped by cultural context to reflect the general wisdom of the day. So, for some people, it's common sense that poverty is the result of a lack of individual initiative, that we live in a world in which free speech can be exercised without negative consequences, and that racism is over. As Gramsci (1971) argued we need to turn common sense into good sense. Unexamined common sense, even the evidence of our own eyes, is a notoriously unreliable guide to action. The most reliable and valid assumptions are crafted from experience that's been critically examined.

Pedagogically this means we have to investigate where our commonsense assumptions come from. Many are in the air of the professional culture we've grown up in, accepted uncritically because colleagues, textbooks, and experts have told us this is how teaching works. When facing a new teaching situation most of us start by asking our elders and betters what to do, but this advice should always be examined as we put ourselves into practice.

Consider the following examples of how commonsense assumptions inform pedagogic action. All these assumptions and their resultant actions are probably familiar to readers, particularly those who see themselves as student-centered, progressive educators. After each example of a commonsense assumption I give a plausible alternative interpretation that calls its validity into question.

Commonsense Assumption—Visiting Small Groups

After you've set small groups a task it's common sense to visit them because this demonstrates your commitment to helping them learn. Visiting groups is an example of respectful, attentive, student-centered teaching that keeps groups on task. It shows students you're committed to their learning and take your role seriously.

Alternative Interpretation

Students experience the teacher visiting their group as a form of surveillance. The closer the teacher gets to a particular group, the more the students in that group start to perform as "good," purposeful, task-oriented students. They disdain silence, dreading that if the teacher stumbles on a group that's not talking he or she will assume the students are sloughing off, confused, or mentally inert. The pauses, thinking time, and hesitations necessary to thoughtful analysis are abolished and eager talk becomes the order of the day. Visiting student groups is also perceived as checking up to see whether students are doing what they were told to do. This comes across as insulting to students, implying that you don't trust them enough to follow directions.

Commonsense Assumption—Stop Lecturing

It's common sense to cut lecturing down to a minimum because lecturing induces passivity in students and kills critical thinking.

Alternative Interpretation

A critically enlivening lecture can, as Freire (Shor and Freire, 1987) acknowledged, be a wonderfully stimulating experience. It can open up exciting new intellectual territory, clarify complex concepts, and challenge students to rethink familiar assumptions. When lecturers question their own assumptions and consider alternate viewpoints they model critical thinking for their students and set a tone for learning. Lecturing is also a very effective way of providing the foundational grounding in an unfamiliar subject area or skill set that students need before they can start to think critically about it.

Commonsense Assumption—Students Learn Best through Discussion

It's common sense that students learn best through group discussion because they feel that their personhood and experiences are respected. Discussions increase students' engagement with a topic and foster active learning.

Alternative Interpretation

Discussions are alienating for students who feel they look or sound different. Racial and cultural minorities, working-class students, those for whom English is not a first language, introverts, and those who need time to think through ideas before speaking all see group discussion as an ordeal in which they need to perform appropriately to earn a good grade. Students aren't prepared well for discussion in high school, and the only models of discussion in the wider political culture they know provide little time for pause, silence, or careful listening.

College discussion groups reflect power dynamics and communicative inequities in the larger society and provide a showcase for egomaniacal grandstanding. Very often they're seen as pointless, held only because the teacher feels "now we should have some group talk." They're also often experienced as counterfeit. It looks as though everyone has an equal chance to speak and all voices are welcomed, but students know that some views are definitely off the table as far as the teacher is concerned. They're often insidious and manipulative, apparently free and open but really being skillfully managed to end at a predetermined conclusion.

Commonsense Assumption—Teaching Is Mysterious

It's common sense that teaching is essentially mysterious. If we try to dissect its chemistry or understand its essence, we kill its necessary unpredictability. Attempts to break it down to its component elements or best practices stultify the joyful creativity of teaching.

Alternative Interpretation

Viewing teaching as a process of unfathomable mystery removes the necessity to think deeply about what we do and how best to introduce students to complex new knowledge or skill sets. Any serious inquiry into practice appears reductionist and asinine. The teaching as mystery metaphor can thus be a convenient shield for incompetence. It excuses teachers from having to answer such basic questions as, how do you know when you are teaching well? How do you know what and when your students are learning? How could your practice be made more responsive? Seeing teaching as mysterious works against the improvement of practice. If good or bad teaching is seen as a matter of chance then there's no point trying to do better. The teaching as mystery metaphor also closes down the chance of teachers sharing knowledge, insights, and informal theories of practice because mystery is, by definition, incommunicable.

Commonsense Assumption—Longevity Brings Wisdom

It's common sense that teachers who have been working the longest have the best instincts about what students want and what approaches work best. If my own instincts as a novice conflict with what experienced teachers tell me, I should put my instincts aside and defer to the wisdom of long-standing teachers' experiences.

Alternative Interpretation

Length of experience doesn't automatically confer deepened insight and wisdom. Ten years of practice can be one year's worth of distorted and poorly interpreted experience repeated ten times. The "experienced" teacher may be caught within self-fulfilling interpretive frameworks that remain closed to any alternative interpretations. I have known colleagues who keep explaining away poor evaluations of their teaching by students as "one-offs" or the result of students not yet being able to see the "big picture." Alternatively, as each new set of poor student evaluations comes in, it only serves to confirm the teacher's belief that a programmatic glitch is to blame. So experience that's not subject to critical analysis is an unreliable and sometimes dangerous basis for giving advice. "Experienced" teachers can collude in promoting a form of groupthink about teaching that distances them from students' reactions and bolsters their own sense of superiority.

These assumptions are, in certain situations, entirely valid. At different times and in different situations I've fervently believed in all of them and acted in ways informed by them. Their apparent clarity and truth explain why they're so widely accepted. And, in certain contexts each of them is indeed totally accurate. For example, declarations that I'll learn from my students are much more accurate if (1) the students are well beyond the novice level and have a good grounding in the topic and (2) they've already worked with me and trust my basic competence. But depending on the situation, there are also quite plausible alternative interpretations that can be made of each of them.

Most assumptions teachers act on are not wholly right or wrong. Their accuracy and validity alter depending on circumstances. So visiting groups is indeed helpful if I've explained why I'm doing it and students know me well enough to realize it's not an act of surveillance. Similarly, lecturing doesn't work as an enlivening model of critical dialogue if students are so well versed with the material that they're already talking this way with each other. Likewise, students tend to like discussions that specify nonverbal measures of participation and introduce protocols that secure widespread participation.

Central to all reflection is the attempt to see things differently. In this section I've tried to show how assumptions and taken-for-granted understandings can be challenged by very different readings of experience. Reflective teachers probe beneath the veneer of common sense to investigate overlooked dimensions to their practice. One of the most interesting of these is power.

Assumptions of Power

Power is omnipresent in classrooms and a focus on understanding its dynamics is one of the things that make reflection critical. Informed by the critical theory tradition, "critical" reflection is interested in how power manifests itself in the classroom, how it moves around an educational setting, when its exercise opens up new possibilities, and when it closes them down. Such reflection also seeks to understand what constitutes an ethical and justifiable use of teacher power.

Part of a critically reflective focus is on clarifying how power relations in the outside world reproduce themselves in the classroom unless there's a deliberate attempt to stop this happening. As already mentioned, students most used to having their voice heard outside classrooms dominate discussion inside them. Ideas broadly accepted as true in society at large automatically induce resistance to any critiques of them. Classroom norms of how to please teachers, how furniture should be arranged for optimal learning, or what productive small-group work looks like are all learned in K–12 schooling. How students communicate across racial, gender, and cultural differences and how they cluster in affinity groups based on those differences are structured by life experiences outside.

Teacher and student identities outside the classroom also complicate life within it. In predominantly white institutions white teachers are given more credibility than teachers of color. As an older white male I can admit to mistakes with little fear of consequences. Indeed, my owning up to errors is usually read as a sign of endearing vulnerability: "how courageous of you to share your foibles and mistakes with us!" Colleagues of color and female colleagues are much more likely to have their missteps interpreted as affirmative action giving jobs to incompetent and unqualified minorities.

As a white teacher I also expect to be viewed with hostility and mistrust by mostly African American groups. I don't take this personally. In a white supremacist world it would be strange if this weren't the case. Given the actions of the white power structure a new white teacher like me will probably be regarded suspiciously. This is nothing to do with me, Stephen Brookfield. It's to do with what my skin color and phenotype represent to people of color. Earning any sort of trust or respect will only happen over time and maybe not then. Just as white students will likely view instructors of color as anomalies or the result of faulty affirmative action policies, so students of color will likely regard white instructors as inherently racist.

Focusing reflection on power also raises the whole dimension of teacher power. How does the institution authorize positional power? When do students think teachers exercise their power in helpful and ethical ways? When do they judge teachers to be acting in arbitrary and unjustifiable ways? What happens when teachers attempt to "give away" their power and work in a student-centered fashion? What does it look like to "empower" students, and is that even possible?

A particular interest of mine is understanding the complicated dynamics involved in trying to democratize the classroom. What does a truly inclusive classroom look like—one in which everybody has an equal chance to participate? How can you democratize something when you have all the positional authority? After all, the institution requires you to judge the quality of student work and award the final grade, something students are always well aware of. As a student said to my co-teacher and me about twenty years ago, "your so-called democracy is hypocritical because you can always fail us" (Baptiste and Brookfield, 1997, p. 34).

When power is concerned I've become aware of many instances in which I thought I was working in ways that students found empowering and supportive only to discover the opposite was the case. Actions and practices I believed to be unequivocally democratizing were experienced as manipulative surveillance. In this section I explore two of these: the circle and the teacher as a fly on the wall.

The Circle

One of my most provocatively disruptive investigations has been into the way students experience being put into a circle. Realizing this is not the benign, wholly relaxing, and empowering experience I assumed it to be has been like a little bomb of dissonance shaking up some of my long-settled understandings.

The very first day I went into teaching I became a furniture arranger. If it was at all possible I would get to class early to move the chairs out of their arrangement in neat rows and put them into a circle. I also learned, after some tense confrontations with facility staff members, to move them *back* into rows at the end of class. This is how janitors and custodians expected it to be and woe betide if you didn't conform.

Why would I spend so much time on pedagogic feng shui? Well to my way of thinking the circle is a physical manifestation of democracy, a group of peers facing each other as respectful equals. I assume the circle draws students into conversation and gives everyone an equal chance to be seen and heard. This respects and affirms the value of students' experiences and places their voices front and center. In my own teaching, the circle has mostly been an unquestioned given. I've assumed that when students walk into a classroom and see the circle they heave a sigh of relief and say to themselves, "thank goodness I'm finally in a situation in which my voice counts and my experiences are valued." I've also assumed that having my chair in the circle signifies that I'm one of them and reduces the power differential between us.

Using the circle was a knee-jerk part of my practice for the first twenty years of my career. I remember riding the New York subway in the1980s to teach summer school in July and August and emerging drenched in sweat as from the fires of hell. Then I'd get to class to find the air conditioning was out of order. But, as always, I would conscientiously move tables and chairs into the best approximation of a circle I could manage. As the sweat trickled down my back or into my eyes I would say to myself, "the students will really appreciate being treated like adults." A little frisson of self-congratulatory pride would ripple pleasurably through me even as I began to feel faint from heat exhaustion. I'd give myself a mental pat on the back for being a truly respectful, humane, and democratic teacher.

But I also spent much of my first twenty years teaching in the concurrent role of student or learner. During the first ten years of my teaching career I went through graduate school as a part-time student. I acquired two diplomas, a master's degree, and a doctorate from four different universities during that period. So I spent a lot of time in class as a student. Then, when I was a newly minted PhD I was expected to attend professional conferences and participate in professional development as an indication of service and commitment to the academic field. So I spent many hours sitting in chairs at academic conferences.

Throughout all these diplomas, degrees, and conferences I had the same reaction every time I walked into a room and saw the chairs arranged in a circle. I would hear a voice saying, "oh no! Not the circle!" and realize it was mine—in my head. Seeing the circle my energy would drop and my anxiety rise and I'd think, "now I'm going to have to 'share' with strangers as we exchange our ignorance for no other reason than that we're supposed to." I would also send a telepathic request to the teacher or presenter pleading, "why can't you just let me sit at the back, listen and absorb. When I feel ready to contribute I'll do so. But don't force me into speaking before I'm ready."

Then I'd get home from my student class or conference attendance, fall into bed exhausted, and get up the next morning for work. With no sense of irony or disjunction I would arrive at the center early, arrange the chairs into a circle, and think Carl Rogers was channeling through me as I created a genuinely student-centered, empowering learning environment. I somehow managed to disregard completely the lens of my own autobiographical student experience of the circle as unjustified coercion. As we shall see later in this book, rejecting the lens of personal experience as idiosyncratic and unreliable is very common.

It took two other lenses to open me up to the realization that the circle might not be the welcoming and helpful furniture arrangement I'd imagined. The first was the lens of students' eyes. After two decades teaching I finally got round to making a serious effort to find out how students were experiencing my classrooms by implementing the Critical Incident Questionnaire described in chapter 6. The regular anonymous feedback I received from students indicated that circles were experienced in far more complicated ways than I'd imagined. Students started talking about feeling like they were "being watched" in the circle, about there being "nowhere to hide" from the censorious gaze of their peers and the teacher. They said they felt most distanced in class when being "forced to speak" in the circle and how puzzling it was to have to share ignorance with a group of strangers.

Then the lens of theory kicked in. The ideas of the French cultural critic Michel Foucault (1980) were becoming widely known and I started to read applications of his ideas that analyzed classrooms as arenas of power (Ball, 2013; McNicol Jardine, 2005). A very helpful resource was Gore's *The Struggle for Pedagogies* (1992).

It was all laid out there. Rearranging furniture does not rearrange power relations. Students suspicious of academe who have been burned by previous educational experiences will mistrust the circle and be wary of entering it until they've come to trust the teacher. To them it'll be an arena of heightened surveillance in which, not knowing what's expected of them, they'll say or do the wrong thing in a way that's visible to all. So walking into a room and seeing the chairs set out that way will be intimidating not welcoming, aggressive not respectful.

I still use the circle as a class seating arrangement because I like there to be clear sight lines and I want everyone to feel they have the same opportunity to use nonverbal signals to let me know they want to contribute. But now, in what I hope is a critically informed way, I tell students why I arrange chairs this way. I say that just because it's a circle doesn't mean that I'm expecting people to speak and that they have a right to silence. I share that I won't assume that people who speak are smarter or more committed than those who don't and that I'm one of those who usually stay silent in a circle, at least initially. I need time to feel comfortable in a new group and to think and process ideas before I speak my understanding of them. I also need to be sure that the teacher is creating an environment in which saying the "wrong" thing won't be pounced on as a sign of ignorance or unpreparedness.

It's been interesting to see that, at least in my own classrooms, reassuring people that I won't assume their silence to signify inattention or carelessness has had the effect of galvanizing speech. The confident extroverts talk anyway but it seems there's less of a risk perceived by quieter students in saying the "wrong" thing. It also probably helps that I distribute a grading for participation rubric at the start of the semester that describes multiple ways for people to demonstrate participation without saying too much.

The Teacher as Fly on the Wall

I've always believed that the best kind of classroom is one in which students are in control of their learning. By that I mean that they conceive and conduct their own learning projects, make their own connections between disparate ideas, and raise their own questions that they proceed to answer through self-initiated discussions. A lot of this orientation comes from my own preference for self-directed learning. In college I skipped as many lectures as possible, read the assigned texts on my own, and studied old exam papers to prepare myself for finals.

I also came of age professionally at a time when Paulo Freire's *Pedagogy of the Oppressed* (Freire and Bergman, 2000), Carl Rogers' *On Becoming a Person* (1961), and Ivan Illich's *Deschooling Society* (1970) were first being widely read. It was a heady intellectual bouillabaisse, a pinch of education as the practice of freedom, a soupçon of nondirective facilitation, a dash of teaching as a subversive activity, and a big dollop of dialogic learning. Not surprisingly, when I came to do a PhD my study explored the independent learning of working-class adults who had become experts in different fields despite leaving school early with no qualifications.

My formation as a teacher thus comprised a powerful trifecta of perfectly integrated assumptions.

Paradigmatic Assumption

People learn naturally in a self-directed way.

Prescriptive Assumptions

Good teachers should set the conditions for people to conduct their own learning, serve as resource persons when requested, and say as little as possible in discussions.

Causal Assumptions

Using learning contracts enhances self-directedness, saying as little as possible encourages students into voice, telling students to design the curriculum builds confidence and is experienced as liberating.

This trifecta boiled down to a simple injunction: get out of the way of students' learning as quickly as possible. I believed my natural teaching position was on the sidelines, shouting out encouragement when possible and providing assistance when asked. The metaphor I would most often invoke was that of the fly on the wall. To my mind the best classes would be those in which students didn't even notice I was in the room. They would be so engrossed in practicing new skills or exploring new knowledge that my presence would be entirely forgotten. If a class discussion comprised only student talk and my voice was silent throughout, then that would be the optimal kind of dialogue I was seeking.

Teachers like me who are committed to a vision of student-centered learning will do some very predictable things. We'll put students into groups, give only minimal instructions about what should happen, and then retreat from the scene to let students work as they wish. Our retreat, however, is often only partial. We rarely leave the room entirely for long periods of time because that would indicate we don't care about what students are doing. Instead, we sit at our desk or off in a corner observing groups getting started on their projects. In our minds we're ready to be called on to assist learning at a moment's notice.

In class discussions we'll refuse to say too much for fear of influencing or prejudicing what students are thinking. We want students to reason for themselves, not copy our thinking. So we turn students' questions back on them, asking students to hazard their responses to the question they've just asked of us. The power of the assumption that people are naturally self-directed learners and that institutions and bureaucracy only get in the way of this innate impulse leads us to do as little as possible for fear of corrupting a purely inner-driven process.

After forty-five years I'm still very drawn to this vision of teaching and believe it has a lot of truth. But three of the four lenses available to me—my personal experiences, students' feedback, and theory—have challenged and complicated it in multiple ways. I know from personal experience that when I'm in a class, conference session, or professional development workshop I hate it when the first thing that happens is being put into a small group. I'll tolerate icebreakers but before participating in a more substantive group event I need some early input from the educator or leader. This helps me judge whether or not she or he can be trusted, is competent to lead the activity, is likely to give me something relevant or useful, and so on.

Sometimes I accept having my questions turned back on me, but when I'm genuinely clueless I find that strategy pointless. If I ask a question it's because I'm deeply interested in finding out someone else's own thinking on the matter in the hope that will help me learn something new. It seems like inauthentic game playing to have someone refuse to answer and instead ask me what I think. If I'm expected to answer a leader's questions, shouldn't he or she be expected to answer mine?

The lens of students' feedback has taught me that activities I introduce with the intent of democratizing participation still involve people watching me closely. As an example I think of Chalk Talk (Brookfield and Preskill, 2016). Chalk Talk is an exercise in which students and the facilitator write responses to a common question on a black- or whiteboard. It's intended to help visual learners and to democratize class participation. One of the most interesting comments students make when the posting is done and we start to talk about the resultant graphic is how they noticed the one or two posts I put up there, the question I raised, and the lines I drew. They say they assumed my post represented the correct response or right answer and so consequently they strove to respond to my posts. So an activity in which I feel I've merged into the background is actually one in which students watch me closely.

In class discussions I prefer to say as little as possible. I see my role as establishing the conditions under which good discussion happens and then letting the process go where it may. My responsibilities are to make sure protocols and ground rules set to promote inclusiveness are followed and to ask generative questions. But if a discussion ends with me saying virtually nothing I'm typically pleased by how that demonstrates students have had total control over the day's session. My whole mission is to be unnoticed and unobserved. I want to blend in with the wallpaper, to become a fly on the wall.

For many years I believed that I had succeeded in this process of photoshopping myself out of teaching and learning classroom dynamics. It was only when I started collecting students' feedback on my courses that I realized how naive I was being. The situation of students forgetting entirely that I was even in the room is something that happens relatively rarely. It's pretty much totally absent from whole-class discussions, even those in which I say almost nothing. As I'm listening to students' comments I'm always being watched for my reactions. Am I smiling and nodding or frowning? Do I make eye contact or look away? Do I write down students' comments or is my notepad or screen blank? Does my saying nothing in response to a comment mean I'm withholding approval or does it signify tacit agreement?

Because of students' preoccupation with wondering what my silence really means I believe it's better to give some regular, albeit brief, indications of what's on my mind. If you know something of how students view silence you're in a much better position to ensure that your fly-on-the-wall presence has the helpful consequences you seek. You'll learn when, and how much, to disclose and the confidence-inducing effects of such disclosure. You'll also know when keeping your own counsel leads to students doing some productive reflection and alternatively when they're paralyzed with anxiety regarding your withholding responses to their comments.

Finally, analyses of classroom interaction informed by theory of critical pedagogy (Darder, Mayo, and Paraskeva, 2015; Kirylo, 2013) remind us that acting as the fly on the wall can actually disempower students, even as you think it's bringing them into voice. Standing back and not intervening in a conversation allows for the reproduction of differences of status and power within the classroom. We can close the classroom door to avoid being surveyed by a prowling department head, but we can't close the door to history, power, and culture.

Students who are members of minority groups and whose past experiences have produced legitimate fears about how they'll be treated in academe may hold back. Out of a fear of being browbeaten by the teacher or by students of privilege, or from a desire not to sound stupid because of their presumed ignorance of academic language and conventions, some students may elect for silence. Also, students who are introverts or those who need time for reflective analysis may find the pace of conversation intimidating. In this instance inequity caused by the intersection of personality and culturally imposed preferences (Cain, 2013), rather than that caused by race, class, or gender, distorts what seems to be a free-flowing conversation. Being a fly on the wall only serves to perpetuate existing power differentials.

Conclusion

In this chapter I've tried to concretize what it looks like to unearth assumptions of power.

Creating a circle and acting as a fly on the wall are done for emancipatory effect to equalize participation, acknowledge students as equals, and create inclusive environments. Both practices flow from the prescriptive assumption that good teachers democratize classrooms. Yet assuming a simple cause-and-effect connection between doing these practices and having students experience them as liberating is extremely problematic. On the contrary, they can end up marginalizing some students, creating a mistrust of teachers and leaving students feeling the subjects of surveillance.

In the case of the circle and the fly on the wall, critical reflection has also led me to a new understanding of justifiable power. I need to state my reasons for using the circle (to create good sight lines), acknowledge students' right to silence, and reassure people that their silence won't be construed as lack of diligence or intelligence. I must also create protocols to allow all learners to participate. In the case of the fly on the wall I need to explain my role and my use of silence and intervene regularly to comment on how I think the class is going. In chapter 3 I examine the second kind of distinctive assumptions that critical reflection attempts to uncover: hegemonic assumptions.

3

Uncovering Hegemonic Assumptions

Critical reflection is reflection informed by the critical theory tradition, and central to that tradition are two ideas: power and hegemony. In this chapter I want to reexamine the concept of hegemony outlined in chapter 1. In particular, I want to explore some widely held hegemonic assumptions embedded in "common-sense" understandings of teaching.

To recap very briefly, hegemony is the process by which an existing order secures the consent of people to the legitimacy of that order, even when it disadvantages them greatly. In the wider society hegemony serves to stop people challenging the status quo. Major economic recessions or depressions are seen as being as unpredictable and uncontrollable as natural weather phenomena, such as blizzards, typhoons, or hurricanes. People batten down the hatches, make do with whatever supplies are at hand, and wait it out till the weather clears. When massive layoffs threaten or public facilities (schools, hospitals, day-care centers, parks) close, people "make do." Growing up in England we had a phrase—"mustn't grumble." Essentially this meant that because you couldn't do any-thing about most misfortunes in life you might as well accept them stoically and get on as best you can within the constraints of the situation.

When hegemony is in place the system purrs along smoothly with no threat of revolution or insurrection. Essentially it stops people grumbling. Convince people that the world is organized for their own good and that inequality is a normal and natural state of affairs, and you have the perfect system of social control. However, when people start to question whether or not their own taken-for-granted beliefs really are the immutable laws of nature they imagine, then hegemony is threatened.

Insert the notion of hegemony into the discourse of critically reflective teaching and you create a particular project: uncovering hegemonic assumptions about teaching. Such assumptions meet three conditions:

- They're accepted as representing commonsense truth and are widely regarded as accurate depictions of teaching and learning dynamics.
- They're viewed by teachers as working to support their best interests.
- In actuality, they harm teachers and serve to keep an irrational and injurious system intact.

Hegemonic assumptions are typically paradigmatic, so much a part of who we are that when they're challenged we respond, "that's not an assumption, that's just the way things are!" Uncovering these kinds of assumptions on our own is incredibly difficult. This is because we read our experiences in such a way as to bolster our long-standing analysis of how the world works. When bad things happen we explain them away as the unpredictable workings of things we can't understand, the fault of our ineptitude, or the vicissitudes of fate. The only way a deeply ingrained perspective on experience is challenged is if some external event jerks us out of our comfort zone, some little bomb of dissonance shatters our habitual rationales for doing the self-destructive things we do. These are the "disorienting dilemmas" that transformative learning theorists (Taylor and Cranton, 2012) refer to so frequently.

The four lenses of critically reflective teaching are all important sources of disorienting information. Students' comments, colleagues' critiques, or reading a new and surprising analysis of a familiar situation can interrupt our habitual narratives in a productively disturbing way. Personal experience sometimes shocks us in a visceral and emotional way. In the rest of this chapter I review some common assumptions of teaching that I regard as hegemonic and show how these are challenged.

I Must Motivate My Students by My Charismatic Singularity

Similar to many hegemonic assumptions this springs from a place of compassion. When students seem not to share our primal enthusiasm for our subject we often respond by striving to create in them the same passion for learning it that we feel. Boiled down to its simplest statement, we say we wish to motivate students.

The idea of motivating students is typically embedded in an individualistic conception of learning. The idea is that somehow, by sheer force of our own example, we can create an interest in something that didn't exist before. Two ideas are at play here. First, there's the notion drawn from medicine of determining the pathology of a disease, in this case the absence of motivation. Here an appropriate diagnostic response is to inject a dose of motivational fluid into the patient. If we uncover the particular inhibitor to the learner feeling a natural state of motivation, and then administer the appropriate drug that will lower this inhibitor, we'll release the motivational endorphins lying dormant in the learner's cells.

Second, there's the idea of charismatic singularity. Here we take it on ourselves to be such an exemplar of excited engagement in our subject that students, through some sort of pedagogic osmosis, will absorb our level of interest. To use another medical analogy, our passion will be communicated like an airborne virus resulting in students breathing in the spores of our contagious enthusiasm.

This idea meets all the conditions of a hegemonic assumption. First, it's broadly accepted as a commonsense idea about good teaching. When I've asked teachers to tell me what they'd most like their students to say about their courses, one of the most frequent responses is that they want students to feel that their instructors generate excitement in learning. Second, it's an assumption teachers usually interpret as working in their best interests. We remember with pleasure teachers who awakened our own interest in learning and often cite them as the inspiration for our choice of teaching as a career. Third, it's an assumption that, without our knowledge, harms us and serves the interests of those who wish to keep a system intact.

How can this assumption be deemed harmful? The answer lies in its individualistic crafting. According to this assumption teaching and learning are framed as a relationship between an individual student or particular group of students and an individual educator. The question of how to encourage learning is thus reduced to ensuring that the specific dynamics of a particular classroom are correct. And at the heart of these dynamics is determined to be the presence, or lack thereof, of charisma displayed by the teacher. All the responsibility for creating a motivated learner falls squarely on the teacher's shoulder. If you're a sufficiently charismatic performer you'll ignite your students enthusiasm for learning. If not they'll remain disinterested and apathetic.

This understanding of successful teaching completely sidesteps the reality of broader social conditions. It regards the classroom as a bubble, totally isolated and unaffected by the culture, history, economics, and politics in which it's situated. In reality, the world a student brings into the classroom is a social, political, cultural, and economic one. Students are not just individual cognitive centers or information-processing mechanisms. Despite the undoubted importance of research into brain chemistry, we need to understand students in terms of their social locations and identities.

Take the strength of gender, racial, or class formation as examples. Before even opening his or her mouth an instructor of color walking into a predominantly white classroom has the history of racism and white supremacy framing students' perceptions of their teacher's competence. As teachers of color report (Tuitt, Hanna, Martinez, Salazar, and Griffin, 2009), they're sometimes initially viewed as secretaries and custodial staff members. Even when it's clear they're the teacher they're viewed as being there only because of affirmative action guidelines. The same is true for a woman teaching a predominantly male class who faces the ideology and history of patriarchy. None of these teachers needs to say or do anything to create these complex responses in students. The simple presence of their body is enough.

Switch racial identities and have a white teacher facing a multiracial class, and another complex set of responses, also framed by the reality of racism and white supremacy, are called forth. Here the instructor is likely to be viewed as a representative of power as usual and viewed with suspicion borne of history and experience. Again no words are spoken; identity says everything. As Yancy has shown, the black gaze on whites (Yancy, 2012) and the white gaze on blacks (Yancy and Guadalupe Davidson, 2014) is strong and enduring.

When social class is concerned, accent and vocabulary are typical determinants of class location. Even in a racially homogenous class the history of classism inserts itself immediately into the proceedings. When an upper-class teacher faces a working-class group of students, or in the reverse situation, class identity frames all subsequent interactions. A working-class teacher has to prove she or he belongs in academe. An upper-class teacher has to prove he or she has the best interests of working-class students at heart. This is why five decades ago Paulo Freire in the original publication of *Pedagogy of the Oppressed* (Freire and Bergman, 2000) urged middle- and upper-class teachers to commit class suicide.

Given the power of history, politics, and culture it's insane for any teacher to imagine that he or she can walk into a classroom and overturn centuries of racial, gender, and class exploitation. Students' resistance to learning is clearly generated by many factors, but prime among them must be students' social locations.

If I as a white teacher, I think I can walk into a room of students of color and, by the sheer force of any charismatic energy I might summon, turn their suspicion into enthusiastic endorsement, I am hurtling into hurt. Yet, this is precisely what I have done for most of my career.

So the assumption that teachers can create motivated students by the power of their charismatic energy is deeply harmful. Subscribing to it means you constantly blame yourself for being unable to convert students into eager advocates of learning. Several images come to mind when I think of the naivety of this assumption. I'm in a kayak paddling furiously as I try to turn an ocean liner around. I'm in a pickup truck with my bumper against the Rockies, gears screeching as I attempt to move them further westward. These are metaphors of exhausted futility. Measuring your success as a teacher by how well you create motivated students through your personal efforts leads to a life of demoralized failure.

Whose interests are served by this assumption? Well, as is typical with hegemonic assumptions, we must start with the system. Viewing teaching as the activation of charismatic singularity cultivates the view that student success depends on the teacher. This makes it easy to imagine that change is extremely simple. If students are underperforming just fire existing teachers and hire better ones. This protects the system from critical examination and means that structural inequities are ignored. Everything is down to the individual teacher; good teachers produce motivated learners who excel in taking tests and poor teachers produce disinterested students who fail.

This *Stand By Me, Dead Poets Society,* or *Dangerous Minds* model of teaching elides the need to fund education properly, reduce class sizes, provide proper infrastructure, and support staff development. If the responsibility for learning comes down to whether or not you possess the requisite charisma then legislators can dismiss requests for resources.

It's All under Control

If there's one thing I've learned about teaching it's that I have far less control over classroom events than I assume. Yet the concept of teachers being able to control learning undergirds pretty much all evaluation. Purposeful intentional teaching generally seeks to guide students toward predetermined learning outcomes that are then measured by some kind of assessment protocol. Behind this organizational practice is the notion that control over classrooms and learning is possible. As a young adjunct instructor moving from college to college I was often told to establish control early on and then ease up as the term progressed. I learned to put a lot of pressure on myself to appear cool, calm, and collected and never to appear flustered. Inside I was a roiling sea of nervous anxiety but externally I was Mr. Unflappable, or at least trying to be.

Yet every time I initiate a class discussion, try out a new activity, or make any attempt to get students to think critically I know that the extent of my control over what happens is questionable. And the more I use classroom-response systems to find out what students are thinking the more I realize I often have no idea at all about their inner mental landscape. I remember copresenting a session one afternoon in England recently and asking the audience what needed to happen next for us to be able to help students think more critically. The social media tool I was using that day—TodaysMeet (www.todaysmeet.com)—lit up with comments essentially saying, "Tea PLEASE!" Here I was thinking minds were dealing with the intricacies of critical thinking, when in fact they were focused on beverages.

When I move into analyzing a contentious issue such as racism I know I'm entering an essentially chaotic universe. So-called hot topics (Nash, LaSha Bradley, and Chickering, 2008) hit raw spots and generate strong emotional responses. The one thing I can pretty much depend on is that very quickly I'll start to feel I'm losing control. Views will be expressed and things will be spoken that will offend and inspire and the conversation will take turns I can't anticipate.

This assumption that it's all under control causes multiple injuries. First, as you struggle to look as though you know what you're doing even as things go awry, your sense of impostorship—the feeling that you're faking it until a "real" teacher comes along—will be overwhelming. If you measure your effectiveness by how well you keep control you're going to feel pretty ineffective for long periods of time. Second, the internal voice telling you to "get things back on track" whenever the class goes in a surprising direction robs you of one of the greatest pleasures of teaching—the "teachable moment." Such moments are ones full of rich surprise. Regarding them as unfortunate aberrations to be shortened or avoided entirely means you lose the option to enjoy unexpected chances to help your students grow.

Having your control questioned can also be very interesting. When students challenge me because what I'm teaching is, in their minds, boring and irrelevant or because I'm acting in a way that seems arbitrary or unfair, this is inherently destabilizing. That destabilization is productively insurrectional. If I respond to every student challenge by cutting it off or stamping it down then not only do I dismiss the legitimacy of student criticisms but also I lose the chance to learn. One of the consequences of seeking feedback from your students is that sometimes they'll tell you things you don't want to hear and that complicate your life. Because the lens of students' eyes is so crucial we *have* to take seriously what this lens reveals. If you ignore or dismiss student critiques because they challenge your sense of control you'll probably never think very deeply about your exercise of teacher power. The same holds true for critiques from colleagues. A colleague asking me why my work was race blind was hardly a question I wanted to hear, but it launched me on a journey from which there was no turning back.

Whose interests are served by the assumption that it's all under control? First are the balance sheets of the many companies producing assessment and evaluation instruments to measure student learning. Rating teachers by how well their students perform on standardized tests assumes that all the teachers involved have equal control over their classrooms. Visit two schools on the same day in pretty much any city—a magnet school on Manhattan's Upper East Side and a neighborhood school in Bedford Stuyvesant perhaps—and the ludicrousness of this assumption is clear. But as long as the system parlays the myth that teachers have enough control in their classrooms for valid comparisons of teachers and schools to be drawn from test results, then these tests are immensely appealing. They parlay into another myth of simplistic measurement. Of course, the profits quickly mount up for companies paid a fee every time a particular instrument is used.

Most college teachers live in a pedagogic demilitarized zone caught between institutional demands and the rhythms of teaching and learning. Bureaucracies assume learning can be neatly managed and packaged—commodified to use the language of critical theory (Brookfield, 2004)—but brains and hearts dictate otherwise. Learning that's complex and demanding never follows a neat institutional design. It goes off in unexpected directions, sometimes takes much longer than anticipated, and requires constant pedagogic adaptation. To assume you can control what's happening in your classroom is to ignore reality.

Washing Clean the Stain of Resistance

Educational institutions, even those funded by the state, operate in a capitalist system. We're selling a product and students, or their parents, are shopping around for the best deal. Institutional brochures and web presences are replete with images of smiling students, usually conversing in multicultural rainbows. The message is clear: learning is fun and satisfying as students reach their potential, be all they can be, and generally self-actualize for four pleasurable years. Banned are images of frustration or struggle, of slogging repeatedly to learn difficult content or skills. Colleagues often complain that so-called millennials (Bonner, Marbley, and Howard-Hamilton, 2011; Knowlton and Hagopian, 2013) bring a sense of entitlement to higher education. They expect learning to be entertaining, to earn automatic As for attendance, and to receive social promotion through a four-year curriculum. If that's true then the enticing websites, glossy brochures, and social media marketing efforts of colleges have a lot to do with it.

In a competitive marketplace, teachers not surprisingly feel the pressure from administrators and students to make difficult and complex learning "fun." I've had teachers at multiple institutions consult me regarding their poor teaching evaluations, received largely because students experience the course as too difficult or challenging. They ask me how to combat student resistance and remove it from the classroom. It's almost as if resistance is a dirty stain that can be removed with some pedagogic detergent: "Wash your classroom free of those stubborn blemishes of student disinterest or apathy!"

Resistance is a complex phenomenon. Sometimes it's completely justified, such as when we neglect to build a case for learning, don't demonstrate our own commitment to it, send conflicting messages regarding its importance, or provide examples that confuse rather than clarify. The truth is that any learning that stretches students beyond where they are, that introduces them to complexity, or that asks them to think critically can pretty much be guaranteed to induce resistance on the part of some students.

A lot of resistance is caused by factors totally beyond our control. Any time learning is institutionally coerced there's a possibility of resistance. Resistance can be linked to students' poor self-images as learners or to a history of being burned by teachers of the subject you're asking them to study. Maybe they're afraid of committing cultural suicide or looking uncool or foolish. And student development theorists frequently document the cognitive struggle eighteen- to twenty-two-year-olds face to move from binary, dualistic thinking to appreciate contextuality (Evans, Forney, Guido, Patton, and Renn, 2010).

Speaking personally I know I focus on students who seem resistant far more than I do on those who appear enthusiastically engaged. In a discussion I'm often worrying about students who aren't speaking rather than listening to those who are. Online I obsess about students who post rarely and briefly. When giving a presentation I'm easily distracted by expressionless faces and start to panic thinking that I've lost the room. Of course, these may not be signs of resistance at all, just deep processing. As a student I often participate little in discussions that I find fascinating, because I'm too busy doing the mental work of listening carefully. I don't make enthusiastic eye contact or nod my head in lectures that I'm taking seriously; instead, I lower my head and doodle. A note pad that's covered in doodles signifies deep engagement and cognitive processing on my part.

But there's no denying that every teacher sooner or later faces overt resistance in college classrooms. Students often have no qualms in asking, "why do we need to know this?" or "will this be on the test?" They'll try to bargain you down on the number of pages in a homework assignment paper or the number of posts to the chat room required of them. They can also sabotage you by refusing to ask or answer questions. Sometimes I hear students say I'm asking too much of them, that there's too much reading, too many assignments, and too little time. When I stress the need to think critically and develop their own independent judgments regarding a difficult issue I'm often asked to say what the correct opinion or response really is. In discussions of racism I have had students accuse me of being racist, of my seeing race everywhere when it's really not an issue, and of creating a classroom environment in which they can't say anything without fear of seeming prejudiced.

The assumption that it's your responsibility to remove student resistance completely overlooks the fact that resistance is a natural rhythm of learning. Any time you push students to confront complexity, increase their skill level, or think more critically you're going to get substantial pushback. To interpret that as a sign of bad teaching is insane. In fact, if you're *not* getting resistance, you're probably not doing your job. Your responsibility is not just to support students but also to challenge them.

Similar to any hegemonic assumption, the belief that we must wash away the stain of resistance in order to consider ourselves good teachers is one many of us eagerly embrace, but it's one that harms us. If resistance is an essential rhythm of significant learning and completely predictable, then its presence can legitimately be regarded as a sign of your pedagogic effectiveness, not the opposite. If you put pressure on yourself to remove it then you're setting yourself up for permanent failure. I say it again: resistance is completely natural, indeed necessary. Plus, because it's often caused by factors totally outside your control, you're often powerless to affect it. So you can't, or shouldn't, want to remove resistance. Of course you want to respond to it in a way that keeps students engaged in learning. But don't automatically conclude that because it's there you've somehow failed.

As with most hegemonic assumptions, the interests this assumption serves are institutions and organizations set up to perpetuate themselves and to expand their reach. If learning can be sold as a perpetually joyful and smoothly enervating increase in students' command of knowledge and skill then the customers keep rolling in. No president, provost, or board of trustees ever instructs alumni relations, admissions, or the development office to send a message to prospective students that studying at their college will be a long, hard slog full of difficulty and involving painful self-appraisal. So the fiction is maintained: "come to us and be bathed in the warm glow of permanent self-actualization!"

The Perfect-Ten Syndrome

Many teachers take an understandable pride in their craft wisdom and knowledge. They want to be good at what they do and, consequently, they put great store in students' evaluations of their teaching. When these are less than perfect—as is almost inevitable for the reasons explored in the last assumption—teachers assume the worst. All those evaluations are forgotten and the negative ones assume disproportionate significance. Indeed, the inference is often made that bad evaluations must, by definition, be written by students with heightened powers of discrimination: "if they're critical of me they must realize I'm only one step ahead of them." Conversely, good evaluations are thought to be produced by students who are half-asleep.

This constant inability to receive uniformly good evaluations can lead to feelings of guilt concerning one's supposed incompetence. When we keep these evaluations to ourselves (as is typical given the privatized culture of many college campuses) the sense of failure becomes almost intolerable. We're convinced that we're the only ones who receive bad evaluations and that everyone else is universally loved. In this way an admirable desire to do good work, and the assumption that good evaluations signify this, turns into a source of demoralization. Once again, a belief that seems self-evidently good becomes hegemonic, harming us in the process.

A critically reflective teacher recognizes the error of assuming that only the receipt of uniformly good student evaluations signals the presence of good teaching. She knows that the complexities of learning and the diversity of college classrooms mean that no action a teacher takes can ever be experienced as universally and uniformly positive. She knows, too, that teacher assessment and performance-appraisal mechanisms that reward perfect scores don't serve students' interests. For one thing, good evaluations are sometimes the result of teachers pandering to students' prejudices. Teachers are almost bound to be liked if they never challenge students' taken-for-granted ways of thinking and behaving or if they allow them to work only within their preferred learning styles. Because letting people stick with what comes easy to them is a form of cognitive imprisonment, one could argue that anyone who consistently scores a perfect ten is just as likely to be doing something wrong as something right.

So whose interest does the perfect-ten assumption serve if not that of students and teachers? Primarily, it confirms the belief of those with a reductionist cast of mind that the dynamics, complexities, and contradictions of teaching can be reduced to a linear, quantifiable rating system. Epistemologically challenged people like this sometimes end up in positions of administrative and legislative power. Believing that learning and teaching are one-dimensional phenomena, they carve curricula into discrete units and create standardized objectives that are meant to be context and culture proof. In their minds teaching becomes the simple implementation of centrally produced curricula and objectives. Good or bad teaching then becomes measured by how closely these are followed and implemented. Call it the "Pearsonization" of American higher education; the way that Pearson Education PLC (the corporation producing widely adopted tests in over 70 countries) fundamentally shapes how learning is assessed and how schools and teachers are evaluated.

The perfect-ten syndrome also makes life easier for those who have the responsibility of deciding which members of their staff are to be promoted. All they need to do is consult student ratings because according to this assumption the best teachers are obviously those with the highest scores. This turns professional advancement into a contest in which the winners are those who get the most students to say they like them. Judging teaching by how many people say they like what you do supports a divisive professional ethic that rewards those who are the most popular. Administrators who use this ratings system are not venal or oppressive. They are tired and burned out from making an unworkable system look like it's working. So if a neat solution (giving promotion to those with the highest scores on student evaluations) appears to a difficult problem (deciding who of their staff advances) we can hardly blame them for embracing it.

Deep Space Nine: The Answer Must Be out There Somewhere

For many teachers the first response to encountering a problem of practice is to look for a manual, workshop, or person who can solve it. Students refusing to learn? Buy a book on dealing with resistance to learning. Classes full of students with different racial and cultural identities, ethnic backgrounds, ability levels, and experiences? Enroll in that summer institute on dealing with diversity. Running discussions that are dominated by a handful of confident, articulate students? Go and see how that colleague across campus whom everyone raves about creates democratic classrooms.

All these resources for dealing with problems are useful and necessary. I myself have written books that have dealt with resistance to learning, have run workshops on dealing with diversity, and have invited colleagues to watch me teach, so I don't want to decry the importance of doing these things. But I do want to point out that although reading books, attending workshops, and watching colleagues can give you some useful insights and techniques, it's wrong to assume that at some point in these activities you'll inevitably stumble on the exact answer to the problem you're experiencing.

To think this way is to fall victim to a fundamental epistemological distortion. This distortion holds that someone, or something, out there has the knowledge that constitutes the answer to our problems. We think that if we just look long and hard enough we'll find the manual, workshop, or person who will tell us exactly what we need to do. Occasionally I suppose this might just happen. But much more often than not, any ideas or suggestions we pick up will have to be sculpted to fit the local conditions in which we work. And that goes for all the suggestions I make in this book on how to become critically reflective.

Unless we challenge this epistemological distortion we risk spending a great deal of energy castigating ourselves for our inability to make externally prescribed solutions fit the problems we're facing. It might never occur to us that what needs questioning is the assumption that neat answers to our problems are always waiting to be discovered. It can take many demoralizing disappointments as our application of rules, protocols, and models misfire before we realize the fruitlessness of the quest for standardized certainty. Once again an assumption that we think represents commonsense wisdom—that if we look long enough we'll find the neat answer to an intractable problem—becomes hegemonic. As each promised activity or process fails we berate ourselves for our failure to implement the "solution" we've discovered correctly or for falsely diagnosing our problem in the first place.

Methods and practices imported from outside rarely fit snugly into the contours of our classrooms, and difficult problems never have simple, standardized solutions. At best, they call forth a multiplicity of partial responses. The assumption that complex problems of practice, such as creating an inclusive classroom that teaches students about racism, can be dealt with by following standardized guidelines serves the interests of those who accrue power, prestige, and financial reward from designing and producing these guidelines. Consultants, authors, and production companies rarely say of their products, "these might be useful but only if you research your local conditions and adapt what is here to your own circumstances." Neither do they advocate a mixing and matching of their products with elements from others marketed by their rivals. The promise that somewhere someone will take care of our problems for us removes from our shoulders the tiresome responsibility of having to research our contexts critically.

We Meet Everyone's Needs

When asked to explain why they've made a particular decision, administrators will often justify what they've done by saying that they're meeting the community's, the faculty's, or the students' needs. Likewise, teachers will say that the best classes are those in which every student feels his or her needs have been met. The assumption that good teachers meet all students' needs all the time is guaranteed to leave us feeling incompetent and demoralized. Because meeting everyone's needs is impossible we enthusiastically set ourselves up for failure, the sure sign of a hegemonic assumption.

One problem with the meeting-needs rationale is that students' articulation of exactly what those needs are is sometimes done in a distorted and harmful way. For some students the primary need is an easy A with the least possible effort. Others define their need as staying within their existing comfortable ways of thinking, acting, and learning and avoiding any topic that comes with trigger warnings. Someone who expresses a need of never being challenged in college is not in the best position to judge what's in his or her own best interests. So although meeting everyone's needs sounds compassionate and student-centered it's pedagogically unsound and psychologically demoralizing. Clinging to this assumption causes us to carry around a permanent burden of guilt at our inability to live up to this impossible task. What seems to be an admirable guiding rule for teachers, and one that we're all tempted to embrace, ends up destroying us.

Who is served by this assumption? Primarily those who believe that educational processes can be understood and practiced as a business. Higher education becomes a marketplace in which different companies (colleges) compete for a limited number of customers. Private colleges depend on tuition revenue to survive but even state colleges need to attract and graduate large numbers of students if they're to continue to secure funding from the legislature. Under such circumstances keeping the consumers (students) happy enough so that they don't buy the product (education) elsewhere is the bottom line for institutional success. Those who survive because they have enough consumers are viewed, by definition, as doing a good job. And one way to entice paying customers is to promise that you will meet their needs.

The meeting needs assumption means that we devote a lot of energy to keeping the customers satisfied. We definitely don't want them to feel confused or angry because we have asked them to do something they find difficult and would rather avoid. But this view simply ignores pedagogic reality. As has already been pointed out, anytime someone attempts to learn a challenging or complex theory, or anytime people are pushed to think critically, an ambivalent mix of feelings and emotions is prompted, in which anger and confusion are as prominent as pleasure and clarity. The most hallowed rule of business—that the customer is always right—is often pedagogically wrong. Equating good teaching with how many students feel you have done what they wanted is a dead end that prevents significant learning.

I Can Fix Racism (Sexism, Classism, Ableism)

Zeal and righteous outrage animate many teachers eager to use education as a way to change the world. Turning on the pilot light of your anger at the clear injustice and inequity you see all around gives you the necessary energy to get through days when you'd otherwise feel your work was meaningless. But, as Myles Horton (1997) was fond of saying, you can't let the slow burn of anger consume you in its fire. Burning out is a danger all activist-oriented teachers face as they try to effect social change from inside the academy.

As with several of the hegemonic assumptions we've examined, the assumption that "I can fix racism" harms teachers by inducing enormous guilt when external factors prevent this from happening. If you've gone into teaching fired with an antiracist passion it's demoralizing in the extreme to confront the reality that neither colleagues nor students share this passion. I've spent many hours in conversations with colleagues who feel like quitting because they don't seem to be getting anywhere despite their best efforts. Just as they think they're making progress with a group of students someone says something in class that makes them realize that nothing really significant is happening. They report taking one step forward only to fall two steps back as racist views are expressed in a class where they felt change was taking place.

The I-can-fix-racism assumption overstates the individual power of teachers. "Isms" such as racism, classism, sexism, and ableism are historically produced and systemically embedded. They comprise beliefs and practices entrenched in the culture and reinforced through lifelong socialization. People can push back against these dominant ideologies by naming and challenging them and they can strive to educate students and each other about how to take effective antiracist action. But they can't be fixed by individual agency. A systemic function can be altered only systemically, through, for example, revolutionary political parties or well-organized social movements.

Obviously I'm not saying it's pointless to engage in antiracist work in academe. I spend a lot of time and energy in this work myself and I don't consider it futile, naive, or ill-intentioned. I do it because it's the right thing to do but without any expectation that it will make much difference. Of course I hope it will have some small but significant consequences, but I try not to measure my efforts by how far I've fixed institutional racism. It's hard enough to work on combatting the racism I carry in myself, without thinking I can fix it in anyone else, let alone a whole system.

When you use the kinds of critically reflective lenses outlined in this book you tend to start thinking in big-picture ways and get a better understanding of the constraints to and limitations of your action. Critical reflection helps you situate your classroom and your practices in the structures and systems of the outside world. Although we might like to think that we exercise sole authority over our classroom domain, the reality is that everything we do is framed by history, politics, and culture. Once we start to think structurally we're quick to see that our individual actions, although important and valuable, can't fix systemic problems.

I suppose some might find it pessimistic and demoralizing to realize that their actions will have much smaller consequences than they'd like. To me, however, it's a necessary corrective that helps you stay in this work when not much seems to be happening because of your efforts. I think of it as a kind of critical optometry: getting a new pair of glasses that reveals everything that's going on rather than just what's in front of you.

The I-can-fix-racism assumption serves the interests of institutions that perpetuate racism. If you convince people that instituting a faculty development program, creating a new office of diversity, or changing mission language will address racism in a way that removes the problem from organizational life, then you can convince yourself that the issue has been effectively addressed. Setting up mandatory workshops on dealing with racism or requiring all faculty members to read *Why Are All the Black Kids Sitting Together in the Cafeteria?* (Tatum, 2003) make it appear that serious change is happening. I've visited many campuses where the college or university concerned has created a diversity office run by the only person of color on the senior leadership team. This looks good in institutional brochures but it doesn't fix the problem of embedded systemic racism. That will only be the case if everyone in the institution, from the trustees to the custodial staff, engage in a sustained analysis of the racism embedded within hiring practices, budgetary processes, curriculum, staffing, and myriad daily institutional interactions.

Lest it be thought I'm saying that workshops, appointments, or changes to the mission statement are a waste of time, I want to emphasize that this is *not* the case. I run lots of workshops on teaching about racism and wholeheartedly support efforts to diversify the institution's personnel or to refocus the mission. But I also know these things won't fix racism. They're the daily bread of activism that often leads to desirable and worthwhile small changes. But fixing racism is the job of movements and parties and something that probably will never be fully realized.

At the very least it will take decades to conduct a sustained, painful, and raw societal self-study supported by massive structural change in economic, legal, and political systems. So although introducing racial issues into the classroom, meeting with student groups, and teaching courses on race is important and necessary work, we should abandon the idea that doing these things will fix racism. Address it, absolutely, but don't assess your effectiveness by how much you fix it in individual students, let alone the department, division, or institution.

Conclusion

Hegemonic assumptions are elusive in their ordinariness. When we're immersed in a system that shapes our instincts and responses it's hard to see how it harms us. One key to unraveling hegemony lies in the collaborative process of critical reflection with colleagues explored in chapter 7. When you're running in circles and caught inside a closed loop, it takes questions from someone outside that loop to jerk you into a realization of its insanity.

In this chapter and the ones preceding it I've done my best to define what constitutes critically reflective teaching. To recap, critical reflection happens when we unearth and challenge assumptions that undergird our actions and practices, primarily by viewing those through the four lenses of students' eyes, colleagues' perceptions, personal experiences, and theory. What makes reflection critical is its grounding in critical theory and its consequent focus on illuminating power and uncovering hegemony.

It's time now to start examining the nuts and bolts of the practice of critical reflection, particularly the way that each of the four lenses can be used to uncover our assumptions. In chapter 4 I provide an overview of how these lenses work.

4

The Four Lenses of Critical Reflection

Assumptions are slippery little things that usually can't be seen clearly by an act of self-will. One particular metaphor comes to mind whenever I think of someone trying to uncover their assumptions by deep introspective analysis and that's being in a clothing store. When you're out on the floor trying on your new jacket you have only one mirror view—the front on view you see every day. But step into a changing room with side mirrors and suddenly you see how you look from multiple perspectives. You gain a fuller picture of yourself, one that represents the ways you look in a 360-degree perspective.

The only way we can become aware of our assumptions, particularly ones we've missed or never been aware of, is to view what we do through the equivalent of the side mirrors in the clothing booth. We need to be able to see ourselves from unfamiliar angles. No matter how much we think we have a full and accurate picture of our practice we're always stymied by our personal limitations. It's impossible to become aware of our own interpretive filters by using those same interpretive filters. This is as futile as a dog furiously chasing its tail.

To some extent we're all prisoners trapped within the frameworks we use to assign meaning to our experience. A self-confirming cycle often develops in which our assumptions shape our actions that are then interpreted to confirm the truth of those assumptions. But the four lenses of critical reflection each illuminate a different part of our teaching. Taken together they throw our assumptive clusters into sharp relief by providing multiple perspectives on what we think and do. As already outlined in the opening chapter, these lenses are students' eyes, colleagues' perceptions, theory, and personal experience. In this chapter I want to outline what using each of these lenses entails.

Students' Eyes

In *The Skillful Teacher* (Brookfield, 2015b) I argue that the most important pedagogic knowledge we teachers need to do good work is an awareness, week in, week out, of how our students are experiencing learning. Without this knowledge we are working largely in the dark. In order to make good decisions about the ways we organize learning, construct assignments, sequence instruction, and apply specific classroom protocols we need to know what's going on in students' heads. This is the essence of student-centered teaching: knowing how your students experience learning so you can build bridges that take them from where they are now to a new destination.

Discovering how different students in the same classroom see us is one of the most consistently surprising elements in any teacher's career. Applying one or more of the many classroom assessment techniques available (Butler and McNunn, 2006; Earl, 2012) helps us get inside students' heads and see the classroom as they do. Each time you do this you learn something.

Sometimes the data is reassuring, such as when you find that a method or exercise you employ has the effect you intend for it. It's just as important to know when your assumptions are broadly confirmed as it is to know when they're in error. I need to know that my students are hearing what I want them to hear and seeing what I want them to see. For example, knowing how much students learn from a relevant personal story has encouraged me to work autobiographically whenever it makes sense to do so. Similarly, having learned that students appreciate my constantly talking out loud about my classroom process, I pay special attention to explain the rationale for each new classroom activity before we go into it.

At other times we're stopped in our tracks to discover the diversity of meanings students read into our words and actions. Students hear as imperatives comments we've made unthinkingly that have no particular significance to us. Answers we give off the cuff to what seem like inconsequential questions are later quoted back to us to prove that now we're contradicting ourselves. What we think is reassuring behavior is interpreted as overprotective coddling. What we deem as an inspired moment of creativity on our part that builds spontaneously on an important teachable moment is seen as inconsistent or confusing. What we regard as a lighthearted remark is appreciated by some but seen as an insult by others.

The chief dynamic to consider when using the lens of students' eyes is that of power. Because of our power to award grades and sanction student progress it's not surprising that people are understandably reluctant to be honest with us. Teachers who say they welcome criticism often react very differently when they actually receive it. Some students will have learned that giving honest commentary on a teacher's actions can backfire horribly. It takes a courageous or foolhardy individual to suggest in class that teachers have unwittingly stifled free discussion, broken promises, or played favorites. And, I have to say that given the egomania of some academics, student paranoia is completely justified.

What will help teachers get accurate information from students is anonymity. Students who are genuinely sure that their responses are anonymous are much more likely to tell the truth. So when you request honest and anonymous feedback from a particular class you must demonstrate that you have no idea who is saying what. After students have seen you openly discussing their feedback on the class several times they may decide you're trustworthy enough to speak honestly with you. But never assume that students believe your assurances that you welcome critique, even if you're totally sincere. You need to model a non-defensive gratitude for student criticisms for a sustained period before people will start to take you seriously.

The importance of responding non-defensively to anonymous student feedback is crucial. I've seen far too many colleagues react to criticisms by immediately trying to explain them away. They might not say outright that the students are wrong, but they'll correct students by saying that the point of a particular exercise was clearly not understood, or they'll re-justify why an activity that's been criticized was actually worth doing. In terms of teaching, and in leadership generally, this is an absolute no-no. When you receive negative criticism, even if you think it's fundamentally misguided, you need to start by thanking people for the time they spent giving the criticism. Then, if any part of the criticism is unclear you should ask for people to volunteer clarification, assuring them that no one has to identify him- or herself as the source of the criticism.

When the criticism opens up a new perspective for you then that should be acknowledged. If it highlights a problem that you haven't been aware of you should explain how you're going to try to deal with it. If the criticism asks you to do something that you feel is fundamentally wrong, then you stand your ground by explaining and re-justifying why you can't do what's requested. In leadership classes I often get asked to stop harping on race and have to keep clarifying that for me being aware of racial dynamics is a crucial element of effective leadership. But I try never to blame students for feedback or get irritated with its naivety. It's crucial that you show you take it seriously even when you fundamentally disagree with it.

Sometimes teachers protest that soliciting student feedback takes far too much time and means they can't adequately cover all the content that students need to know in order to move forward in their studies. To this point I always respond the same way. If getting students to understand content correctly is your main job, then the only way you can do this job is to keep checking in that this is happening. Just asking students, "are you following me?" or "is that clear?" is pretty worthless. I can count on the fingers of one hand the times in my life when I've seen students say the equivalent of "actually, no, we don't understand what you're saying." Students will be wary of publicly admitting that they're confused or not following your explanations. But if you institute regular opportunities for students to provide anonymous information on how they're understanding content you'll be much better placed to know whether or not you need to revisit some earlier material, re-explain something, or quicken the pace.

The only way we can know if students are learning what we intend for them to learn is by checking in with them. Sure, you can wait for a midterm exam to find out that things have gone awry, but isn't it better to know as soon as possible that students aren't understanding the all-important content? That way you can adjust or take remedial steps before things get worse and too much time has passed. This deliberately utilitarian justification neatly sidesteps the usual "all this participatory stuff is fine if you had the time but I've got too much content to cover" argument I often hear.

The lens of students' eyes has been the most important of the four critically reflective lenses in my own career and that's why I begin with it. When you understand the different ways students view your practice it can open up productively disturbing insights for you. Assumptions that you believed to be self-evidently true are sometimes shown to be without real empirical foundation.

When it comes to understanding the power dynamics of classrooms I don't see how you can possibly know what these are without regular anonymous student feedback. Many times I've been stopped in my tracks by student comments regarding the exercise of my authority, particularly when I think I'm being transparent, but students see me as shifty or evasive. I've also come to understand the essentials of an ethical use of authority much better: the need to respond non-defensively to criticisms, the need to model my own engagement in any risky activity I'm asking people to do, and the importance of self-disclosure. To me the lens of students' eyes is the Rosetta stone needed to decode assumptions of power.

Colleagues' Perceptions

The presence of critical friends is at the heart of the critically reflective process. A critical friend is someone who strives to help you unearth and check your assumptions and opens you up to new perspectives about familiar problems. When we hit experiential bumps in the road of life or encounter the disorienting dilemmas beloved of transformative learning theorists, the first thing many of us do is run to our best friends. Your truest friends are those who stand by you when you're in trouble. They provide a sympathetic ear as you talk out whatever grief or frustration you're going through. Sometimes this helps you come to new insights about your situation and discover how to deal with it.

The best teaching colleagues are critical friends. They'll encourage you to describe a problem as you see it, take the time to ask you questions about it, and suggest different ways of thinking it through. Institutions may force us to teach solo, and staff meetings may focus on policies, personnel, and organizational difficulties, but in corridors, cafeterias, and sometimes online the real work of teaching is shared. The biggest difficulty I faced as a part-time, adjunct teacher was not having a trusted group of colleagues, or even a single person, I could talk to about the things I was experiencing. Without the need to pay rent I never would have made it through that first year.

Talking to colleagues unravels the shroud of silence in which our work is wrapped. It's one of the many reasons why I prefer team teaching (Plank, 2011). To have a colleague who helps you debrief the class you've just taught and who alerts you to things (positive and negative) you've missed is extremely helpful for your own efforts to check your assumptions about what's happening. In reflection groups talking about classroom dynamics that you think are unique to you usually prompts colleagues to disclose how they negotiate those same dynamics. Sometimes they'll describe a very different interpretation of a situation than the one you hold. This helps you check, verify, or reframe the assumptions you've brought to your own analysis of it.

Some of the best conversations I've had with colleagues concern the nature of resistance to learning. Because I'm a driven, type A personality, I want to do good work and teach classes full of eagerly motivated students. Throughout my career I've had a specific image of a good class. It's one in which everybody says something, there are no awkward silences, students ask provocative and pertinent questions, and there are multiple nonverbal indications of student engagement. People sit on the edge of their chairs leaning forward, their eyes ablaze with enthusiasm, interspersed with frequent nods of recognition, and smiles of appreciation. This unrealistic and naive image is so far removed from what actually happens in most of my classes that I'm constantly fixated on why students seem to be resisting the learning I'm urging on them.

Over the years colleagues have suggested to me some very different readings of, and perspectives on, student resistance. I've realized that students' resistance to my efforts is sometimes grounded in events that happened before I showed up. For example, one year I taught a course that had been identified with a much loved-teacher who didn't get tenure. Not surprisingly, I got a frosty reaction from students in the department. Even if I don't receive a startling new insight from a colleague on why students seem disengaged it's helpful to know I'm not alone. Pretty much every time I ask a colleague to help talk me through a problem I'm facing, that colleague tells me how she or he is also dealing with it. At the very least this makes me feel I'm not a total impostor.

Faculty learning communities—groups of colleagues from across the disciplines coming together to explore a shared problem—provide another avenue of collegial feedback (Felton, Bauman, Kheriaty, and Taylor, 2013; Lenning, Hill, Saunders,

Solan, and Stokes, 2013; Palmer and Zajonc, 2010). During the writing of this book I co-led such a community that focused on exploring racial dynamics in college classrooms. From disciplines as diverse as biology, theology, physics, and art history we shared experiences of both white teachers and teachers of color dealing with expressions of racism in our classes and also approaches to raising racial issues with reluctant students.

In my experience the best teacher-reflection groups are those composed of people from multiple disciplines: art history to engineering, management to theology. Discipline-specific groups have an initial ease but often come to early conclusions. Multidisciplinary groups quickly discover that the problems they face are remarkably similar: how to work with underprepared students, how to sequence curriculum, how to design assignments that test student knowledge accurately, and so on. But the specific ways people describe how they accomplish these tasks in their own subjects varies widely. I have found that people are more likely to discover genuinely new ways to think about problems in multidisciplinary work groups than in discipline-specific ones.

To sum up, when colleagues function as critical friends they affirm that our problems are not idiosyncratic blemishes that we need to keep hidden but shared dilemmas. They help us sort out how we frame a problem and whether the problem we're obsessing about is the real problem we need to deal with. They offer multiple perspectives and viewpoints on a situation and help us decide what parts of our analysis or response are valid and what needs reexamining. Although critical reflection typically is conceptualized and practiced as a solo endeavor, it's actually a collective enterprise. A conversation, whether mediated or unmediated, synchronous or asynchronous, in which colleagues are genuinely seeking to understand how you experience a problem and then reflect back to you their own interpretations and reactions to it, is a fantastic way to open people up to new ways of thinking and acting.

Personal Experience

Of the four lenses of critical reflection this is the lens that gets the least respect. This is because western epistemology is still dictated by its Enlightenment roots and the birth of scientism. This epistemology holds that accurate knowledge is created through the application of protocols developed and monitored by a community of scholars alert to individual subjective bias. Truth is established when the accumulation of insights derived from these applications coalesce into a theory explaining a discrete part of the world. The most effective academic put-down is to dismiss a view or proposition as "merely anecdotal," in other words, as hopelessly subjective or impressionistic. Academic research that investigates personal experience through stories (Shadlow, 2013) or scholarly personal narratives (Nash and Viray, 2013, 2014) has a hard time being accepted as legitimate inside the academy.

Yet accounts of personal experience typically move us more than summaries of findings in a research study. Politicians know that you secure support for a policy by embedding your case for it in a personal story. When I think of the factors that shape how I teach, it's personal experiences of particular teachers that come to mind rather than theories I've studied or research reports I've read. Yet when personal experience is dropped into a conversation about teaching it's often prefaced by someone saying, "of course I've got no real evidence for this; it's just my own experience" as if your own experience should be discounted as inherently invalid.

One of the most stringent objections to taking personal experience seriously is that it's unique and therefore ungeneralizable. It's true that at one level experience is idiosyncratic. No one experiences the death of a parent in exactly the same way as anyone else, with the same mix of memories intertwined into the grief and pain. Yet predictable rhythms of bereavement with their dynamics of denial, anger, and acceptance are discernible across multiple lives.

Specific experiences always have universal elements embedded within them.

The fact that people recognize aspects of their experiences in the stories others tell is one of the appeals of the collegial teacher-reflection groups I described previously. This is why support groups for those going through periods of crisis or transition are so crucial. When I describe how I constantly feel like an impostor I can see the light of mutual recognition dawn in people's eyes. As you hear someone telling how he stopped cancer defining his life, responded to depression, struggled with addiction, or dealt with the death of someone she cared about, you'll hear echoes of, and sometimes direct parallels to, your own experience. The details and characters may differ from case to case, but many of the tensions and dilemmas are the same.

Personal experiences of learning are intertwined with teaching practice. All of us gravitate seemingly instinctively toward certain ways of working. Some teachers rely on group work, others on independent study. Some are compelled to stick to preannounced plans; others delight in breaking away from structures and building on unexpected events. I would argue that we can trace the impulse for many of these decisions back to the kinds of situations in which we felt excited or confused as learners. We assume that what worked for us will be similarly galvanizing for our own students. How we've been bored or engaged as learners, what approaches and activities have helped or inhibited our understanding, which of our teachers made a difference for us and which we felt were a waste of space—all these elements are far more influential than we often realize.

Let me use myself as an example. As a student I was a bad test taker. No matter how hard or long I studied, when I entered the exam room my anxiety was so strong it was hard for me to focus. Consequently, I have a history of failing exams. This means that as a teacher I try to introduce multiple forms of student assessment. I always give second chances, am open to renegotiating aspects of the curriculum, and assume that when students say they need more time they're telling the truth. This is directly a result of my own bad experience with closed-book exams.

Or take the way I run discussions. As a student I hated speaking up in discussions and got very nervous when required to do so. I felt I never sounded smart enough or never had anything worthwhile to say. So I'd stay silent and as much as possible let other students take the risk of speaking up. I was actively thinking about the content of what was being talked about and struggling to understand the different viewpoints expressed, but I just hated opening my mouth.

Because of this experience I structure my own discussions in very specific ways. I use a rubric to grade participation that emphasizes listening and responding rather than speaking a lot or sounding smart. My discussion protocols are designed for introverts and contain specific periods for silent reflection. Some have no speech at all. With my colleague Steve Preskill I've written two books specifically on the dynamics and protocols of discussion (Brookfield and Preskill, 2005, 2016) and pretty much every one of the discussion activities we suggest springs to some degree from my personal experiences as a student participating in discussions.

When it comes to investigating student disengagement or student hostility and resistance to learning, personal experience has provided one of the most fruitful sources of data for me. I simply have to ask myself what typically causes me to disengage from activities in conference sessions, professional development workshops, or faculty meetings. The top ten answers are immediate and clear:

- I don't see the reason why I'm being asked to do a particular activity.
- The instructions provided are unclear.
- The time allowed for it is too short.
- The leader has not demonstrated any commitment to the activity.
- I fail to see how this activity will do anything for me or my colleagues.

- I don't have any experience or knowledge that would enable me to participate.
- I've been burned by participating in similar activities in the past.
- I don't trust the leader.
- I don't want to say anything for fear of looking stupid.
- I'm tired and can't be bothered.

None of these reasons for my disengagement are particularly earth-shattering or dramatic. But associated with each of these reasons are some very vivid personal experiences. I recall faculty meetings in which small-group discussions were called on significant matters with hardly any time allowed for deep conversation. I remember task force meetings in which input was asked for but no guarantee that it would be taken seriously was demonstrated. I remember conference sessions in which presenters asked for early input from the audience that would shape the presentation and then delivered what had clearly been preplanned. And I remember small-group discussions in which the leader said all viewpoints were welcome and then made it subtly clear that some were off limits.

It takes no time at all to remember each of these incidents, and they teach me important lessons. I know I have to be very clear in explaining what's going on and why it's necessary and helpful. I have to make sure I model my own commitment to an activity before asking anyone else to do it. I have to allow sufficient time and not feel I have to cram everything that's important to me into a space that feels rushed for participants. I have to make sure a discussion is one that students bring relevant knowledge to. I have to create opportunities for anonymous participation. And I must never make a promise that I'm not prepared to keep.

Theory

The final lens of critical reflection—theory—is the hardest sell. Time and time again I hear teachers say they don't have time to read or that educational theory and research really doesn't have anything to do with the particularities of their classrooms. It's strange to hear a mistrust of theory voiced by educators, but I also understand why they feel that way. As a writer on critical theory (Brookfield, 2004) I'm often frustrated by the way an activist-inclined body of work intended to bring about democratic socialist transformation can be written so obtusely. Similarly, the hostility of some academic journals to strongly personal descriptive writing means that the last place an instructor will go for help with a teaching problem is to the journal shelves in the library. I know in my own trajectory that I spent years while teaching at Columbia University (New York) writing articles pretty much for the sole purpose of impressing the as-yet-unnamed members of my future tenure and full professor committee. It was only after getting tenure that I was free to write books that were meant to be helpful.

Yet reading theory can sometimes feel like coming home. You stumble on a piece of work that puts into cogent words something you've felt but been unable to articulate. Finding a theorist who makes explicit something you've been sensing or who states publicly what you've suspected privately but felt unable to express is wonderfully affirming. Thirty years ago I remember Paulo Freire in a "talking book" with Ira Shor (Shor and Freire, 1987) stating, "You can still be very critical lecturing. . . . The question is not banking lectures or no lectures, because traditional teachers will make reality opaque whether they lecture or lead discussions. A liberating teacher will illuminate reality even if he or she lectures. The question is the content and dynamism of the lecture, the approach to the object to be known. Does it critically re-orient students to society? Does it animate their critical thinking or not?" (p. 40). This clarified what I'd sensed was an overly simplistic element in my analysis of lectures as inherently authoritarian and discussions as inherently democratic.

When I first read Marcuse's (1965) comments on teaching through democratic discussion, it clarified for me some misgivings that had been bubbling under the surface. Democratic discussion's intent is to honor and respect each learner's voice by valuing all contributions. But the implicit assumption that all contributions to a discussion carry equal weight means discussion leaders rarely point out when a contribution is skewed or just plain wrong. In Marcuse's view, the idea of democratizing discussion groups means that "the stupid opinion is treated with the same respect as the intelligent one, the misinformed may talk as long as the informed, and propaganda rides along with falsehood. This pure tolerance of sense and nonsense is justified by the democratic argument that nobody, neither group nor individual, is in possession of the truth and capable of defining what is right and wrong, good and bad" (1965, p. 94).

This brief comment distilled something I'd felt but been queasy about owning up to. It challenged my reluctance to critique students' factual or reasoning errors and sent me on a journey to understand how to point these out without permanently shutting discussion down. Similarly, Baptiste's (2000, 2001) work on the use of ethical coercion in teaching made me realize how power relations are embedded in the most benign requests I make of students. For example, when I ask a group, "can we form into small groups please?" I'm not really asking a question. I'm *telling* the students to form into small groups. Again, my saying, "I'd like us to turn to page 80 if we can, please" is not an expression of personal preference that students can choose to follow or not. It's a direct instruction. Behind my language of facilitation or encouragement to students is a clear exercise of institutional power.

Theory can also crash into your life in a productively disturbing way by unsettling the groupthink arising from cultural norms and shared experiences. Theory that explodes settled worldviews is important because it combats the groupthink that sometimes emerges in collegial reflection groups. Institutionally sponsored groups, even those with members from very different disciplinary backgrounds and teaching very different kinds of students, nonetheless share a common organizational history and culture. Even at a professional conference where you meet strangers from multiple institutions across the world there's still a disciplinary orientation present that defines what gets talked about and which sources of knowledge are taken seriously.

When a book presents an analysis of a familiar situation that catches you off guard and skews your world, this can be creatively dissonant. I've already talked about how reading Foucault (1980) totally changed the way I thought about power in my classrooms. Similarly, reading about the commission of racial microaggressions (Sue, 2010, 2016), or the ways in which white educators engage in preaching and disdaining when working with supposedly less-enlightened whites (European American Collaborative Challenging Whiteness [(ECCW], 2010), challenged my self-image as a "good white person." This work productively disturbed my sense of myself as someone who was largely free of racism and was one of the "good guys" working for racial justice. Instead I began to investigate how racism lived in me and expressed itself through my actions, an investigation that has led me into a long experimentation with narrative disclosure as a tool of antiracist teaching (Brookfield, 2015A).

Conclusion

Since the first edition of this book appeared in 1995 there's been an explosion in programs and protocols that ask teachers to reflect on their pedagogic experiences. It's not uncommon for reflection to be institutionally mandated and for teachers' reflective capacities to be assessed. Although I'm all in favor of critical reflection and love to be involved with colleagues who are collectively hunting assumptions and opening themselves up to new perspectives, I'm troubled by the notion of mandating and assessing reflective practice. It's so easy for this to become instrumentalized and for reflection to be reduced to a reductionistic checklist: "I uncovered five assumptions this week," "I asked for student feedback in three classes," "I read this article in *The Chronicle of Higher Education*," and so on. Additionally, measures to assess teachers' capacity to reflect on personal experience are designed to record how this happens in individuals. This is a direct contradiction to the way teachers and other practitioners describe how it actually happens. In accounts from multiple educational and human services professions (Bradbury, Frost, Kilminster, and Zukas, 2010; Fook and Gardner, 2007, 2013), it's clear this is a collaborative endeavor.

Finally, there's a mandatory confessional tone to much of what passes for reflective practice. In an interesting application of Foucault's (1997) notion of confessional practices, Fejas (2016) points out how performance appraisals ask teachers to gaze into themselves: "to scrutinize their inner selves—that is, to turn their gaze towards who they 'truly are' and who they wish to become" (p. 8). There's a subtle trajectory implied in asking employees to reflect—what we might call the mandated confessional. Reporting in an end-of-year appraisal interview that your reflection has pretty much confirmed what you thought at the beginning of the year, that no new insights into teaching have emerged, and that no perspectives transformed is probably not going to cut it. What's called for is a dramatic transformation along the lines of "I used to hold this erroneous assumption but by reflecting on my practice I've transformed my experience and have a wholly new perspective."

So although I advocate for critical reflection (indeed chapter 5 extols its benefits at length) I'm suspicious of its mandatory measurement. When reflective assessment protocols are determined in advance, and teachers are required to show a suitable level of reflectivity to get reappointment, promotion, and tenure, the collaborative and collective dimension of reflection is entirely lost. Measuring reflection becomes a power play, a way for administrators to control employees by specifying the type of reflection that's permissible or legitimate. Instead of being a collective journey into mutual ambiguity it becomes a means of aligning individual actions and preferences with institutional needs.

The lenses explored in this chapter provide four different ways for teachers to look at what they do. All teachers have access to all of them, though the degree to which they can use a particular one depends on external constraints, the chief of which is time. The larger the class, the more complex is the process of seeing our teaching through students' eyes. Adjuncts shuttling between multiple institutions have little chance to form collegial relationships. Personal experience is easily discounted as subjective and unreliable, and good theory takes time to locate and study. But, as we shall see in chapter 5, when we try to build these lenses into our teaching we do better work.

5

Clarifying the Benefits of Critical Reflection

In this chapter I want to review the claims that can be made for integrating the critically reflective habit into our teaching. Critical reflection is not a means of ensuring alignment with an institutional mission or a way to secure institutional accreditation. The last thing I want is for it to be formulaically applied to keep teachers in line. On the contrary, critical reflection illuminates and challenges subtly hidden forms of manipulation. The case for reflection lies instead in the pursuit of pedagogic, political, and emotional clarity.

Because teachers are caught in webs of power relationships and often embrace assumptions that harm them, the critically reflective habit is a survival necessity. But, given the time and energy the process requires, it's often viewed as an add-on, something that would be nice to incorporate if we had the time but that can wait until things start to slow down (a time that, of course, never arrives). If things seem to be going well and students aren't complaining then critical reflection may seem totally unnecessary. Why bother to do this if everything's ticking along nicely?

It's easy to understand why reflection is often considered to be primarily a problem-solving process that's invoked only when something's not working. Unfortunately this fix-it approach casts reflection as a tool of institutional control to be employed when someone needs remediation or when a skill deficit needs to be addressed. But critical reflection is not a remedial tool; it's a stance of permanent inquiry. Teachers committed to this stance build it into their pedagogic lives. You don't just use the four lenses when something goes awry. Instead, uncovering assumptions becomes part and parcel of what it means to do good professional work.

It Helps Us Take Informed Actions

Teachers worth their salt want to do good work. They want students to understand and apply important content knowledge correctly and to develop a sophisticated command of required skills. If I sequence classroom activities in a particular way to ensure students understand a theory properly, I want to be sure that's what's happening. If I use an example because I think it illustrates a complex idea I want that to be the case. The actions I take are all based on the meta-assumption that they'll help students learn.

Critical reflection raises our chances of taking informed actions. By informed actions I mean those that are based on assumptions that have been carefully and critically investigated. Informed actions can be explained and justified to interested colleagues and students and their rationale can be clearly communicated. If requested, we can set out the experiential and empirical evidence that undergirds these assumptions and the theory that informs them.

Informed actions stand a good chance of achieving the consequences intended for them. They're taken against a backdrop of inquiry into how people perceive what we say and do. When we behave in certain ways we usually expect students and colleagues to read into our behaviors the meanings we intend. Sometimes, however, our words and actions are given meanings that are very different from, and sometimes directly antithetical to, those we proposed. When we've seen our practice through students' eyes and colleagues' perceptions we're in a better position to speak and behave in ways that ensure a greater consistency of meaning.

I don't want to suggest though that critical reflection results in unalloyed clarity. Because of the complexities and ambiguities of human communication, meaning is inherently uncontrollable. Postmodernists remind us of the dangers of logocentrism, of thinking that words have a core central meaning that can be uncovered by diligent inquiry. In fact meaning is a wild chameleon, roaming unbounded across multiple terrains and constantly changing its colors depending on the identities and experiences of its creators. However, I am modernistic enough to believe that we can decrease communicative ambiguities. I don't think we live on isolated islands of experience with no possibility of shared meaning.

It Helps Us Develop a Rationale for Practice

The critically reflective habit confers a deeper benefit than that of procedural utility. It grounds not only our actions but also our sense of who we are as teachers in an examined reality; we know why we believe what we believe. Critically reflective teachers are well placed to communicate to colleagues and students the rationale behind their practice. They work from a position of informed commitment and convey a confidence-inducing sense of purpose. Having a rationale composed of your basic beliefs and working assumptions functions similar to a pedagogic gyroscope. It helps you when you have to make decisions in difficult situations and stabilizes you when you feel swept along by forces you can't control.

This is important because we all find ourselves in situations in which no single response or action suggests itself, and we all feel from time to time that we've been blown wildly off course. In my world this usually happens when I introduce racial issues into a discussion and someone says something that instantly raises the temperature in the room from a comfortably uncertain simmer to a searing, red-hot boil. It's as if an unseen hand has just turned the gas control from off to ignite. In this situation I try to keep from burning up by recalling my guiding beliefs about discussing race: that strong emotions can be expressed, that students are not bullied or shut down, that everyone has the chance to be involved, that agreement or consensus is not the point of a discussion, and that the focus should be on understanding the different experiences that shape the different opinions expressed. I also remember my mantra that I should model risk taking before asking anyone else to do so.

Oftentimes it's my job to remind the group (and myself) of this rationale and the guidelines that flow from it. If critical reflection's purpose is to uncover and challenge power dynamics I need to be ready to clarify for students the rationale informing my own exercise of authority over them. I never deny my institutional power. Instead, I try to clarify how and why I'm directing students' learning and to invite challenges and critiques of that process. Of course doing this doesn't solve the problem of emotions boiling over. Instead it recasts this problem as a predictable and necessary dynamic that will be present in any discussion of hot topics. That reminds people that emotional spillage is the inevitable accompaniment of trying to probe raw and painful issues.

A critical rationale also helps in building a trustful environment. As I make clear in *The Skillful Teacher* (2015b), a teacher's ability to explain what she stands for and why she believes this is important is a crucial factor in establishing her credibility with students. Even students who disagree fundamentally with a teacher's rationale gain confidence from knowing what it is. In this instance knowledge really is power. According to students, the worst position to be in is to sense that a teacher has an agenda and a preferred way of working but to be unsure exactly what these are. Without this information, they complain, how can they trust the teacher or know what they're dealing with?

Although developing a rationale for practice should span a career it's particularly important for junior faculty members in their first year of teaching, for teaching assistants, and for adjuncts. All of these may have a question mark against them in students' eyes concerning their presumed lack of experience. Getting into the habit of explaining why you're doing what you're doing and why you're asking students to engage in a particular activity is one way to establish your credibility. Students say it inspires confidence to see that teachers clearly have a plan, a set of reasons informing their actions. So you need to get into the habit of speaking out loud why you're introducing a specific exercise, changing learning modalities, choosing certain readings, demonstrating skills in a particular way, putting students into groups, or moving into a mini-lecture.

I would venture that it's almost impossible to overdo this activity of talking out loud your rationale for practice. In class feedback I've collected over the years appreciation of this behavior is an amazingly consistent theme. Students repeatedly say how reassuring it is to know that they're in the hands of a trusted guide. This shouldn't be surprising. After all, knowing why doctors wish us to take particular medications is an important element in our trusting that they have our best interests at heart and that they know what they're doing. Knowing why an auto mechanic is suggesting that a certain part needs to be replaced is crucial to our trusting that we're not being conned. The same holds true for teachers. If students are to have confidence in our abilities they need to know, and trust, that there's a rationale behind our actions and choices.

So a critical rationale for practice—a set of assumptions and beliefs borne of examined experience that we consult as a guide to help us decide how we should act in unpredictable situations— is a psychological, pedagogic, professional, and political necessity. That doesn't mean, however, that it's static. As contexts change so do elements of our rationale. For example, after four decades of teaching I've completely rethought my understanding of teacher power and my responsibility to direct classroom process. I've always seen my job as being to help students learn but my understanding of how modeling helps that process came relatively late in my career. So although foundational commitments such as the importance of democratizing classrooms or encouraging critical thinking may remain unaltered, our understanding of how to make those things happen changes and evolves.

It Helps Us Survive the Emotional Roller Coaster of Teaching

Twenty-first century teaching is a roller coaster. Teachers are under pressure to teach larger and larger classes and to deal with astonishingly diverse groups of students drawn from equally multiracial communities. They work in a world in which technology changes daily. The need to curtail spending while maximizing student revenue pushes administrators to require more online teaching. Some students manifest a culture of entitlement in which they view the teacher's responsibility as being to keep learning fun with no need for students to struggle and slog through complexity. Whether in a tenured line or on an annually renewable contract, teachers know they have to secure favorable student evaluations to keep a job. And they have to do all these things while publishing and serving their institutions and their professional fields. Furthermore, faculty members of color are also expected to educate their white colleagues about racism.

Not surprisingly, a lot of teachers feel they work at the center of a hurricane, tossed this way and that by whatever winds prevail most strongly at any moment. Administrators double your class size or "accelerate" a program, cutting the instructional time by half. Students show up with a degree of hostility you can't fathom or overwhelm you with endless individual requests for assistance and petitions to raise their grade. Questions take you off guard, technology doesn't function thereby destroying your lesson plan, or a small cabal of students railroads the class preventing anyone else from participating. Although a degree of unpredictability keeps you on your toes and can be pleasingly capricious, to be permanently tossed around like a cork on a roiling sea induces permanent motion sickness.

If we've never researched our assumptions through the four critically reflective lenses we have available we have the sense that our world is essentially chaotic. Whether or not we do well seems to be largely a matter of luck. Lacking a reflective orientation we place an unseemly amount of trust in the role of chance. We inhabit what Freire (Freire and Bergman, 2000) calls a *condition of magical consciousness*. Fate or serendipity, not human agency, appears to shape whether or not things go well in class. The world is experienced as arbitrary, as governed by a whimsical god.

When we think this way we're powerless to control the roller coaster ebb and flow of our emotional responses to work. One day a small success (such as a student asking a good question) causes us to blow our level of self-confidence out of all proportion. The next, an equally small failure (such as one bad evaluative comment out of twenty good ones) is taken as a devastating indictment of our inadequacy. Teachers caught on this emotional roller coaster, where every action either confirms their brilliance or underscores their failure, cannot survive intact for long. They get off the roller coaster by either withdrawing from the classroom or suppressing their emotions.

One of the biggest killers of morale is the sense that our efforts are in vain. To labor diligently to no apparent effect destroys the soul. Pouring your whole being into a committed attempt to change students and feeling as if none of that effort makes any difference leave you demoralized and hopeless. But using the lens of students' eyes gives you a more accurate sense of what's really happening in your classrooms by illuminating the small changes and incremental gains taking place.

For example, in the middle of lectures I often feel I've totally lost students. Blank faces and a lack of questions from a group leave me feeling powerless. I'm tempted to tell a joke, pull up a YouTube video, or put them into small groups for no other reason than I'm having a pedagogic panic attack and want to make it look like something's happening.

But sometimes I've often found that what I assumed was total disengagement actually masked a reasonable level of interest. By asking for questions to be posted on www.todaysmeet.com or by using a classroom research technique such as the Critical Incident Questionnaire (CIQ) I get a quick snapshot of what students are thinking. Sessions that I've assumed were total duds have received good feedback from students who wrote about the way they were helped to understand concepts they've struggled with or how a new piece of information clarified something that had previously been confusing.

The lens of colleagues' perceptions also alerts me to things I've missed in class, such as comments students make, questions they ask, or answers they provide. Before I team taught I used to think I had total recall of pretty much everything that happened in class. Now I know that I miss an awful lot and that I can't trust the evidence of my own eyes when I'm trying to gauge whether or not something is working. A colleague's perspective can help me distinguish between situations that are genuinely disastrous and those in which an interesting variety of contradictory student responses are present.

It Helps Us Avoid Self-Laceration

Teachers who want to do good work are often prone to self-laceration. By that I mean that they automatically blame themselves if students seem not to be learning. These teachers (and I'm one of them) feel that at some level they're the cause of the anger, hostility, resentment, or indifference that even the best and most energetic of them are bound to encounter from time to time. Believing themselves to be the cause of these emotions and feelings, they automatically infer that they're also their solution. They assume the responsibility for turning hostile, bored, or puzzled students into galvanized advocates for their disciplines brimming over with the joys of learning. When this doesn't happen (as is almost always the case) these teachers allow themselves to become consumed with guilt for what they believe is their pedagogic incompetence.

In my own case impostorship and a tendency to self-deprecation often cause me to conclude I'm failing. Combine these with an unreasonably inflated image of what a successful class looks like (no silence, students on the edge of their seats, a brilliantly charismatic teacher) and you have a perfect trifecta for the presumption of constant failure. I've consistently fallen prey to the myth described by Britzman (2003) that everything depends on the teacher. This myth holds that whatever happens is the result of the teacher's actions. If the class goes well it's because the teacher's been engaging, energetic, paced instruction well, and used appropriate examples. If it goes badly it's because she or he has been sluggish, boring, misunderstood students' readiness for learning, and spoken confusingly. Because I subscribe to this myth I'm constantly berating myself for not producing a stream of engaging classrooms.

Viewing work through the four lenses of critically reflective practice brings a much-needed counterbalance to the effects of this myth. Being aware of the complex and sometimes contradictory nature of students' responses to the same classroom event helps keep the effects of your actions in perspective. The more you look through the lens of students' eyes, the more you realize that multiple worlds exist in the classroom. Students bring vastly different experiences, readiness for learning, personalities, racial and cultural traditions, and abilities to any particular activity. Student feedback that illustrates this reality stops you falling into the trap of thinking that you're controlling every response.

Similarly, even the most cursory reading of theory on student learning makes you aware of the multiple models of student development, information processing, identity creation, and cognition that exist. Understanding how difficult it is for students to make the transition from binary and dichotomous reasoning to thinking dialectically and contextually has made me much more aware of the difficulties in developing critical thinking (Brookfield, 2012). Colleagues who understand the pedagogic complexities of working with diverse groups can also talk me down from my snap hysterical judgment that I should quit teaching because things suddenly spiraled unpredictably out of control.

A healthy sense of perspective regarding the limits of your own influence is an ontological survival necessity for any teacher. Keep thinking that everything depends on you and self-laceration will be your constant friend. Being aware of the complexity of your world can initially be unsettling, inducing an analysis of paralysis. If so much is out of our control then what's the point of doing anything? But in the long run a clear-eyed view of just how little control we have can keep self-laceration to a minimum.

It Enlivens Our Classrooms

Although this chapter explores the benefits of critical reflection for us as teachers, it's important to note that it affects students, too. One of the most important of these concerns the way it helps students to think more critically. In my own research into critical thinking (Brookfield, 2012) students' report that teacher modeling is crucial in helping them learn to think critically. When it comes to students' learning how to practice this skill it seems they constantly look to us to see what the process looks like. They also say that we earn the right to ask them to think critically by first doing it ourselves. So before we ask students to unearth and research their assumptions we must show how we're attempting to do the same thing.

Teachers engaged consistently in critical reflection have multiple opportunities to model the process for students. The more we provide examples of how we're checking our assumptions about the subject we're teaching, or assumptions about the way we construct the syllabus and run the class, the more students appreciate our modeling of criticality. For example, the CIQ I describe in chapter 6 involves teachers regularly reporting out students' feedback. As I do this I disclose which of my assumptions were confirmed by their comments and which were challenged. I also introduce any new issues or perspectives that students' comments brought to my attention. These often cause me to change how I'm running a particular activity or to drop or add exercises. Here students see how a critically reflective stance continually reshapes thinking and practice.

Critically reflective teachers activate their classrooms by providing a model of continuous inquiry. By openly questioning their own ideas and assumptions—even as they explain why they believe in them so passionately—they create a climate in which accepting change and risking failure are valued. By inviting students to critique our efforts—and by showing them that we appreciate these critiques and treat them with the utmost seriousness—we deconstruct traditional power dynamics and relationships that stultify critical inquiry. A teacher who models critical reflection on her own practice is one of the most powerful catalysts for critical thinking in her own students.

It Keeps Us Engaged

One of the problems many of us face as the years pass by is our teaching becomes stale. As we travel further and further from our first tension-filled days in class, and as we become more and more confident in our content knowledge and our ability to anticipate students' questions or reactions, it's easy to relax to the point where predictability and even boredom take over. Semesters come and go, we get older, gain promotion, and sometimes get tenure. In such circumstances we risk going on automatic pilot teaching the same content, using the same proven exercises, assigning the same texts, and setting the same assignments. A certain emotional flatness sets in, followed by a disinterest in the dynamics of our practice.

When we practice critical reflection this staleness quickly dissipates. We discover that things are happening in our classes of which we had no awareness. Actions we thought were transparent and unequivocal are seen to be perceived in multiple and sometimes contradictory ways by students and colleagues alike. Books give us new takes on familiar dilemmas that we thought were impenetrable, colleagues offer us ways of dealing with problems we had not thought of before, and students constantly surprise us with their privately felt (but not publicly voiced) reactions to our practice.

Teaching in a critically reflective way keeps us alert. It's mindful teaching practiced with the awareness that things are rarely what they seem. For faculty members in mid- or late career, introducing the critically reflective habit into their lives can make the difference between marking time until retirement and being genuinely engaged in the classroom. For example, I began conducting weekly inquiries into how students experience learning in my classrooms in the early 1990s after receiving tenure and a full professorship at Columbia. Since then I've found out some amazing things that have surprised me:

- Students find appropriate autobiographical disclosure to be enormously helpful in understanding complex concepts.
- Publicly reporting and discussing students' criticisms of my teaching has led to end-of-course evaluations mentioning the word *trust* for the first time.
- My silence is perceived in multiple and contradictory ways.
- The how of teaching and leadership (the ways you treat people) is often more important than the what (the specific content or actions you're responsible for teaching).
- My identity as a white male means my actions (such as admitting to errors) are perceived in very different ways than those of my colleagues of color and female faculty members.
- Constantly explaining why you're running a class the way you are builds credibility in students' eyes.
- Deliberate periods of silence are very important for a lot of students who appreciate the time to process new information and formulate responses.
- Members of a teaching team disagreeing in front of a class is one of the most exciting moments for students.

- I regularly commit racial, gender, and ableist micro-aggressions.
- Authority is not necessarily authoritarian.
- My power never leaves the room.

These insights have had a significant impact on my teaching. I've gotten into the habit of working in a more self-consciously autobiographical way when that's appropriate. I've also forced myself to introduce a meta-commentary on my teaching, constantly explaining why exercises are set up the ways they are and why I'm asking students to do something at a particular time. Silence is far more prevalent in my class than in the first two decades of my teaching. And if I can't team teach a course I'm constantly pushing for colleagues to come in for brief visits so we can model a critical dialogue for students.

These insights have also complicated my life. I'm much less confident about trusting the evidence of my own eyes. When my wife asks me, "how did class go?" I usually answer "it's hard to tell" or "I need to read the CIQs to know what went on." Knowing how racism and patriarchy keep reproducing themselves in my actions has productively troubled me. I'll often stop in the middle of class and say to students, "you know that was a microaggression I committed right there" or "wow, what an unexamined exercise of power that was!"

These days the best part of any teaching day is often when I get to read students' anonymous comments on their CIQs. Usually I can't even wait to get to the office to read them. I linger in the room as new students file in for the class after mine curiously scanning my students' responses. I want to know how they experienced specific exercises and the degree to which my own perceptions of what went well and what misfired match theirs. In the past I'd often leave a class session thinking "that was okay" and that was that. Now my teaching has become a fluctuating and evolving focus of study. I'm constantly surprised by what I find, sometimes disappointed, and sometimes proud. But I'm never bored.

It Models the Democratic Impulse

What we do as teachers makes a difference in the world. In our classrooms students learn democratic or manipulative behavior. They learn whether independence of thought is really valued or whether everything depends on pleasing the teacher. They learn either that success depends on beating someone to the prize using whatever advantage they can or on working collectively. Standing above the fray by saying that our practice is apolitical is not an option for a teacher. Even if we profess to have no political stance and to be concerned purely with furthering inquiry into a discrete body of objective ideas or practices, what we do counts. The ways we encourage or inhibit students' questions, the kinds of reward systems we create, and the degree of attention we pay to learners' concerns all create a moral tone and a political culture. This is just as true in an accountancy or calculus class as it is in a social justice seminar.

Teachers who have learned the reflective habit know something about the effects they're having on students. They're alert to the presence of power in their classrooms and to its possibilities for misuse. Knowing that their actions can silence or activate students' voices, they listen seriously and attentively to what students say. They deliberately create public reflective moments when students' concerns—not the teacher's agenda—are the focus of classroom activity. Week in, week out, they make public disclosure of private realities, both to students and to colleagues. They constantly try to find out how students are experiencing their classes and then to make this information public. Their actions are explicitly grounded in reference to students' experiences, and students know and appreciate this.

For all these reasons critically reflective teaching is inherently democratic. Democracy is not always the exercise of majority vote. In fact there are multiple conceptions of democratic process, including the *Parecon* (Albert, 2004) principle that those most affected by the consequences of a decision have the greatest say in making it. For me democracy is an ever-widening conversation regarding how best to steward community resources for the good of all. It requires the widest possible range of voices to be included and the consideration of multiple perspectives on an issue or decision. It also emphasizes the pursuit of perspective taking (Mezirow, 1991) or intersubjective understanding (Habermas, 1979), that is, doing your level best to understand viewpoints different from your own.

If democracy is conceived as a decision-making conversation in which participants strive to be as open to as many different ideas and experiences as possible, then the connection to critical reflection is clear. Both processes require people to see things through multiple lenses and to be ready to question their habitual assumptions depending on the new ideas and viewpoints they encounter. And both stress people changing their thinking and their actions based on exposure to new information. So anytime you involve students and colleagues in the critically reflective process, you're striving to realize the democratic impulse in the classroom. Similarly, when you show students how you're constantly checking out your own assumptions and looking at your practice through the four lenses you have available, you're modeling a commitment to democracy for them.

It Increases Trust

One of my clearest memories as a graduate student was meeting my doctoral supervisor for the first time to get feedback on my PhD proposal. At that initial meeting he gave me some bad news. My methodology, he told me, had to be completely redesigned.

Essentially the methodology I was proposing (a survey question-naire) did not fit the question I was seeking to answer (how do working-class adults who have left school with no formal qualifica-tions come to be recognized as regional or national experts in a par-ticular field of endeavor?). He encouraged me to use a new form of qualitative research known as grounded theory. This sounded very imprecise and unacademic to me. Interviewing people and then changing the focus of your study based on what you're discovering? Surely you can't get a PhD for doing that!

The interesting thing was that when he put this enormous roadblock in my way I didn't feel resentful or that I was on the receiving end of some kind of power play. To the contrary, I knew he was doing this in my own best interests. The way he gave his direction somehow convinced me he was on my side. For example, he spelled out all the reasons why a positivistic survey question-naire wouldn't help me get at the information I needed to answer my research question. He explained the different methodological options he'd considered and clarified their advantages and draw-backs. He helped me understand the assumptions that informed my choice of a survey questionnaire methodology and showed me how those assumptions needed reappraisal. In doing so he helped me to realize that the reason I chose the method I did was essen-tially because I assumed this was what scholarly rigor looked like. My acceptance of the groupthink governing what counts as legiti-mate educational research was framing my choices and decisions.

This same dynamic was repeated multiple times over the three years during which my doctoral advisor and I met regularly. I would bring my latest work to him and he would question me about the assumptions underlying my construction of data collection instru-ments, interpretation of findings, and my decisions regarding next steps in the research. Often he'd introduce me to a new author's work or to a concept I'd not considered, constantly expanding my perspectives. His questions would point out contradictions or omissions in my thinking, requiring me to go back and reconsider much of what I'd already done. But none of this made me angry. In fact, the contrary was the case. I came to trust him.

Coming to trust another person is the most fragile of human projects. It requires knowing someone over a period of time and seeing their honesty modeled in their actions. Done well, critically reflective teaching models the conditions in which people can learn to trust or mistrust each other. Teachers who take students seriously and who treat them as adults show that they can be trusted. Teachers who go to the trouble of soliciting regular anonymous student feedback, reading it carefully, and then responding to it in a non-defensive way are far more likely to be trusted than those who never share with students how class feedback has confirmed or challenged their assumptions. Teachers who encourage students to point out how teachers' actions are oppressive and who seek to change what they do in response to students' concerns are models of critical reflection. Such teachers are those who truly are trustworthy.

Conclusion

This chapter has built a case regarding the importance of the critically reflective process. I have tried to argue that viewing our practice through the four lenses we have available to us is pedagogically helpful, emotionally necessary, and politically significant. I should also acknowledge, however, that the process is inherently destabilizing. It often complicates our lives by revealing the complex diversity of our classrooms. It brings us a more sophisticated awareness of the workings of power. And, in focusing on hegemony, it puts us on high alert for times we're being manipulated. In chapter 6 I examine in much greater detail the first of these destabilizing lenses—that of students' eyes.

6

Seeing Ourselves through Students' Eyes

Of all the pedagogic tasks teachers face, getting inside students' heads is one of the trickiest. It's also one of the most crucial. When we start to see our classrooms and our teaching through students' eyes we become aware of the complex and sometimes contradictory perceptions students have of the same event. If we know something about the range of symbolic meanings our actions have for students, we're better able to judge how to behave in a way that has the effects we're seeking. For example, when we know that our silence is never meaningless or innocent to students (it implies approval or condemnation, and it's confusing or helpful depending on the student or task) we're reminded of the need constantly to say out loud what we're thinking. Or, if students tell us that they like the way that specific discussion protocols democratize participation, we make sure we use these regularly. In this chapter I want to argue that seeing ourselves through students' eyes is the best way to unearth the power dynamics of college classrooms and help us recognize hegemony.

Students' Eyes and Student-Centeredness

Gathering information about the effects of our teaching on students is probably something that most of us feel we do already. After all, many colleges require faculty members to hand out to students some kind of standardized evaluation form at the last meeting of a course. Students are asked to comment on items such as our clarity of exposition, pacing of the class, or responsiveness to questions. We usually get to see the results of these evaluations, and information from them is then used in decisions concerning our reappointment, promotion, and tenure.

Although any data on our practice is helpful, this approach suffers from two drawbacks. First it's summative, after the fact. If the form tells us that something important needs to be addressed we have no chance to do so with the current group of students. There's nothing more frustrating than finding out after a course has finished that you've been using confusing examples, that students don't feel prepared for finals, that you rarely make eye contact, or that you speak much too fast. Yes, you can work on remedying these things with the next group of students that comes along, but the group that's bothered by them has gone. So although end-of-course student evaluation-of-teaching (SET) forms are certainly one source of useful data information, they're irrelevant in terms of daily pedagogy.

Second, it's hard to know exactly what SET forms measure. As Stark and Freishtat's (2014) evaluation of SETs observes, "We don't measure teaching effectiveness. We measure what students say and pretend it's the same thing. We calculate statistics, report numbers and call it a day" (p. 9). Summative SET forms often leave us in the dark regarding the dynamics and rhythms of learning because they focus mostly on students' perceptions of the externals of teacher performance, such as clarity of expression, frequency of evaluation, or organization of lectures.

I'm not advocating that we abandon SET forms, only suggesting that we don't overemphasize their significance. I take these forms seriously and am always pleased when students say they've found a course useful or that I'm a good teacher. But in terms of the business end of critical reflection—the daily effort to see what we do through students' eyes and to use that information to confirm or challenge our assumptions about what's helping learning—they really have no effect.

Striving to see what we do through students' eyes is at the heart of student-centered teaching (Watts, 2016; Weimer, 2013). By student-centered teaching I don't mean polling the class about what people want to learn and then doing what you can to support those expressed wants. I mean instead (1) designing whatever you want to teach informed by what you've found out about student experiences, ability levels, racial and cultural identities, and so on and then (2) constantly researching their responses to learning and making continuous adjustments based on what you find out.

Student- or learner-centered teaching is discovering as much as you can about your learners so you can craft an instructional sequence that takes them deep into territory you feel they need to explore. It's all about building bridges that connect where they are now with where you wish them to go. You can't create appropriate links between past experiences and new material if you don't know what those experiences are. And, unless you have information about how students are learning and which activities are helping them learn, you can't make good choices about what to do next in class. Knowing something of how students experience learning helps us create connections between their previous knowledge and skills and where we want to take them. Researching students' perceptions of our actions and words alerts us to problems and mistakes that otherwise we might miss. It also tells us what's working and why. This, in turn, means we can make more accurately grounded decisions about how and what to teach.

Some awareness of how students are experiencing learning is the foundational, first-order knowledge we need to do good work as teachers. Without this knowledge all the pedagogic skill in the world means very little because that skill is being exercised in a vacuum of misinformation. This contention is generally accepted in the scholarship of college teaching and learning as evinced by the impressive body of work on evidence-based teaching (Buskist and Groccia, 2011), classroom response systems (Bruff, 2009), and classroom assessment techniques (Dana and Yendol-Hoppey, 2009). More recently social media (Joosten, 2012) have been adapted as a tool for teachers to gain knowledge about how their students are processing information in the middle of a class.

The Unwitting Diktat: An Illustration of Power Dynamics

Students' perceptions are especially helpful to us when it comes to surfacing issues of power. Seeing situations through students' eyes illuminates how power dynamics permeate and structure all their interactions with us. No matter how carefully we monitor our actions we can never really know their full impact on students. Events, words, and decisions that to us mean very little are sometimes taken as highly significant expressions of our power and authority by students. Let me give an illustration.

I once taught an introductory-level course designed to introduce students to a new program of study. I did so with what I thought was a pretty sophisticated awareness of how patterns of interaction structured by participants' race, class, and gender quickly emerge in class discussions unless a deliberate intervention is made to stop this happening. Early in the course I said that I didn't want anyone to take up a disproportionate amount of airtime and suggested that one way to do this was to have a "three-person rule." This rule states that once someone has said something she or he can't speak again until at least three other people have spoken. The only time this rule can be contravened is if the original speaker is explicitly invited to say more by another member of the group. I asked what people thought of this idea. There was no particular response to my proposal that I remember so I dropped the idea.

Six or seven weeks later I was reading the CIQ responses for that week's class. Out of eighteen completed forms there were five mentions of how students were finding it increasingly difficult to speak in the group. These students reported how they thought I was continuously stifling discussion. I was staggered. Here I had been priding myself on my awareness of the traps of antidemocratic discourse and my expertise in dialogic process. Yet it seemed that I had created exactly the consequence that I had been seeking to avoid. Several students were clearly feeling inhibited from speaking by my apparently arbitrary exercise of teacher power.

When I reported the CIQ feedback to them at the next week's class I asked students to tell me why some might feel inhibited about speaking up. Turns out they had been slavishly following the three-person rule since the time I had airily mentioned it and then assumed it had been rejected. What I believed had been a suggestion that had fallen flat on its face had been heard by them as a diktat, a teacher imperative. As a consequence they had been strenuously monitoring their own speech and feeling frustrated at the constraint I had imposed on their participation.

I had no awareness that some students were observing what they felt was an unfairly imposed rule. If the CIQ feedback had not been available a power dynamic that was oppressive and unhelpful would have continued to influence how students spoke to each other and to me. A group of students would have continued to feel angry at what they saw as my attempt to shut them down and I would have been wholly unaware this was happening.

In the rest of this chapter I want to propose a number of methods you can use to become a phenomenological detective and get inside students' heads. Doing this enables you to draw a primitive but useful map of the emotional and cognitive topography of your classrooms. I then describe in detail one instrument—the CIQ— that's been particularly helpful to me in finding out what is really going on in my classrooms.

The One-Minute Paper

The one-minute paper is one of the best-known classroom research techniques. Students are asked to spend one minute writing a quick response to a specific question asked about the subject matter covered in class that day. The one-minute paper can be used at the beginning of class to prep for discussion or to orient students toward the theme of the lecture. When used this way students can be asked to write a response to questions such as, "why is the topic of today's lecture important?" or "what's the most important question we need to address in today's discussion?" Time then needs to be allotted for students to share their responses with each other or with the teacher.

When used at the end of class (which is how I use it) the one-minute paper assesses students' comprehension of ideas covered in the discussion or lecture. Here students are asked questions such as, "what was the most important idea or insight that you learned today?" or "what new information on this topic took you by surprise today?" The teacher uses students' responses to decide how to structure the next class, what points need revising, and so on.

The one-minute paper also encourages students to start thinking about where they go next with their learning. After a discussion my one-minute paper question is usually, "what issue was raised in class today that most needs addressing next time we meet?" Themes that emerge from these papers can then be used to begin the discussion the next time the class meets.

The Muddiest Point

In the muddiest point exercise students are asked to jot down their response to a question along the lines of "what's the muddiest point in the material covered in class today?" Variations on this question are "what's the most confusing idea we addressed today?" or "what information was most poorly explained today?" These last two questions are appropriate for lecture or discussion-based classes. In demonstration-based teaching in labs or skills-building classes I ask, "what process was most confusingly demonstrated today?" or "what's least clear for you about how to implement the technique we practiced today?" The muddiest point provides an indication of what needs to be reviewed next time the class meets. Depending on what the responses reveal, we can judge whether the level of confusion is roughly what we'd expect at this stage of the course or whether we need to take a serious look at slowing down the pace of the class in order to revisit earlier concepts or skills.

The Learning Audit

In the learning audit students are asked to respond to three questions at the end of the last class of the week:

- What do I know now that I didn't know this time last week?
- What can I do now that I couldn't do this time last week?
- What could I teach others to know or do that I couldn't teach them last week?

The origins of this instrument lie in students' complaints that they're learning nothing, making no progress, getting nowhere. It's pretty depressing to hear students say this, particularly if you sense it might indeed be true. However, another interpretation of these complaints is also possible. Perhaps small incremental learning gains are being made without students noticing this is happening. In completing the audit, learners sometimes realize that more is going on than they'd assumed. Over several weeks students can review their audit responses and notice that by putting together the small things they're able to know and do at the end of each week some cumulative progress has occurred.

Clickers

Clickers enable students to register their vote regarding the accuracy of a series of statements. A statement or number of statements is put on the screen and students are given a few seconds to click on the one they most agree with or think is the most valid. In his interviews with college teachers who used clickers Bruff (2009) noted how these were viewed as a stimulus to critical classroom discussion across the disciplines. For example:

- A psychology professor asked students to vote on the high, medium, or low construct validity of articles, used these responses as a prompt to classroom discussion, and then called for another round of votes.
- A chemistry professor developed reason-focused questions that asked students to vote on why molecular reaction rates increased as the temperature of a reaction increased.
- A pharmacy instructor asked students to choose from different treatment options and vote on the best insulin regimen to treat a patient newly diagnosed with type 1 diabetes.
- An anthropology professor asked students to provide definitions of the term *civilization*, added one or two of his own, and then asked students to vote on the best definition (Bruff, 2009, pp. 89–93).

In each of these examples the point is not the vote but the discussion that follows afterward. The vote is merely a way to engage students with content by asking them to make their best choice from multiple possible options. The critical analysis emerges only in the discussion of why they made the choice they did, the reasons why they found certain evidence most compelling, or why they judged particular arguments to be more persuasive than others.

Social Media

My own orientation to teaching is critically pragmatic. I will use whatever I feel works in a situation, no matter how much colleagues may sneer at it or think me weird. So I'm happy to use social media and to encourage students to take out smartphones, tablets, and any other hand-held devices they have. I do this because I have so many students who just prefer to communicate this way. If I'm really striving to see the classroom through their eyes I need to use tools that they feel comfortable with. Trying to keep millennial students from sneaking looks at hand-held devices is about as useful as King Canute telling the tide to stop coming in.

There are three specific instructional reasons why I like to use these media:

To Democratize the Classroom

On social media it's much harder for a small clique of students to dominant the discussion and dictate its direction. Nobody's voice is louder on the screen. Those who don't usually get heard have as much chance of their contribution determining the direction of the class as anyone else.

To Allow Public Recognition and Inclusion

Everyone's comments are visible to everyone else so students can see their contributions getting exposure. As someone interested in encouraging participants to acknowledge what different group members bring to a discussion it's been interesting for me to see how much appreciation is expressed as students respond to comments on the screen.

To Acknowledge Students Who Are Introverts or Who Speak English as a Second Language

Introverts need time to think of how to express a reaction or pose a question, and social media provides them with that time. Students whose first language isn't English also appreciate the pause for thought that accompanies the use of social media. It gives them the chance to experiment with getting their phrasing and vocabulary just right.

TodaysMeet

TodaysMeet is a form of back-channel communication, that is, a flow of immediate information from students that provides a sense of how they're reacting to the class. It's essentially an electronic chat room on which students can ask or answer questions, provide reactions, and raise issues as soon as they occur to them. For me the big advantage of TodaysMeet is its anonymity. When students log on they create whatever identity they like—a nickname, a random set of numbers, a sports team, and so on. This means that they can ask questions or post responses without the fear of public embarrassment that would stop them speaking up in class. I've found this tool to be particularly helpful in getting students to post questions that reveal they don't understand the basics of a topic—something they would usually hold back from doing for fear of looking stupid.

Typically I get to the classroom a minute or two before students arrive and go to the TodaysMeet website (https://todaysmeet.com) to create a room for that day. Creating a room is easy. You simply add a word or abbreviation describing that day's topic after the TodaysMeet URL. So, if I'm teaching a class on the concept of hegemony that day I create a room with the URL https://todaysmeet.com/hegemony. That page stays active for a week so we can post follow-up comments after class is finished.

Once the students are all in class I tell them the TodaysMeet URL for that day and ask them to log onto the page. When they get there they're asked to create an identity for themselves and I stress that this should be anonymous. I explain to the group that I've created the page for them to pose questions that occur to them at any time and I promise to check the feed every quarter of an hour so that I can deal with questions posed. I also use this as a discussion starter by posting a question to the class and then asking them to respond. I allow 30 seconds or a minute of thinking time before asking students to post their comments. Because the feed is public and everyone can see all the postings I usually talk about the different ways people answered the question and then use these responses to move into a whole-class discussion.

TodaysMeet is particularly good at surfacing power dynamics and taking the emotional temperature of hot-button discussions. When talking about racism or sexism many students never open their mouth because they want to be politically correct and not say the wrong thing. But with a clearly anonymous online tool they'll make comments and raise issues they would have considered too dangerous to speak out loud in verbal discussion. When discussing racism I have seen multiple provocative and pertinent comments posted on the live class feed that I've never heard spoken aloud in class. People can disclose their own racist instincts and commission of microaggressions without the fear of public shaming that would accompany a verbal contribution. That disclosure then allows me to take the verbal discussion into deeper waters.

Finally, this tool provides a safe channel for students to criticize me directly. If anyone feels my power is being exercised arbitrarily or if I'm breaking a promise, comments to that effect will invariably show up on the live feed. This is useful because it enables me to clarify why I'm insisting on a particular activity or to reappraise whether I'm throwing my weight around in an unjustifiable way. Sometimes students will jump in to "save" me from criticism and I can stop them from doing that. I need to model a non-defensive consideration of criticism.

Of course the risk of anonymity is the lack of accountability and the concomitant opportunity for people to insult each other, be sarcastic, or make generally inappropriate comments. I feel the advantages of anonymity generally outweigh these drawbacks. It's also interesting to see that students will take each other to task over negative posting etiquette in ways that typically don't happen with classroom speech.

The Critical Incident Questionnaire

The Critical Incident Questionnaire (CIQ) is the instrument that has been the most helpful in enabling me to see the classroom through students' eyes. It's a quick and revealing way to discover the effects your actions are having on students and to find out the emotional highs and lows of their learning. Using the CIQ gives you an insight into what's working and what's misfiring, what you should keep and what you should discard, and how different students experience the same classroom activity in varying ways. It's good at illuminating misunderstandings of content and difficulties in applying new material and also provides you with running commentary on the emotional tenor of each class you deal with. You can download this free from my home page: http://www.stephenbrookfield.com.

The CIQ is a single-page form that's handed out to students once a week at the end of the last class you have with them that week. It takes about three to five minutes to complete and students are told *not* to put their name on the form. If nothing comes to mind as a response to a particular question they're told to leave the space blank. They're also told that at the next class you'll share the group's responses with them.

There are five questions on the form:

- At what moment in class this week did you feel most engaged with what was happening?
- At what moment in class this week were you most distanced from what was happening?
- What action that anyone (teacher or student) took this week did you find most affirming or helpful?
- What action that anyone took this week did you find most puzzling or confusing?
- What about the class this week surprised you the most? (This could be about your own reactions to what went on, something that someone did, or anything else that occurs.)

Students are given the last five minutes of the last class of the week to complete this form. As they exit the room I ask them to hand the form to a student volunteer who then gives them to me. If individual students bring their forms to me I redirect them to the volunteer collecting them that day.

As soon as time allows I read through the forms looking for common themes. For a class with thirty to thirty-five students this usually takes about twenty minutes. I look for comments that indicate problems, confusions, and anything contentious. Major differences in students' perceptions of the same activity are recorded as well as single comments that strike me as particularly profound or intriguing. This then becomes the basis for the questions and issues I address publicly the next time we're together.

If I have time I post a summary of the comments to the learning management system (LMS) the college uses. If I'm too busy to do that I wait until the start of the first class of the next week. I tell students I've conducted an elementary frequency analysis and that anything that gets mentioned on 10 percent of the forms will be reported. I also let them know that I reserve the right to report single comments I find to be particularly revealing or provocative.

Students know that the only comments I won't report publicly are those that identify other students in a personally disparaging way. I tell students that if such comments are included on the form I'll reframe them as general observations or dynamics the group needs to address or communicate them in a private, confidential conversation with the student concerned. Such conversations are usually with students who are reported on the CIQs to be dominating the class or behaving in an obnoxious manner. If students have made comments that have caused me to change how I teach, I acknowledge those and explain why I'm making that change. I try also to clarify any actions, ideas, requirements, or exercises that seem to be causing confusion. Criticisms of my actions are reported and discussed.

If contentious issues have emerged we talk about how these can be negotiated so that everyone feels heard and respected. Quite often students write down comments expressing their dislike of something I'm insisting they do. When this happens I know I must take some time to reemphasize why I believe the activity is so important and to make the best case I can about how it contributes to students' long-term interests. Even if I have spoken about this case before and written it in the syllabus, the critical incident responses alert me to the need to make my rationale explicit once again.

I am such a strong advocate of CIQs because of the clear benefits their use confers. Let me mention a few of these very briefly.

Detecting Problems before They Get out Of Hand

Using CIQs helps teachers detect early on in a course any serious problems that need addressing before they get out of hand. Since I began using this form more than twenty-five years ago I've never had a class explode in unexpected mutiny. There's been mini-revolts but none of them have caught me by surprise. I've always had a pretty good idea from the CIQ responses that the uprising was coming and that's helped me prepare to deal with it when it happened.

Justifying Why You Use Different Teaching Approaches

CIQs help me justify to students why I use a variety of activities and approaches in my classes. Each time I report the spread of responses on the previous week's forms a predictable diversity emerges. A particular activity—say a small-group discussion or a visiting speaker—is chosen by one group of students as being incredibly helpful and engaging and by another group as a waste of class time. As I read out these responses I emphasize that my recognition of this diversity lies behind my own efforts to use a range of teaching methods and materials. If different people learn differently then I need to vary my approaches as much as possible to make sure that for some of the time in class each person feels as if he or she is learning in a style that feels comfortable, familiar, and helpful.

Helping Resisters Realize They Are in a Minority

One or two troublesome students who constantly complain and always object to class exercises you've arranged can effectively sabotage a class by exercising an influence hugely disproportionate to their number. The CIQs provide the troublesome students, the teacher, and the other learners with a realistic assessment of the degree of resistance that really exists in a class. When a majority report how they are engaged with, or helped by, the same activities that one or two object to, this stops you from overestimating the extent of the resistance and making lots of adjustments that aren't really necessary.

Using CIQs with Small and Large Classes

Teachers often raise the problem of how to use this method with small and large classes. The largest group with which I've used it had about 250 students. Most of my classes have between twenty and thirty-five people enrolled. If you're teaching classes considerably larger than that, I'd still advocate that the method be tried but that you read only a portion of the responses each time. It's not realistic to think that a teacher with a class of one hundred or so students can do a weekly analysis of a considerable amount of qualitative data. However, asking a fifth of the class (a group of twenty or so students) to complete the CIQs at each meeting is much more manageable, and you still get some valuable insight into what's going on.

Another approach is to have everyone complete the forms and then to ask for volunteers to collect some of the forms and summarize the main themes that are reported. The students who volunteer to do this are excused from doing that week's assignment or a portion of it and also given maximum points for it, so there's usually a flood of people offering to do this. In the group of 250 I worked with I had ten volunteers summarize the responses of twenty-five of their peers. I then read those ten summaries to prepare my CIQ report.

I use a variant on this approach when I'm working with very small classes or with groups I've taught for a long period of time. Because it's easier in these situations for me to recognize handwriting or to see the order in which students hand in their forms, there's a risk of students clamming up because they think I'll be able to identify individual contributions. To prevent this happening a student collects the forms and summarizes the responses. Again, this student is excused from part of that week's homework. Although I know the identity of the student who provides the summary of group members' responses, that person is simply the reporter or conduit for the group members' responses. I have no idea who made which of the comments that appear.

Letter to Successors

An interesting way to discover what students feel are the most crucial elements in your teaching is to ask them to identify what they think are the essential things new students need to know and do as they enter your classroom. The Letter to Successors exercise asks students to compose a letter that will be sent to new students who are entering the same course the next time it's offered. The letter documents the departing students' insights about how to survive the experience. I often use this exercise as the last things students do in a course.

After these letters have been written privately and individually I ask students to form small discussion groups and to read them to each other. Group members look for common themes that are then reported back in a whole-class plenary session. Because responses are given by a group reporter, anonymity is preserved and no one is required to say anything about a particular concern unless he or she wishes to do so.

Here are the instructions:

In this exercise I want you to write a letter to the new students who will be in this course next year. I want you to tell them—in as helpful and specific a way as possible—what you think they should know about how to survive and flourish in the class. Some themes you might consider writing about are as follows:

What I know now about this course that I wish I'd known when I came in

The most important things you need to do to keep your sanity in this class

The most common and avoidable mistakes that I and others made in this class

The words that should be on your screen saver telling you how to make it through this class

Feel free to discard these themes and just write about whatever comes into your head around the theme of survival.

These letters are used as part of new student orientation the next time the course is taught. I'll also post them on whatever LMS is being used so incoming students can get a sense of what they're in for.

Conclusion

This chapter has explored the first critically reflective lens of students' eyes. Most of the techniques described don't need a lot of time and some (TodaysMeet is a good example) are pretty much instantaneous. But even if some take time away from the all-important coverage of content, the payoff from using them is enormous. You can know if students are understanding content only by getting constant feedback from them throughout the course. You can't know if your approaches to helping them learn this content are working unless you hear each week from them. And you have no hope at all of understanding the power dynamics in the room, including your own exercise of power, unless you get trustworthy information from students about this.

7

Learning from Colleagues' Perceptions

Critical reflection is best practiced as a collective endeavor, a collaborative process in which people gather to ferret out assumptions, challenge groupthink, and consider multiple perspectives on common experiences. If you're lucky enough to have colleagues who are willing to help you think through the nuts and bolts of your daily practice then you have a fantastic resource available to you. This is why one of the best things institutions can do to support good teaching is simply provide opportunities for people to talk with each other about what they're doing in the classroom. A collaborative and critical analysis of experience can help teachers generate good responses to the problems they face.

In applying critical reflection to the analysis and resolution of teaching problems we can learn a great deal from the ideas and practices of the adult educator, Myles Horton (1997, 2003). Myles was the founder of the Highlander Folk School in Tennessee, and he spent his life as an activist educator working with labor unions, the civil rights movement, and various grassroots organizations. Although known chiefly for his social activism he also worked out a theory of how to help people learn from their experience. "Helping people learn what they do" is his succinct description of what I've tried to do in my own attempts to get teachers to learn from their experiences. When I heard Myles speak this phrase to a group of educators in New York I was taken immediately with how it captured what I saw happening in the best kind of critical conversation groups. People share experiences and analyze these together to help them deal with problems they face.

Talking to colleagues about what we do helps us in significant ways. Colleagues can be critical friends reflecting back to us images of how we're perceived that help us confirm and also challenge assumptions we hold about the best ways to encourage learning, exercise power ethically, create democratic classrooms, or uncover power dynamics. Sometimes conversations with colleagues confirm the accuracy of assumptions we've held privately but not articulated because we feared they contradicted conventional wisdom. At other times we realize that our taken-for-granted assumptions might not be as accurate as we thought.

By asking us questions colleagues can help us notice things we've missed and suggest aspects of our practice that need further scrutiny. When we describe a situation to colleagues it often takes only a couple of questions from them about the evidence informing our reasoning to set us off on new analytical paths. Colleagues can provide alternative perspectives on situations we thought we'd analyzed correctly by offering us different readings of students' behavior or power dynamics. When they share their own examples of what we thought were idiosyncratic problems they help us realize the commonality of pedagogic experience. This breaks down the isolation we feel. For example, whenever I talk about my own sense of impostorship or my feelings of powerlessness in the face of student silence, I typically have colleagues tell me that that's *exactly* how they feel.

Finally, colleagues can suggest new possibilities for our practice. In my experience teachers are a helpful bunch. Get a group of them chatting in a corridor, car park, cafeteria, or professional conference and there'll be lots of talk about how to address common problems. And if one of them asks for help with a specific situation they'll either receive an avalanche of suggestions or an empathic confirmation of how tough the problem he or she is facing really is.

Creating Critically Reflective Conversations

When teachers talk together about individual or shared problems, however, there's a very common dynamic that quickly develops. One person will describe her struggle to teach a difficult unit, explain a particular idea, get students to participate more, or respond to the diverse ability levels in a class. Immediately the rest of her colleagues will talk about what they did in a similar situation, what responses they've found useful, and what exercises or activities she might find useful. In zero to sixty seconds, similar to a pedagogic *Fast and Furious* film clip, they move from diagnosis to solution.

This response is predictable and understandable. When you hear colleagues describing a problem they face you naturally want to say, "try this" or ask, "why don't you do A or B?" That's what good friends do, right? They solve other friends' problems. But offering an immediate response in a spirit of empathic support misses the chance for the kind of critical analysis of the problem that might uncover a wholly different set of suggestions. The exercises outlined in this chapter are all designed to stop this rush to premature analysis, judgment, and solution.

It's also easy for conversations with colleagues to become self-reinforcing exchanges of prejudices. I've seen this particularly in "blame-the-student" conversations in which colleagues swap stereotypical conceptions in an unproductive form of groupthink. People say "today's generation doesn't read," "they don't know where the library is," "there's a generational short attention span: you've got to entertain them every minute," or "they lack the basics of good thinking." Reaching back to the good old days and contrasting them with the unsatisfactory state of digitally reared students may make people feel a little better in expressing a shared frustration, but it doesn't really help us uncover hidden assumptions or consider things differently.

Also putting teachers into a group won't necessarily increase the amount of critical reflection in the world. Sooner or later talk will predictably turn to how administrators don't understand teaching and how institutional procedures prevent us working properly. Moreover, if the institutional culture is one that rewards apparent perfection and punishes public disclosure of private error we're hardly likely to spring enthusiastically into conversations that highlight our problems. After all, academic performance appraisals rarely celebrate a history of making mistakes. You tend to get a good rating by reporting on the exemplary, error-free performance of your role.

There's also the problem that the professional conversations we most frequently engage in—those that happen in department meetings—aren't usually models of critically reflective analysis. Typically they focus on institutional procedures or bureaucratic necessity: for example, what does our department need to do as part of the upcoming accreditation visit? How do we deal with students who've racked up multiple incompletes? What's our departmental contribution to the strategic plan? Any suggestions for how we can shave another 10 percent off our departmental budget? There's often a lot of posturing, point scoring, passive-aggressive hostility, and power plays going on. And it's clear that racism and sexism are present. I can honestly say that the department meetings I've participated in which a critical and sustained conversation about the dynamics of learning and teaching occurred can be counted on the fingers of one hand.

In the wider society models of critically reflective conversation hardly abound! In political "talk" shows we see only hostile binary advocacy with each side doing its best to prove the truth of its perspective and destroy its opponent's legitimacy. Even when well-intentioned people get together to work on a common problem it's so easy for someone to ask a question in the wrong way or make a passing remark that antagonizes someone else. Members of the dominant culture like myself miss the microaggressions we're committing in mixed-race, -gender, or -class groups. In a politically divided culture in which hegemony tries constantly to confirm the legitimacy of dominant ideas and voices, it's easy to fall into patterns of communication that reproduce and reinforce external inequities. Indeed, unless a deliberate intervention is made to structure the process differently, the chances of critical conversation happening are almost zero.

For all these reasons certain conditions need to be in place when colleagues get together to talk:

- A sustained attempt to keep the focus on uncovering assumptions, particularly those having to do with power and hegemony
- A constant effort to bring into the discussion as many different perspectives on the topic as possible
- An acknowledgment of the importance of each person's contribution, irrespective of seniority, status, or institutional role
- An agreement to try out conversation protocols that are designed to be inclusive and to hold off a premature focus on one stream of analysis or one response to a problem

The techniques described in this chapter are all designed to realize these conditions. I've sequenced them in order of complexity, beginning with ones designed for groups just starting the reflective journey and ending with ones intended for more established groups.

Start-up Sentence Completion

I'm not a big fun of icebreakers, finding most of them embarrassing and pointless. This is partly a result of my natural shyness and partly because I don't see the point of telling people what kind of animal represents my personality or sharing something that no one else in the group knows about me. If nobody knows that fact it's probably because I've worked hard to conceal it from the world! Whenever I meet with a group for the first time I use instead some simple starting exercises aimed at prompting initial reflections that can serve as the grist for the mill of discussion.

One approach is to ask group members to finish one or two sentence starters. These starters are deliberately broad so as to encourage the widest range of possible responses. They're also positively framed to highlight topics people are comfortable talking about. I don't want group members to feel that the first thing they have to do is confess mistakes or reveal secrets.

Here are some examples of these sentence completion statements:

- I know I've done good work when . . .
- I know students are learning when they . . .
- The quality I most admire in a teaching colleague is when he or she . . .
- Good teaching is all about . . .
- If there's one piece of advice I'd give to someone starting to teach in my area it's that . . .

Sentence completion can be done in groups or electronically via TodaysMeet. The responses shared suggest points of connection among different disciplinary-specific teachers. Right off the bat several themes usually emerge. One of the most common responses to "I know students are learning when they . . ." has to do with the quality of questions students ask. Many teachers say that they know learning is happening when students raise good questions that encourage the introduction of new relevant information or that take an analysis or demonstration to a deeper level of complexity.

A slightly more reflective set of sentence-completion prompts can be used when people have been meeting for some time and you judge that a degree of familiarity and mutual trust has developed:

- When my students talk about my class when they're out of my earshot I'd most like them to say that . . .
- In my teaching life the accomplishment that I'm most proud of is . . .
- If I could turn back the clock and talk to myself on my first day of teaching I'd say . . .
- The mistake I've learned most from is when . . .
- The instructional problem I spend most energy trying to solve is . . .

With this set of questions it's important to let people take a minute or two to think about the question and search their experience before responding. I always answer the questions myself as part of this exercise and I share my responses along with everyone else. However, I don't usually go first—an exception to my usual practice of beginning by modeling what I want people to do. That's because I don't want to establish early on a normative template of what people feel they ought to say.

Beginning the Conversation with Critical Incidents

If people are unused to critically reflective conversation you can't expect them to do a deep dive into personal disclosure or power analysis the first time they meet. After sentence-completion statements, one of the most common ways newly constituted groups ease into conversation is by talking about high and low points of the past week or month of their teaching lives. Sometimes these have happened the day of or the day before the group meets, which always gives a spice of immediacy to the discussion.

When I'm facilitating an initial meeting I usually begin by asking people to focus on the following two topics:

- Think over the last few weeks of your teaching. What was the moment when you were closest to thinking or feeling "this is what teaching is all about!" or "this is why I teach!" or "this is a good day's work!" Where and when did this incident happen? Who was involved? What was it specifically that made this such a good moment?
- Think over the last few weeks of your teaching. What was the moment when you were closest to thinking or feeling, however fleetingly, as if you'd fallen short, were incompetent, or ought to quit teaching? Where and when did this incident happen? Who was involved? What was it specifically that made this such a distressing moment?

Sometimes we begin by talking only about the positive incidents. At other times we consider both together. In line with my belief that I ought to model my own commitment to the process I usually start by disclosing my own responses to these questions. Asking people to begin by sharing moments they're proud of is very deliberate. When you begin to surface assumptions regarding power dynamics and hegemony it's very easy to fall prey to a pessimistic despair as you realize the complexities you're dealing with. A sense of powerlessness develops if all you do is focus on intractable problems, unresolved dilemmas, and institutional and societal barriers to change. We need to celebrate the good things that happen, the small victories and unexpected breakthroughs that keep us engaged in this work.

During the initial round of sharing a particular incident often captures the group's attention and we start to explore it further. People ask for more specific details of an event and then talk about similar or allied experiences. If it makes sense I usually try to get people to settle on a common dynamic they want to explore more deeply. For example, if several of the initial critical incidents talk about moving students from dichotomous to multiplistic thinking—some illustrating the difficulties of doing this, some recounting successes—then that becomes the theme for the day.

Chalk Talk

This exercise was developed by Hilton Smith (Smith, 2009) of The Foxfire Fund. Chalk Talk is a silent and visual way to engage in discussion without speaking. It takes maybe five to ten minutes and is a good way to unearth the concerns of a group of people before building an agenda for further exploration. The technique serves to create a visual record of group concerns that suggests what issues to focus on next. Here's how it works:

- Write a question in a circle in the center of the board— for example, "What problem most drains your energy as a teacher?" Place markers or several sticks of chalk by the board. Bring everyone out of his or her seats to stand next to the board.
- Explain this is a silent activity and that when people are ready they should write a response to the question directly on the board. They're also free to write responses to what others have written, to pose questions about comments already posted, to answer questions posted, to draw lines between responses on different parts of the board that seem to connect, or to indicate startlingly different responses to the same question, and so on.
- You as instructor also participate by drawing lines connecting comments that seem similar or contrasting, by writing questions about a comment, adding your own thoughts, and so on.

- When a suitably long silence ensues or the board is getting full ask if people are done. Once everyone's finished posting move into conversation about the whats on the board. Are there one or two clusters of responses that get a lot of mentions? If so, they're probably good starting points for collegial conversation. When a range of different responses to a particular issue emerges this signifies it'll probably be ripe for exploration.

I like Chalk Talk for several reasons. One is that it has never badly misfired! Another is that it always produces contributions from far more people than would have been the case had I thrown the question out to the group and asked for comments. Often well over half the group posts something in a ten-minute Chalk Talk session, compared to the 5 to 10 percent of students who would have dominated a group discussion. It also honors silence and enables introverts to order their thoughts before posting. Of course, those same introverts may feel inhibited about writing something while everyone is watching. But because in Chalk Talk there are usually several people up at the board writing simultaneously, this isn't too much of a drawback.

The Circular Response Method

Sentence completion, critical incidents, and Chalk Talk are all opening activities to be used in the early stages of a group's life together. Once people are starting to get comfortable with each other it's time to move into more complex forms of discussion. The Circular Response exercise was developed in the 1930s by the adult educator Eduard Lindeman (Brookfield, 1988) to help community groups prioritize their concerns and settle on a manageable agenda. Its intent is to democratize group participation, to promote conversational continuity, and to give people some experience of the effort required in respectful listening. Because it's more complex I usually hold this in reserve until a group has met a few times and some level of trust and familiarity has developed. And if a group is falling into a very predictable rut in terms of who speaks most often this shakes things up nicely. Here's how it works:

- People sit in a circle where everyone can see each other. The optimal size for this exercise is eight to twelve participants so it works well for teacher-reflection groups.
- You or the group poses a question, perhaps, "how can we make our classrooms more inclusive?" or "what constitutes an effective exercise of power?"
- The process has two rounds of conversation. In the first round each person in turn takes up to a minute to respond to the issue or question that the group has agreed to discuss. When someone is speaking in this first round there are no interruptions allowed.
- Once the first person has spoken in the opening round whoever sits on the speaker's left goes next. However, the second speaker is not free to say anything she wants. She must incorporate into her remarks some reference to the preceding speaker's comments and use these as a springboard for her own contribution. To help ease the anxiety new speakers feel about responding to the person before them they are told to take a few moments to think about their response before contributing. There's absolutely no expectation that someone will spring straight into speech after the previous speaker has stopped talking.
- The new contribution doesn't have to be a précis or an agreement; it can be an expression of dissent from the previous opinion. If someone can't think of anything to say about the preceding speaker's comments then he talks about why it's hard to respond; perhaps because the contribution was expressed in unfamiliar language,

referred to experiences that are unfamiliar, or dealt with content the new speaker knows nothing about.

- This process moves around the circle with every new speaker using the previous person's contribution as the prompt for whatever he or she wishes to say.
- The first round of conversation ends where it started—with the opening speaker. Only this time the opening speaker is responding to the comments of the person who spoke before her.
- When this first round of conversation is over the group moves into open conversation with no more ground rules. Anyone can speak, there's no order of contributions, interruptions are fine, and people can ask questions, seek clarifications, or offer new ideas.

Whenever I've used this exercise I invariably observe that in the first round of conversation heads lean in as each person watches how his or her contribution to the discussion is responded to. This is really an online threaded discussion happening synchronously in a face-to-face setting. Unlike an online environment, however, you don't need to wait for hours or days to see what someone will do with your comment.

Bohmian Dialogue

Based on David Bohm's *On Dialogue* (1996), this is a process for getting groups to talk and think together more deeply and coherently. It's designed to create a flow of meaning among dialogue participants by getting people to build on one another's ideas creatively and freely. Bohm recommends forty members as the optimal group size so that a true diversity of experience and opinion is present. Most collegial conversation takes place in much smaller groups so I've adapted this process to smaller groups of ten to fifteen.

The process starts by participants identifying an issue or topic of mutual interest. Examples might be how to get students to talk about power and privilege, how to deal with domineering students, or how to improve the quality of discussion. Members agree to do some preliminary study of the chosen issue by reading some common materials or viewing the same video.

When the group meets, members form into a circle and the convener explains the meaning of dialogue: it's the creation of a flow of meaning among the participants, there are no winners or losers and no attempt to persuade or convince, the focus is on understanding what people actually say without judgment or criticism, and the object is to develop collective thinking. It's anticipated that people will have radically different opinions but that these will be expressed as precisely that: as different takes or perspectives prompted by a contribution.

One person at a time speaks and while that person is speaking people listen intently. The convener participates by making contributions. She also steps in to remind people of the ground rules when participants start trying to convince or rebut each other or when the conversation turns into a debate. Optimally, everyone takes on that responsibility.

There's no pressure to respond immediately to the opening question posed. People are encouraged to stay silent and to speak only when they have something to say or a thought is prompted by another's comment. Silence is viewed as indicating that people are actually thinking. If it's helpful, participants can close their eyes or look at the floor, though others love to give nonverbal support and eye contact.

The process continues for as long as seems optimal. Bohm recommends two hours but I've used this in much briefer chunks of time. It ends with participants sharing what they came to understand more deeply.

Initially there's often some resistance to this process because of its apparent looseness, so it's important to explain that this is designed to build a conversation organically, from the ground upward. Because it's meant to stop members from quickly falling into a pattern of trying to convince dissenters, I've found it very appropriate for working with groups that meet to consider racial issues and tensions.

Critical Conversation Protocol

The Critical Conversation Protocol is designed to accomplish the core purposes of critical reflection: to uncover assumptions and to consider multiple alternative perspectives. In this protocol I ask that people play one of three possible roles—storyteller, detective, or umpire.

> *Storytellers* make themselves the focus of critical conversation by describing some practice, dilemma, or experience they need help in understanding. Their problem situation becomes the focus of the conversation.

> *Detectives* help the storyteller come to a more fully informed understanding of the assumptions that frame his or her thinking and practice. They also try to provide alternative interpretations of the events described and to suggest information or lines of analysis that have been missed.

> *Umpires* agree to monitor the conversation with a view to pointing out when people are talking to each other in a judgmental way. They also keep the group focused on the discrete stages in the exercise.

All participants in the group play all three of these roles at different times. Each time a new conversation is held the members switch roles so participants all have the chance to be the storyteller and umpire at least once and the detectives several times. The idea is that if this exercise is done multiple times, the behaviors associated with each role gradually become habitual.

The exercise has five discrete stages to it and the person chosen to be the umpire has the responsibility to make sure the stages are followed in sequence. The umpire is mostly a nonspeaking role. She interjects only if the group is going off track or if she judges that someone is breaking the ground rules for the exercise. Here's how the activity proceeds:

1. The storyteller tells the tale. (10 minutes)

    Storytellers open the conversation by describing as concretely and specifically as possible an incident from their practice that for some reason is perceived as a problem. It's usually recalled because it's particularly frustrating and leaves the teller somewhat puzzled by its layers and complexities. Perhaps the dynamics of a teaching team are seriously dysfunctional. Maybe students resist attempts to get them to think critically. A small group of students may be dominating the class or storytellers might be concerned about the way teacher power is being exercised.

    Storytellers describe the incident in their own words without any questions or interruptions. Their colleagues, who are in the role of detectives, attend very carefully. They try to imagine themselves inside the heads of other people featured in the story and to see the events through their eyes. They're listening to identify the explicit and implicit assumptions the storyteller holds about what are supposedly correct, taken-for-granted practices. Some of these assumptions will be causal, some prescriptive, and some paradigmatic. There's a particular intent to detect assumptions regarding power dynamics and to uncover hegemony.

2. The detectives ask questions about the story. (10 minutes)

    Once the storyteller has finished speaking, the detectives are allowed to break their silence to ask him or her any questions they have about the problem, dilemma, or situation just described. The detectives are searching for any information that will help them uncover the assumptions they think the storyteller holds. They're also looking for details

not provided in the first telling of the story that will help
them relive the events described through the eyes of the other
participants involved.

Detectives must observe certain ground rules when asking
questions of the storyteller. They can only ask questions
that request information ("can you say more about . . . ?" or
"can you explain again why you decided to . . . ?") and they
can't phrase questions in ways that pass judgment ("are you
seriously telling me that you . . . ?" or "why on earth would
you . . . ?"). Their questions are asked only for the purpose
of clarifying the details of what happened. Detectives must
refrain from giving their opinions or suggestions, no matter
how helpful they feel these might be. They can ask only one
question at a time and must avoid asking multiple questions
masquerading as a single request for information. They must
never give advice on how the storyteller should have acted.

As the storyteller hears the detectives' questions she tries
to answer them as fully and honestly as possible. She also
has the opportunity to ask the detectives why they posed the
particular questions they put to her. The umpire points out
to the detectives any judgmental questions that they ask,
particularly those in which they imply that they've seen a
better way to respond to the situation. An example of such a
question would be one beginning "didn't you think to . . . ?"
The umpire also brings the detectives' attention to the ways
in which their tone of voice as well as their words risk driving
the storyteller into a defensive bunker. Essentially the umpire
serves as the storyteller's ally, watching out for situations in
which the storyteller might start to feel under attack.

3. The detectives report the assumptions they hear in the storyteller's descriptions. (10 minutes)

When the situation, problem, or dilemma has
been fully described, and all the detectives' questions
have been answered, the conversation moves to the

assumption-reporting phase. Here the detectives tell storytellers, on the basis of their stories and responses to questions, what assumptions they think the storytellers hold.

This is done as nonjudgmentally as possible as a reporting-back exercise. The detectives seek only to state clearly what they think the storyteller's assumptions are, not to judge whether those are right or wrong. They're asked to state these assumptions tentatively, descriptively, and nonjudgmentally, using phrases such as "it seems as if . . ." or "I wonder if one assumption you might be holding is . . . ?" or "Is it possible that you assumed that . . . ?" They state only one assumption at a time and do not give any advice about the way storytellers *should* have acted in the situations described. The umpire intervenes to point out to detectives when she or he thinks they're reporting assumptions with a judgmental overlay.

4. The detectives give alternative interpretations of the events described. (10 minutes)

The detectives now give alternative versions of the events that have been described, based on their attempts to relive the story through the eyes of the other participants involved or drawing on their own similar experiences and relevant theory. These alternative interpretations must be plausible in that they're consistent with the facts as storytellers describe them. When appropriate, detectives should point out how power or hegemony plays itself out in the different interpretations they're giving.

The detectives are to give these interpretations as descriptions, not judgments. They're describing how others involved in the events might have viewed them, not saying whether or not these perceptions are accurate. They're speculating how the situation might look when viewed from a different intellectual framework, not saying that this is the one the storyteller should have used. They avoid giving any advice.

After detectives have offered their alternative interpretations storytellers are allowed to give any additional
information that would challenge these. Storytellers can ask
the detectives to elaborate on any confusing aspects of the
interpretations they offer. At no time are they expected to
agree with any interpretations provided.

5. Participants do an experiential audit. (10 minutes)

Finally, the ground rules cease to be in effect any longer
and the detectives can give whatever advice they wish.
Storytellers and detectives state what they've learned from
the conversation, what new insights they've realized, what
assumptions they've missed or need to explore further,
what different understandings they have as a result of the
conversation, and what their conversation means for their
future actions. The umpire then gives an overall summary of
the ability of participants to be respectful listeners and talkers
and also gives his or her personal perspective on the story.

Although this is a heavily structured and artificial exercise, the
intent is for these dispositions to become so internalized that the
ground rules and structure eventually become unnecessary. And,
although I've presented this as a neatly sequenced exercise with
five discrete stages, the reality is that of course it isn't! Throughout
the conversation detectives think up new questions they want to
ask that will help them unearth assumptions and provide alternative perspectives.

The most frequent job the umpire usually has to do is step in
when people give advice in the guise of asking questions, reporting
assumptions, or providing alternative perspectives. We're so culturally conditioned to move straight from being told the problem
to providing the solution that the intermediate stages of critical
reflection are completely forgotten.

I've used this protocol with thousands of practitioners in multiple settings. It seems to be infinitely adaptable and is really very

simple to use, providing the ground rules are clearly understood and enforced. One caveat needs to be said, however. This should never be attempted without an initial teaching demonstration of how the process works. When I do this I play the roles of umpire and storyteller. In the umpire role I often wear a red baseball cap because I need to put a red light on to stop detectives from being judgmental, bombarding the storyteller with questions, and offering advice. I wear a green cap when I'm playing the role of storyteller, because I've received the green light to tell my story. And throughout I take questions on why the protocol is arranged the way it is.

Conclusion

Conversations among colleagues can easily be derailed by institutional politics or turn into venting sessions that leave people without any new insights into their habitual assumptions or heightened awareness of the different perspectives that could be taken regarding their teaching. But if conversational protocols are adopted that are designed to elicit the widest array of viewpoints and that focus on power dynamics and hegemony, we raise the chances of something useful happening. Colleagues are the people who know our dilemmas and problems the best from their having walked the same experiential paths we do, so using them in a structured effort to help us uncover our assumptions is an obvious step.

In recent years the idea of faculty learning communities (FLCs) has become popular on college campuses (Cox and Richlin, 2004). Sometimes these are disciplinary-specific (Buch and Barron, 2012) but more often they cross departments and divisions (Lenning, Hill, Saunders, Solan, and Stokes, 2013; Sipple and Lightner, 2013). As I wrote the second edition of this book I co-convened an FLC on racial intersections in the classroom and was privy to conversations that embodied critical reflection as people tried to understand their own racism and consider the effects of their positionality on different students. We all shared the desire to understand the workings of racism in our classrooms but we inhabited different racial identities and had different disciplinary allegiances. Within FLCs there's a clear opportunity to try out some of the exercises outlined in this chapter.

Another chance for us to use the lens of colleagues' perceptions arises when we're members of teaching teams. In a teaching team you have the built-in critical mirrors of colleagues who can consistently provide alternative interpretations of what's going on in your classroom. Embedding critical reflection in a team-teaching process is the topic we turn to in chapter 8.

8

Team Teaching as Critical Reflection

Similar to most teachers, I usually teach solo. In many ways this is very convenient. Within the constraints imposed by the institution I am pretty much the sole decider of matters of content, process, and evaluation. If I want to change the pace of a class or suddenly introduce a new exercise I don't need to consult anyone. There's no time spent in planning or debriefing meetings and no negotiations with colleagues over the grades particular students should receive. It's cleaner and less complicated than working as a team.

But the seeming efficiency of having only to answer to myself is offset by the collaborative benefits and supports I've lost by not having colleagues present. In particular, I miss the chance to consult a critical mirror in real time. Teaching solo means that if I want to understand a problematic situation I have to find a colleague and provide a version of events filtered through my narrative lens. But when I'm team teaching she or he is right there with me experiencing the same situation and noticing things I've witnessed and missed. In this chapter I want to explore in detail how team-teaching colleagues constitute an important part of the lens of colleagues' perceptions.

Team teaching, properly done, is something I'm passionate about. The "properly done" caveat is crucial, however. Team teaching is not two or three people agreeing to carve up a course into discrete solo sections—you do this month then I'll do the next—so that each person conducts 50 or 30 percent of the sessions. Properly conducted, team teaching involves all members of the team planning the course; writing the syllabus; specifying learning objectives; planning, conducting, and debriefing the class; and evaluating student work. This takes far more time than teaching solo. You need to coordinate, discuss, and decide multiple matters as a group, something that adds considerably to your faculty load (Pharo et al., 2012).

Obviously within that structure leadership roles vary so that different members of the team take the lead in teaching certain content, drafting particular assessment rubrics, or running specific exercises. But every team member is in class all the time so that she or he can complement and support whatever the lead teacher is doing. This model of teaching parallels the work reality most students will face. In the information age, working in project teams is the norm, so it makes perfect sense for our pedagogy to mirror that reality.

I'm such a proponent of the team-teaching method because of my own experiences working in teams at multiple institutions over the past four decades. I've also made it a point to observe teaching teams in action outside of my own discipline. As chroniclers of team teaching (Eisen and Tisdell, 2000; Plank, 2011; Ramsey, 2008) often point out, this approach has benefits for students and teachers. One of the most important is the way it offers a wonderful opportunity for critical reflection. Teaching colleagues can offer different perspectives on a class, interpret classroom events in multiple ways, help us recognize our assumptions, and offer helpful analyses of why things did or didn't work.

Colleagues who are right there in the room with us notice things we miss. No solo teacher can expect to have an auctioneer's eye that records every gesture, body change, or movement in the class. For example, when I'm trying to explain something as clearly as possible or when I answer a student's question, I usually look at the floor or up into the middle distance. I avoid eye contact with a questioner because I'm trying to come up with the clearest possible sequence of words to convey a particular meaning. I actually have one colleague who closes his eyes whenever he strives to explain a point! Looking at faces I get distracted pondering the meaning of a blank gaze, smile, or eyes cast downward. So I simply stop observing students so as to clear my head and come up with the most helpful response.

In such situations I miss an enormous amount of what's going on. I fail to notice students who are trying to get into the conversation and I don't see how the questioner is responding to my answer. A teaching colleague who is not taking the responsibility for leading the class at that particular moment can serve as a second eye watching out for cues I've missed. This is particularly helpful in alerting me to students I've overlooked who wish to contribute in some way.

I always look forward to a team-taught class in a way that's absent when I'm working solo. When I'm on my own I pretty much know what I'm going to do and say. Occasionally students' questions can take me by surprise and I find myself explaining something in a new way that just seems to pop into my head. But these moments are pretty rare. In a team, however, there's always an element of the unanticipated waiting in the wings, and that makes the class more enjoyable for me. My teaching partner can interrupt me, ask a difficult question, or take things in an interesting new direction. I also know I have someone watching my back, pedagogically speaking, a partner who can jump in to help me out when something I'm trying seems to be stalling.

Providing Emotional Grounding

Similar to a lot of teachers I know I'm very hard on myself. I usually leave class feeling that I've fallen short. Sometimes things have seemed too sluggish, sometimes I can't seem to get students to participate, and sometimes a question takes me completely by surprise and I can't craft a good response. Part of this is my own impostorship, my feeling that I'm faking it and that sooner or later people will realize that this boy from Bootle (the part of inner city in Liverpool where I was born) doesn't deserve to be a professor. Part of it derives from my own sense of commitment, my desire to be as helpful and useful as possible to students. This striving for perfection means I'm doomed to live in a state of imagined perpetual failure.

I remember coming home one evening and feeling embarrassed about being unable to control a flashpoint moment in class when tempers led to a raw expression of emotions. I walked around my house literally hitting myself on the head shouting, "stupid, stupid, stupid." This was before Chris Farley created an interviewer character on *Saturday Night Live* that would ask a guest an obvious or wrong question and then do the same thing. And it definitely wasn't done for comic effect. I was fully intent on punishing myself, on administering the self-laceration described in chapter 5.

One part of suffering from clinical depression and anxiety (as I do) is that I'm always expecting things to go wrong. I live on the edge of imagined calamity, seemingly one word or gesture away from having things spiral out of control. When it comes to assessing how well a particular class session has gone, I focus on the people who never participate, on the questions I feel I didn't answer well, or my lack of charismatic energy. This expectation of disaster fuels my belief that I'm not smart enough to be in academe, meaning I often exit the classroom convinced I've been a failure.

This is a demoralizing way to spend a career! What keeps this self-lacerating tendency under control has been the chance to co-teach several courses. A colleague who has just conducted the class with me is able to provide a reading of it unaffected by my built-in expectation of disaster. Of course co-teaching colleagues don't provide an objective rendering of what just happened because they're also working with perceptual filters they've constructed out of their own experiences. But, unless they're depressives suffering from impostorship, they won't see things exactly the way that I do. They'll probably assign more charitable meanings to students' silence than I would; as, for example, signifying that they're grappling intently with difficult material. Maybe they'll notice signs of engagement I've missed: nods of recognition, smiles, and so on.

I've found the presence of a co-teacher curbs my habitual tendency to interpret things that are happening in the worst possible way. Because I anticipate catastrophe in the classroom there's always a part of me looking to confirm that disaster is indeed happening. But colleagues will usually provide a different version of what they saw as the most significant events that day. They don't necessarily downplay or contradict the truth that I saw, they just tell a different story. Their recounting of the class picks out things I paid no attention to and they interpret students' actions in ways I hadn't thought of.

This has been an especially interesting dynamic in courses in which I've been the white member of a multiracial teaching team working with a multiracial group of students. Caught as I am in my white identity I can completely misread the intent of students of color. If someone from a different racial or cultural background is expressing themselves using vocal tones, gestures, or language I'm unfamiliar with, it's hard to judge what these all mean. Because I'm used to seeing myself as un-raced, it took me a long time to realize the truth of an African American co-teacher's comment: "to students of color everything is seen in racial terms." As we shall see in chapter 12 multiracial teaching teams can model very effectively how to surface the different assumptions and perspectives that instructors of different racial identities bring to the table.

Even when a co-teacher essentially agrees with my gloomy interpretation of a particular class, this is not always as demoralizing as you might imagine. This is because when colleagues perceive a session as not going well they usually provide examples of similar classes they've conducted in the past. This helps combat the sense of isolation solo teaching induces. To struggle through a day when you're by yourself feeling you've completely misjudged what would galvanize a group of students is an awful experience. You ask yourself, "how can I call myself a teacher?" or at least I do. But when a colleague endures this agony and then shares similar past experiences with you you're reassured that you're not uniquely pitiful. To hear someone you respect describe exactly the same sense of helplessness you've just experienced is very reassuring. It's one of the most important benefits of co-teaching.

Modeling Critical Reflection for Students

Read mission statements of colleges and universities and the development of critical thinking is frequently mentioned. My own institution, the University of St. Thomas in Minneapolis–St. Paul, is a case in point. We say we wish to develop morally responsible citizens who think critically, act wisely, and work skillfully for the common good. Yet, given the overwhelming predominance of solo teaching, students have very little exposure to seeing teachers model critical thinking. Some of us use tricks to simulate a critical conversation with ourselves, such as the "Clint Eastwood chair" (Brookfield, 2012), when, after you've presented an argument from a particular seat, you move to a different chair and direct a critique of your remarks to your empty seat. But nothing beats seeing a teaching team bring very different perspectives to their understanding of a topic and exploring and critiquing each other's assumptions in front of a class.

This modeling is crucial given the difficulty, well-documented in research on student development (Evans, Forney, Guido, Patton, and Renn, 2010; Jones and Abes, 2013), of helping students move from dualistic and binary right-wrong thinking, through multiplicity, to arrive at a stage of informed commitment. This process involves learning to live with contradiction and disagreement, something Basseches (2005) explores in his work on the development of dialectical thinking in young adults. He reports how difficult it is for students to hold two contradictory ideas in tension without needing to decide that one is definitively correct and one clearly wrong.

A teaching team can model how to explore this dialectical tension by stating opposite positions on an issue and then demonstrating how each member strives to understand the other's viewpoint. Members can summarize each other's arguments, check that they've understood these correctly, and ask questions designed to elicit why these views are held. A transformation of faculty members' understanding sometimes happens in front of people's eyes or at least a readiness to hold contradictions in some kind of congenial tension.

A teaching team also embodies critically reflective process when team members talk out loud the way they see themselves working together. In my past teams we typically start off the course by talking about the content strengths each of us has and what we look to gain from working with each other. We talk about our different personalities and how these manifest themselves in our decision making and in how we run the class.

For example, my sometime teaching colleague Steve Preskill loves the energy of whole-class discussion while I'm always anxious to move to small-group exercises. As good friends for over twenty years we also have an ease joking with each other. From feedback, we know we need to tell students just how much we communicate through teasing, lest it seem we're engaged in a passive-aggressive attempt to belittle and sabotage each other. Students from Southeast Asia can read Western teasing as disrespectful animosity, so it's important to acknowledge in advance that joking about each other is a Western cultural trait signifying affection. In England, where I grew up, you know who your best friend is by the fact that she or he is the one you tease the most mercilessly.

One of the best opportunities to model collegial critical thinking happens when a teaching team reviews data provided by students using the various instruments and approaches described in chapter 6. For example, when instructors give the weekly Critical Incident Questionnaire (CIQ) report to students, they share how students' comments challenged and affirmed assumptions they held about the best ways to support students' learning, teach material engagingly, pace the class, deal with questions, and so on. Very often the same set of comments challenges assumptions of one team member while affirming those of another. A particular CIQ notation takes one instructor by surprise yet is old news to another.

In the conversation accompanying this summary of the previous week's CIQ results, different instructors have a chance to model critical thinking. A racially charged comment will produce different responses from members of a multiracial team, and an observation on gender dynamics will lead to some productive conversation in a mixed-gender team. It's intriguing for students to see professors stopped in their tracks by reports of what students consider an unethical or arbitrary use of teacher power. Different team members can provide their individual responses to problems students have raised and then try to negotiate a solution the team can agree on. People usually have to give something up and move from a fixed position to arrive at "something we can all live with."

Recently my membership in a male-female teaching team enabled me to model an intentionally critically reflective conversation. After the first class session of a course my colleague said she'd noticed a change in my communicative tone toward the end of the session. I'd taught the course many times before but it was the first time for my colleague. At the beginning of the evening I'd scrupulously used *we* when referring to decisions about course organization, process, and content. By the end of the evening I was confidently answering students' questions by saying *I* and assuming authorship of the decisions.

My colleague waited until the students had exited the room to point this switch out to me. She said she didn't want to embarrass me publicly by referring to it in front of the students. I told her it would have been terrific if she'd done that, because it would be a wonderful illustration of how patriarchy worked. I had no awareness of how I'd slipped into an automatic presumption of authority and was assuming I'd been working in a suitably equitable way. My perspective on the evening was that it had been collaborative and collegial.

We resolved to begin the next class meeting telling students of this conversation and did exactly that. It enabled us to illustrate some very complex power dynamics to students. I was able to point out how it demonstrated a very specific instance of patriarchy, the ideology that holds that men should be entrusted with decisions for the whole community because of their superior reasoning power, strength, and logic unsullied by emotion. Even though I believed I was working in a non-patriarchal way, that ideology had its hooks so firmly into me that I moved into *I* language with no awareness of that fact.

My colleague then spoke of how patriarchy also framed her response to my action. In the moment she didn't want to embarrass me by calling me out in front of the students. To her this was an instance of the self-censorship women engage in when interacting with male colleagues. At some deep level she didn't want to be seen as the "uppity" female making waves with the male "Endowed Chair" (my institutional title). She also felt the societally imposed need to take care of me by not calling me publicly to account. So, despite teaching courses on feminist perspectives and self-identifying as a strong feminist she pointed out how in this instance she also was ensnared by patriarchy.

The two of us talking through this dynamic in front of, and with, the students was far more powerful than one of us telling the story at a later date as an example of patriarchy in action. The real-time modeling of discussing how gender or racial power dynamics manifests themselves in teaching teams provides a powerful example of critical thinking in action. This is why any course designed to foster critically reflective abilities and dispositions really needs to be team taught.

Negotiating Vulnerability

Critical reflection's emphasis on unearthing and scrutinizing assumptions entails a strong element of vulnerability. After all, there's always the possibility of you discovering that assumptions you'd taken for granted for a long time are actually misguided, based chiefly on unexamined "common sense." Alternatively, you may be alerted to versions of familiar problems or dilemmas that take you completely by surprise, revealing analytical approaches to understanding that you'd never been aware of. It's chastening to discover that you've been reading a situation wrongly for many years and that your response to it has omitted a significant perspective. Public disclosure of error requires a level of vulnerability many of us feel disinclined to exhibit.

But displaying vulnerability is much easier if this is done within a team that has developed a level of trust. In her account of team teaching a course at Luther Seminary in St. Paul, Ramsey (2008) argues that the degree to which a team-taught course is helpful for student learning is the degree to which the team members trust each other. It seems to me that the trust Ramsey speaks of undergirds critical reflection. We can't take the risk of questioning another's assumptions or providing a very different perspective unless we trust that our partner will welcome the questioning and expression of difference.

Displaying vulnerability is more likely to happen if people feel that their expression of this behavior will be supported. In a patriarchal culture asking for help is not something men are brought up to do. Even in a gendered profession such as teaching, awards and approval tend to go to those who do everything in an apparently exemplary manner. I have never seen a "professor of the year" award go to someone who admitted to regularly getting it wrong and asking for help. The award usually goes to the charismatic performer, skilled at inspiring students and displaying a dazzling command of different pedagogic approaches.

Working with colleagues inevitably entails a degree of vulnerability. In their account of co-teaching an interdisciplinary science course, Ouellett and Fraser (2011) emphasize this reality. Ouellet comments how "I've found that I have to be both vulnerable and confident to make it work . . . to be open to compromise with and critique my partner, and yet be confident enough to stand on my own and take the best of the critique forward to influence my teaching" (p. 32). Fraser writes of his fear of having a knowledgeable and capable colleague in the room watching him and of how "there is a real vulnerability that makes me strive to ensure that my information is up to date and correct in every detail . . . (and) to make sure my teaching style and pedagogy were flawless" (p. 33).

Disclosing errors in judgment and action is one of the most effective ways of demonstrating critical reflection. But it's also one of the hardest things to do. Publicly revealing parts of myself I don't particularly like is not pleasant. But I force myself to do this because students and colleagues tell me this is helpful. Over the years some of the most dramatically positive student feedback on CIQs has pinpointed moments when I gave an unplanned autobiographical example of making a mistake, getting something clearly wrong, or finding out something about myself I'd rather not have known. Learning how memorable these asides and autobiographical excursions are for students I've tried to be more and more intentional about building them into my teaching rhythm.

Some disclosures are relatively insignificant, such as admitting that I struggle with a lot of the critical theory I read. I usually feel like an impostor trying to understand critical theory texts and conclude that they're intended for people smarter and more sophisticated than me. Just owning up to repeatedly reading a paragraph from Foucault for half an hour and having no idea what it means is reassuring for many students to hear. Of course I then have to justify why making the effort in the first place is worthwhile!

Others are more substantial and probably cost me more. I remember doing a presentation with my friend and colleague the late Elizabeth Peterson (1996) in which we were trying to model a black-white, female-male dialogue. Elizabeth was an African American woman and I'm a white European American man. Part of that dialogue involved me documenting some of the learned racism that manifested itself in what seemed like instinctive decisions. I talked about how I catch myself holding back from challenging students of color and realize my so-called concern masks an embedded racist paternalism that says that "they" can't take a "strong" challenge from a white person. I spoke about how I find myself quickly granting paper extensions to black students and can only assume it springs from a white supremacist judgment that because black students are not as intelligent as white students, of course they'll need more time to complete their work (Peterson and Brookfield, 2007).

I don't like the fact that I have a lot of learned racism in me and that I'll struggle with this until I die. It's never going to go away and I'll never become the "good white person" I used to think I was. I've had to force myself to confront this part of me and to talk publicly about it. But that act of enforced vulnerability is made much easier when it's done as part of a team-taught course, particularly if my colleague is a person of color. I can check with my colleague if I've just committed a racial microaggression against him or her and my colleague can point out whole swaths of research or literature I'm unaware of or perspectives and interpretations that never occurred to me.

Making uncomfortable personal disclosures and asking colleagues to help you understand the assumptions informing the actions and situations you describe is difficult. It needs to be modeled by senior figures who have something to lose and it's best done in a team setting. Students need to see us do this with colleagues first before being invited to do it with each other. Displaying this kind of vulnerability is a very powerful dynamic to observe and is usually remembered more vividly than other classroom events. It's at the heart of the best critically reflective conversations.

Vulnerability is the flip side of trust. The more we trust our colleagues the more we are willing to reveal our vulnerability to them. Speaking for myself, there have been precious few environments in my life when I've perceived myself to be in a trustful relationship, particularly at work. But my team-teaching experiences are overwhelmingly like that. There are exceptions—times when I felt that agreements I had made with a partner were then ignored—but they are remembered much less readily than the times I felt I could trust my partner to be a critical mirror.

Learning Risk and Embracing Uncertainty

Building a critical scrutiny of assumptions into our practice and opening ourselves up to multiple perspectives is risky. You never know what you're going to find or how you'll be surprised. Risk and uncertainty are endemic to the critically reflective endeavor so working in an environment where a teaching colleague can debrief experiences with you is very helpful. To me this prospect is delicious, but then I'm at a point in my career where after four-plus decades I feel reasonably confident in my abilities. To discover that I've completely misread a situation is tantalizing rather than demoralizing, a challenge I can get my pedagogic teeth into.

But when I first began team teaching in the 1980s I was much more nervous about having a colleague in the room with me. My sense of impostorship was sky-high and I was afraid of being found out for the inexperienced and ignorant fraud I felt myself to be. I knew I was supposed to welcome collegial feedback and did my best to fake an openhearted delight in being part of a team. But my internal nervousness meant I spent an enormous amount of mental energy trying to impress whoever was my teaching peer.

This meant that I had very little to spare for the students. Instead of thinking through how best to help them acquire a knowledge base and then conduct a critical analysis of that base, I slipped right into performance mode. I was determined to sound and look smart for my colleague, to have an answer for every question, and to be a model of instructional sangfroid.

Over time my co-teachers and I became much more intentional in clarifying what our working relationship was to be. The general agreement was that the lead teacher in any particular moment would be primarily concerned with communicating content accurately and assessing students' understanding of that content. The co-teacher or co-teachers (I taught a lot in pairs and trios) would be on the lookout for signs of student confusion and make sure everyone got a chance to participate. We also agreed to create multiple instructional points when each of us would provide examples to illustrate an idea the other was explaining or to structure mini-presentations in which each of us would argue for different theoretical frameworks. Similar to Ouellett and Fraser (2011), "we were committed to modeling the intellectual and social learning and risk taking we were asking of students" (p. 76).

This kind of collaborative talking out loud of different classroom options or different approaches to problem solving is common in social work (Fook and Gardner, 2007, 2013) and health care (Johns, 2004; White, Fook, and Gardner, 2006). It's also a prime way to teach clinical reasoning to medical interns (Higgs, Jones, Loftus, and Christensen, 2008). For this modeling to work several things need to be in place:

- The conversation must be unrehearsed. If it's planned or scripted the elements of risk and uncertainty are gone.
- The different perspectives that two or three colleagues express must be real, not artificially generated. This must be an in-the-moment conversation.

- Colleagues should ask questions that seek to understand the differences they're expressing, not to convert each other to a particular viewpoint.
- When answering questions people should be ready to state the reasons, evidence, and experience that inform their responses.
- Team members must be visibly open to considering new perspectives and hearing inconvenient information that challenges their assumptions.
- People should be ready to talk about new things they've learned and new insights gained.

Teaching this way involves multiple pauses. When a colleague asks me a question in front of the students and I don't have a good answer on the tip of my tongue, I'll say that I need a moment's pause to think about this before replying. I always try to take plenty of time to think about my response as a way of socializing students to be more comfortable with periods of silence in class. Sometimes I'll end up saying, "you know I don't have a good response for that question, I need to think more about it—can we come back to it later?" Alternatively, I'll state my answer hesitatingly, maybe saying something such as, "I'm not really sure how to answer that, but as a first pass what I'm thinking might be the case is A." Students need models of pause and hesitation just as much as they need confident declarations of your disciplinary authority. Team teaching enables students to see how we stumble, pause, and double back as we try on new perspectives or understandings.

Confirmatory Critical Reflection

One of the traps I often fall into when writing or talking about critical reflection is emphasizing the dramatic moments when old assumptions are exploded, old perspectives shattered, and new identities formed. These road-to-Damascus epiphanies are fun to describe and exciting to experience but they're only part of the story. Much of the critical reflection that takes place in team teaching is confirmatory; that is, it affirms the accuracy and validity of assumptions you've been working under.

For example, I've always assumed that it's better to be open about any power you have and the way you choose to exercise it than to pretend it's not there. Instinctively I've felt that an adult way to treat people you supervise, whether students or colleagues, is to let them know the expectations you bring to your work and the assumptions you operate under. Having researched this assumption in numerous settings it's been broadly confirmed. There's been no transformative moment that's led to a serious reappraisal. But critical reflection has helped me better understand the dynamics informing the practice of transparency such as when it needs to be kept in check and how it's communicated.

Confirming the accuracy of assumptions and getting deeper insight into why they can be provisionally trusted as guides to action is crucial to informed practice. It's just as important as discovering you've missed some vitally important information or overlooked a relevant analytical approach. In teams we have the opportunity to practice confirmatory critical reflection much more frequently and at a deeper level than when we teach solo. The lens of students' eyes can certainly open up the opportunity for confirmatory reflection, but it's harder to get into an extended conversation with students about the meaning of their comments regarding your actions. If students tell you things are going well and that for the moment you've pretty much got it right it seems a tad self-aggrandizing to keep asking "exactly how and why do you think I've got it right?" or "can you say more why my teaching this way is so helpful to you?"

But members of a team are much more likely to see these kinds of confirmatory conversations as useful. This is partly because it's heartening to know that things are going well and that the careful planning and execution of teaching is working out roughly the way you hoped it would. After all, that keeps your sense of impostorship under control. But mostly it's because if you can understand better the dynamics of what works well to help students learn difficult content, contemplate complexity, and grapple with intellectual challenges, then you can do better work in the future as a teacher. This is why the debriefing sessions in a team-taught course are such a crucial opportunity for critical reflection. As you check your perceptions of what happened on any particular day against those of your colleagues you'll discover not only when they broadly confirm some aspects of your work but also how they add new insights into why something went well.

Debriefing sessions are also one of the few times we engage in something that's crucial for morale: giving appreciation. Giving appreciation is one of the least practiced dispositions of higher learning. Working solo, colleagues never see us teaching other than when mandatory observations for reappointment, promotion, and tenure take place. And the tenor of these observations is often remedial: "here's what you need to work on to get to full professor." But when the members of a teaching team take some time to express appreciation for the actions each other takes, it creates goodwill, raises morale, and energizes them to keep going in the face of adversity. Giving appreciation is so important to creating an emotionally cohesive group, yet it's rarely exhibited.

Conclusion

Because critical reflection happens best collaboratively, team teaching is one of the most underused opportunities to practice it in our daily lives. If higher education institutions realized its significance this would have major implications for protocols evaluating teaching. As well as assessing the typical indicators, such as clarity of communication, command of content, frequency of evaluation, and pacing of instruction, we would also be looking at how far the team members practiced critical reflection. To what extent did they model respectful disagreement by providing examples of critical analysis of key topics? How regularly did they share alternative perspectives and engage each other in exploring these? What were examples of questions they asked of each other to understand fundamentally different frameworks and worldviews? What were some of the ways they helped clarify and examine each other's assumptions? Did they demonstrate the giving of appreciation for each other's specific talents and contributions in class?

In chapter 9 we move to the third lens of critical reflection—personal experience. This is probably the lens influencing teaching that gets the least attention, yet, perversely, it often has the most influence.

9

Using Personal Experience

Whether we admit it or not, a lot of us go into teaching to reexperience the primary joy we felt as we first discovered our field. The beauty of the ideas we encountered, the excitement of discovering new intellectual worlds, and the feelings of pleasure that suffused us as we developed new skills are things we want to share with learners. Because we love our subjects and disciplines we want to spend our lives creating environments in which others can similarly fall in love.

The roots of why we teach the way we do are found in a complex web of formative memories and experiences of learning. We remember teachers we loved and hated, imitating those we admired and striving to avoid working in ways that resemble those we hated. We may espouse philosophies of teaching we've learned from professional development workshops, but the most significant and most deeply embedded influences are the images, models, and conceptions of teaching derived from our own experiences as learners.

As we progress through our careers and get further and further from these memories, it becomes harder and harder to recall the visceral dimensions of our initial experiences of learning our discipline. As we get more knowledgeable about and comfortable within our disciplines it's difficult to understand how students can't "get" something that's so clear to us. We forget the butterflies of nervousness or the sheer panic we feel as we take a test or approach a new and difficult learning task.

One of the hardest things for us to do is to imagine the fear that students feel as they try to learn what we teach. If we've been teaching for a long time we've most likely forgotten what it feels like to come to this learning as an uncertain novice. Moreover, because most of us end up teaching what we like to learn, we probably never felt much anxiety about it in the first place. If we teach what we're good at and love, it's almost impossible for us to understand, much less empathize with, students who find our subject boring or intimidating.

What *will* take us straight to this understanding is if we try to learn something that bores or intimidates us in adulthood. Learning we undertake in adulthood provides a rich vein of experience that can be mined for insights into the power dynamics of teaching. Learning something new and difficult as an adult and then reflecting on what this experience means for teaching is a visceral rather than intellectual route into critical reflection. It develops our emotional intelligence and reminds us of the affective components of learning.

Adult learning opportunities provide us with an experiential analog of the terrors and anxieties that our own students are facing as they approach new learning. As people used to orchestrating others' learning we probably won't enjoy feeling frightened, embarrassed, and intimidated when we find ourselves in the role of student. But if we care about helping our own students learn, the experience of struggling as learners ourselves is a kind of privilege. It gives us a gift of empathy that helps us adjust what we're doing to take account of students' blockages and anxieties.

When we try, and fail, to learn something as quickly and easily as we'd like, we experience all the public and private humiliation, the excruciating embarrassment, the fear, anxiety, and pain that some of our own students are feeling. As we endure these feelings and emotions we can reflect on what it is that our own teachers do that alleviates this pain and what they do that exacerbates or sharpens it. How do our teachers make it easier or harder for us to ask for help? Are there actions they take that boost our confidence and ones that kill us inside?

We can also observe how we deal with the experience of struggle on a personal level. Do we try to keep our problems private? What supports and resources do we turn to? Where do our fellow learners come into the picture and under what conditions are we more or less likely to ask them for help? Analyzing this will almost certainly give us some valuable insights into actions we can take with our own students who are struggling with similar feelings.

Noticing the kinds of teaching methods, classroom arrangements, and evaluative options that either make our struggles as learners easier to bear or bring us to the point of quitting altogether alerts us to the kinds of practices that should be a central feature of our own work. We may know, intellectually, that a kind word, a cutting remark, a tension-breaking or inappropriate joke can make a positive or negative difference to fearful students. But it's one thing to know this rationally and quite another to be the victims of a sarcastic aside or the beneficiaries of a respectful acknowledgment. Being on the receiving end of these utterances as learners reinforces our appreciation of their significance.

As you read these words I can imagine you thinking, "nice idea, but how am I supposed to find time to put myself in the position of learning something new and difficult when I don't have enough time to cope with all the things I have to do and teach right now?" Four opportunities suggest themselves as ones in which we can reflect on our experiences as adult learners: graduate study, professional development workshops, conference attendance, and recreational learning.

Graduate Study

Beginning college teachers on any campus are often recent graduates or likely to be finishing advanced degrees, so the experience of being a student is current or recent. Furthermore, the first experience of college teaching that many of us have is when we serve as a teaching assistant (TA) in the department in which we're studying.

Graduate study can thus be an invaluable site for reflection on the dynamics of teaching. As graduate students we're regularly brought face-to-face with the realities of power. Our professors control our scholarly fate and with it our career possibilities. No matter how congenial our relationship with an advisor might be, we know that at the final moment her word goes. Until we find a question and a methodology that she likes we're never going to finish that dissertation. Without her approval of what we want to do we know we're not going anywhere.

Reflecting on how it feels to depend so much on someone's approval is salutary. It should make us much more aware of the power we wield in our own classrooms and how that power is exercised ethically. Noticing the effects of an advisor's approving or dismissive comment about our work gives valuable insight into how our own students experience our judgments and comments on their efforts. This should help us provide more educative evaluations.

The experience of graduate study is, at best, ambivalent. For every professor we encounter who communicates clearly, there's one who glorifies opaqueness. For each class in which we experience a mix of activities involving our intellects, bodies, and emotions, there's one that is rigid and monotonal. For each teacher who demonstrates a concern that students actually learn something, there'll be one who makes it clear that time spent teaching is an annoying distraction from the real business of academe (building a résumé with enough refereed articles to knock the socks off a tenure review committee or to ensure a new job when tenure is denied). And for every teacher who shows it's important to attend and respond to how students are experiencing learning, there'll be one with a breathtakingly arrogant disregard.

Studying how good and bad professors work teaches us a great deal about the interpersonal dynamics of teaching. Yet, despite the opportunity graduate study offers for purposeful reflection on the nature of teaching, many teachers I speak to keep their lives as graduate students and their lives as teachers neatly compartmentalized. On the one hand they regret bitterly having to visit a university campus on a Tuesday night for hours of back-to-back, mind-numbing lectures, the purposes of which are never entirely clear. On the other hand they sometimes proceed unwittingly to reproduce these same behaviors in their own classes on Wednesday morning.

Keeping a regular learning journal of your experiences of graduate study can provide you with some provocative insights and implications for your own teaching. Even if your experience is one of near total demoralization it's still, from one point of view, useful. When you identify what your professors do that you find shaming, depressing, or off-putting you can resolve to make sure those same kinds of behaviors are kept to a minimum in your own teaching. If you feel powerless you can investigate where this powerlessness originates and what happens to make you feel it so deeply. Then you can study whether or not you might unwittingly be reproducing with your own students the very same power dynamics that so overwhelm you when you're in the student role.

Professional Development Workshops

Most college campuses make some effort at arranging workshops, presentations, and institutes for faculty members intended as professional development opportunities. Indeed, many have mandatory faculty days—often at the beginning of a semester or new academic year—at which attendance is required. These are often billed as "celebrations" of teaching, but sometimes having to sit through them is a form of punishment. I speak at a lot of these kinds of days and love to do so. But I learn more about teaching when I'm an audience member than when I'm the presenter. This is because I have the chance to experience, however temporarily, being in something similar to the same situation as that enjoyed or endured by my own students. When I record my own reactions to faculty professional development events I'm struck by how closely the qualities I look for in faculty developers mirror those that college students look for in teachers.

Let's start with my expectations regarding what makes a good workshop leader and what constitutes a good use of my time. First of all, I want those who are organizing the workshop or leading the session to be experienced practitioners who understand the dilemmas, pressures, and problems that I face. I'll take them seriously if I feel I'm going to learn something useful from them that will help me do my work better. I want the institute leaders to have been around the block a few times because this will help them suggest some routes through the typical classroom dilemmas, pressures, and problems I face. I've usually given up valuable time to be at this workshop so convince me early on that you've got something important that I need to know about and I'm hooked.

I want, too, to have my own experiences as a teacher respected. I don't want to be talked down to or treated condescendingly. I pride myself on being able to detect pomposity and self-importance remarkably swiftly so knock off the self-glorifying war stories. However, tell me a story that describes a situation similar to one I'm facing and give me some new ways of analyzing or responding to it, and I'm with you. I also appreciate presenters who strive to respond to what participants say they want, who address complaints, and who are interested in how we're learning. At the same time, I want whoever's leading the session to stand for something. I want to know that person has skills and knowledge to share that he or she considers important.

If college teachers simply thought about what demeaned or affirmed them during their time as participants in faculty development days, and what it was about those days that caught or disengaged their attention, this could provide some very provocative insights for their own teaching. It's clear that there's a remarkable correspondence between the behaviors that both college students and college teachers appreciate in their instructors (Brookfield 2015b).

Conference Attendance

Most of us have the chance to attend conferences in our subject and disciplinary areas, and these can be studied systematically as learning episodes in which our intellects and emotions are engaged or repelled. Even a bad experience can be useful if it alerts us to how we might be reproducing the same behavior in our own classes. I'd say that a lot of my own ability to lecture has resulted from observing some truly awful keynote speeches. From studying our own reactions to conference events we can stumble across some insights that have important implications for our practice.

But catching the fleeting thoughts that arise in conference sessions, coffee breaks, and corridor conversations is not easy. It requires deliberation and structure. A conference learning log can help us focus on what we can draw from conference attendance that will be helpful to our teaching. Whenever we notice something that engages or destroys our interest, or that affirms or insults us, we can jot the details down. Following are some instructions on how to do this that I've developed for myself and colleagues.

Conference Learning Log Instructions

As you attend this conference try and carry a small memo pad or tablet around with you in which you will jot down or type up notes on anything that captures your attention regarding the educational processes in which you're involved.

When you notice something that strikes you as important or significant—something that hits you viscerally and leaves you excited, angry, exhilarated, depressed, or in some other emotional state that's noticeably different from your everyday way of being—jot down the following details:

Note when and where the event occurred, who was involved, and what it was that was so significant about what happened.

If it was, generally speaking, a positive event, note (1) what it was that made it so positive and (2) those things that you do in your own teaching that you think might induce the same reaction in your students.

If it was, generally speaking, a negative event, note (1) what it was that so depressed, annoyed, demeaned, or bored you and (2) those things that you do in your own teaching that you think might induce the same reaction in your students. Also, jot down any thoughts you have on what the people involved could have done differently that would have avoided inducing this reaction in you.

Finally, on the basis of your responses to these items, write down any lessons that you think this experience has for your own practice as a teacher. What might you do differently, add, eliminate, or rethink in your own teaching because of what you've just experienced as a conference participant?

Here's an extract from a conference learning log dealing with my annoyance at having a keynote presenter refuse to give a speech and insist on putting us in small groups.

Conference Learning Log Entry: Spurious Participation

Showed up at PG's keynote speech today, ready and eager to hear his ideas. He's been such an influence and inspiration for me. I was very disappointed at being put into a small group as soon as I walked in and being told to share my experiences with a couple of strangers. I know this is supposed to be good educational practice—participatory learning in action—but I was pretty annoyed anyway. I'd come to hear him and the first thing that happened was I was asked to hear from others. I wonder why I was so annoyed? What he did is what I often do as a way of building cohesion among students and engaging their attention. Yet somehow I felt cheated, not respected. He was asking me to do something without letting me know anything about himself. There was obviously a reason why he was doing this, but he never let me in on it.

What would have helped? Well, if he'd done a better job of explaining why he wanted us to work in groups I might have been more ready to go along. Also, if he'd told me that he would be making a presentation in a short while I might have been able to do the group exercise in better spirit. Best of all, if he had given some scene-setting introductory remarks, and then linked the small-group task to what he'd just said, I wouldn't have felt as cheated.

Lesson for my practice? First, make sure that I don't ask students to give something of themselves to each other before I've given something of myself to them; second, when I use a group activity make sure I explain very clearly what it's designed to achieve; and third, let students know how a small-group task fits in to the overall scheme of a session before asking them to participate.

Recreational Learning

In this section I want to use an extract from my own autobiography as a learner to show how learning something new and difficult in a recreational setting, and reflecting on how this feels, can significantly change how you teach. As a result of the following autobiographical experience several of my causal, prescriptive, and even paradigmatic assumptions about what good teaching entailed were challenged and changed.

I'm in late middle age and getting flabby. Because the climate where I live is so unfriendly I need to find some indoor form of exercise that's weather-free. But doing sit-ups, squat thrusts, and running on the spot is really boring. My wife suggests swimming as a form of good cardiac exercise that doesn't involve jarring any joints. The only problem is I can't swim. My wife suggests I enroll in a swimming class for adult nonswimmers. I protest, saying I don't need it and that I can learn to swim self-directedly; thank you very much.

I explain how I've been working on self-directed swimming since I was in my teens. On each vacation, when the chance arises, I watch people swim in hotel pools, lakes, and oceans during the day and remember exactly what it is that they do. Then, under cover of darkness, when everyone else is asleep or eating, I slip out of my room—like some aquatic vampire—and make my way to the water, a Bela Lugosi figure with a towel rather than a black cape draped around my shoulders. I slide into the pool, lake, or ocean and do my best in near darkness to mimic what I've observed other people do during the bright light of day. Needless to say, I've spent several years floundering (literally as well as figuratively) in this self-directed learning project.

When my wife hears me describe my autobiography of learning to swim she gently points out that my "natural" learning style— self-direction—is, in this case, severely dysfunctional for me. (In spite of this humiliatingly penetrating insight we remain married.) She says that what I'm really afraid of is looking stupid in front of other people. All this self-direction is a cover for my innate shyness and my arrogant conviction that I can learn anything I want without others assisting me. What I need, she tells me, is to switch from my preferred learning style into a situation where I'm getting some expert instruction. I should study swimming with someone who can break down this extremely complex skill into manageable, but increasingly complex, operations. If this happens, she assures me, the confidence I'll derive from mastering some basic skills will lead me to increase my efforts until, before I know it, I'll be swimming. I protest that what she's saying is ridiculous, all the while knowing that she's right, a marital dynamic that continues to this day.

Insight

Sometimes the last thing learners need is for their preferred learning style to be affirmed. Agreeing to let people learn only in a way that feels comfortable and familiar can seriously restrict their development. If I'd stayed within my own habitual pattern of self-directed swimming I never would have moved beyond the point of staying afloat for a couple of seconds.

Meaning for My Practice

I must reexamine my previous belief that good teachers find out the preferred learning styles of their students and then design methods and forms of evaluation that connect to these. I understand this is important to do for some of the time so students connect to ways of learning that are comfortable and familiar. But it's equally important to expose students to ways of learning that are unfamiliar and that make them uncomfortable, at least initially. Good teaching involves broadening the range of learning styles with which students are familiar. No one can spend all their time learning only in the way they like, so providing experience with a range of styles is really in students' best long-term interests. From now on I'll try to mix methods and evaluative options that strike an equitable balance between affirming students' preferred styles and introducing them to alternative ways of learning. My preference for self-directed learning formats must be balanced with more directive and collaborative forms of teaching, learning, and evaluation.

The Story Continues . . .

A few weeks later I'm in a tiny changing cubicle at a swimming pool. It's the first evening of a class for adult nonswimmers and, while I'm stripping down to my swimming trunks, a number of thoughts are darting through my mind. One is that I hate to show my pale, pimply, naked Englishman's body in public. My torso and legs are so skinny and underdeveloped and my stomach is so flabby. Another is that I'm probably the only man in America who doesn't know how to swim. Somehow, my lack of aquatic ability embodies my problems dealing with the world of artefacts and the psychomotor domain in general (I have to ask my wife to tell me which is the Phillips screwdriver in the tool box).

A third thought is that it's taking some nerve for me to show up at this class and make a public admission that I don't know how to swim. I think, "if it's difficult for me to show up at an adult nonswimming class, what must it be like for a nonreader to show up at an adult literacy class? What an act of courage *that* really is!" As I step out from my cubicle to the poolside I look around at the other students in my class. They're all women. Right then and there I know that my suspicion that I was the only man in the whole country who didn't know how to do this was well founded.

Over the next few weeks I splash around in a fairly unconvincing fashion. Matters aren't helped much by one of our instructors. He's a young man whose athleticism, muscles, youth, and aquatic abilities have already prejudiced me against him before he has opened his mouth. He seems to bounce rather than walk into the pool area, a pedagogic version of A. A. Milne's Tigger, the kind of muscular jock I hated in high school. Moreover, he looks eighteen years old, a fact that causes me to reflect ruefully that when teachers and cops start to look to you like adolescents, you're really getting old.

Matters are made very difficult by his teaching method, one I would describe as "charismatic demonstration," which means he believes that by showing us how terrifically well he is able to swim, this will inspire in us an uncontrollable desire to match his exemplary performance. At the opening class, for example, his first action is to jump in the pool at one end, cut through the water with stunning power, aquatic grace, and fluidity, and emerge from the water at the other end. As he levitates out of the water he shouts out, "see how easy it is; that's all there is to it; in ten weeks you'll be doing this, too!"

This creates a crashing dissonance because for me to do anything vaguely resembling what I've just seen is an action so far beyond my comprehension that I feel like throwing in the towel (literally and figuratively). I pull him aside early on and explain that the problem for me—the thing that's really stopping me learn how to swim—is that I hate to put my head under water. Each time I do this I feel like I'm drowning. The universe becomes a white chlorinated haze, with all my usual reference points totally obscured. I'm reminded of how it used to be when as a young boy I was having dental treatment in England and the dentist would give me gas to knock me out entirely. There was the same sense of being out of control and the inability to stop oneself from being submerged by an onrushing smothering force. Putting my face into the swimming pool is as close to a near-death experience as I can have while still remaining reasonably sentient.

I ask him if I can do the backstroke (which will at least ensure that my face is out of the water), but he tells me that the crawl stroke is the stroke of choice and that's what *real* swimmers learn to do. He then says something to me that I forget but his whole body language conveys to me one unequivocally expressed message: "for God's sake, grow up. For once in your life act like a man."

Insight

The best learners—people for whom learning a skill or subject comes entirely naturally—often make the worst teachers. This is because they are, in a very real sense, perceptually challenged. They can't imagine what it must be like for others to struggle to learn something that they've found so enjoyable. Because they've always been successful in their learning it's impossible for them to empathize with learners' anxieties and blockages. I visualize my swimming instructor being thrown in the deep end of the pool at three years of age to find out to his surprise that he actually already knew how to swim. Because he didn't experience the terror I feel at putting my head in water, he can't offer any good insights from his own experiences of learning that might help me keep my fears under control.

Following this line of reasoning I realize that the best teachers are probably those who've achieved their skill mastery, knowledge, and intellectual fluidity only after periods of struggle and anxiety. Because they know what it's like to feel intimidated they're well placed to help students through their own learning difficulties. From now on, when I'm on search committees to appoint teachers, I'll make sure that as

I review candidates' CVs I'll look for academic records that start off relatively undistinguished but that improve over time. That will probably indicate that the candidate has a history of struggle as a learner she can draw on when thinking how to help her own students with their difficulties.

Meaning for My Practice

As a teacher I need to find a way of revisiting the terror most people associate with learning something new and difficult. Only if I do this will I be able to help my students with their own problems learning something that I enjoy teaching. I think about ways I could do this. One would be to bring in students from my earlier classes to talk to new students about the emotional difficulties they faced in their own learning. Another would be to find ways of entering my students' emotional worlds so that I can get some sense of the ways they're reacting to learning; this was a prime reason for developing the Critical Incident Questionnaire. Probably the best way is to put myself in my students' situation of learning a skill that is new and intimidating to me—just like I'm doing here.

Final Scene . . .

One night about half-way through the semester, a colleague in the swimming class to whom I'm complaining about my fears and lack of progress hands me her goggles and says, "try these on, they might help." I slip them on, put my head in water, and the effect is amazing! At a stroke the universe has been returned to me! True, the chlorine sting is still in my nose, but the awful white haze has disappeared. I can see the tiling at the bottom of the pool, the lines marking the lanes, even bubbles from my own breathing. I begin my usual attempt at the crawl stroke, trying to coordinate arms, legs, and breathing, and after a while I feel my hand hit tiling. "Damn," I think to myself, "I thought I could see where I was going with these goggles but I must have swum across the pool again, done a width rather than a length, and all the lap swimmers will be glaring at me for messing up their rhythm again."

I raise my head out of the water and I'm astounded at what I see. I'm at the other end of the pool from where I started a couple of minutes before. I've swum a length, not a width! With this realization I feel a startling jolt of pride, an unalloyed rush of pure happiness. I can't believe it! I thought I'd never see this moment. I've actually swum a length of a swimming pool without stopping at least once to touch the bottom of the pool and make sure I'm still in my depth, all the while pretending that I'm casually treading water. At some level I knew, or thought I knew, that this day would never come. Now that it's arrived I start to think that maybe I'm not the psychomotor dolt I always thought I was and that maybe all aspects of the physical world are not totally closed off to me.

Getting tenure, winning awards for books, having a good round of applause from an audience after a speech, notes of appreciation from students, learning to play the academic game by getting published in prestigious scholarly journals—all these things are nice and affirming, but they pale into visceral insignificance when compared to this moment. By any index, this is a "critical incident" in my autobiography as a learner, a transformative marker event when I looked at myself as a learner in a completely different way and realized a host of new and alternative possibilities for myself.

Final Insights

If it hadn't been for the suggestion of another student that I try on her goggles I'd still be splashing around in frustration. Her insight about how to deal with my fears made all the difference in the world to my learning.

On almost any scale imaginable by which one could measure aquatic excellence, my performance is pathetic. Seniors are zooming past while my own actions are an uncoordinated mess of huffing, puffing, and unsightly struggling. Yet, in terms of my own estimation of the significance this event has in my history as a learner, this means more than anything that has happened to me for quite a time. So, my subjective assessment of how well I've done probably bears no relation to the instructor's external assessment of my efforts. To him I'm still a dismally uncoordinated wimp who expends many more times the amount of energy needed to get down to the end of the pool. But external evaluations mean nothing next to my own sense that I've done something really significant. Swimming that length is a monumental learning achievement of intergalactic proportions in terms of my own autobiography. The instructor would give me a C minus while I'd give myself an A plus. And both grades would, in their frame of reference, be entirely valid.

Meanings for My Practice

I must remember that a student's suggestion that I wear goggles made all the difference to my own progress as a learner. I need to remember that the experts on learning are often learners themselves. Within any learning group students should learn to see each other as resources who can help with learning difficulties. After all, the formally recognized "expert" in the class—the teacher—was of no help whatsoever in getting me past the major blockage to my learning. The person who did most to help me through my anxieties was another learner who'd recently faced the same difficulty. It's just been demonstrated to me how crucial a peer's role was in my own learning.

So maybe when I'm setting up peer learning groups in my own classroom I need to pair up struggling learners with recently struggling learners, because they're the closest, experientially speaking, to each other. Previously I've tended to pair struggling students with high flyers, D students with A students. Now I'll change my policy and pair D students with C students. As an evaluator of students' learning I also need to remember that what I might judge to be a miniscule, insignificant amount of progress by a student—or even a total lack of movement— may be perceived by that person as significant progress. Subjective assessments of the meaning of learning to learners themselves may be very different from the objective assessments of teachers. I need to experiment with self-evaluation methods so students can document— in their own terms—how and what they've learned.

Maybe I should experiment with learning portfolios as an evaluative tool in which students demonstrate and document how far they've traveled in terms of their own histories as learners. I should also start giving more direction on how to write peer evaluations so students can give better feedback to each other.

Joining an adult swimming class is, in the grand scheme of things, a pretty prosaic event. My learning to swim didn't decrease the amount of injustice in the world and it didn't result in any social change. It counted for very little compared to the significant personal learning that people point to as being the most important in their lives. Yet, as a result of this one engagement in recreational learning, I was provoked into challenging and changing some teaching assumptions that I'd viewed almost as axiomatic. Instead of believing that it was my duty to cater consistently to students' preferred learning styles, I now knew I had to try and strike a balance between affirming these styles and making sure that students were exposed to other ways of learning. No longer would I insist on only self-directed modes of teaching and learning.

Instead of believing that the people who could learn something the best were also the best people to teach it, I now knew that naturally talented learners could be perceptually disabled when it came to understanding the source of students' anxieties about learning. This meant that the best learners sometimes made the worst teachers for students in struggle. Finally, I was granted a new insight into the contradictory, yet internally consistent, interpretations that students and teachers could make of the same learning effort. I knew that what to my eyes were apparently minor actions taken by students could, to them, be events of transformative significance. Knowing this made me a more even-handed, empathic evaluator of students and led to my experimenting with forms of self- and peer evaluation.

Conclusion

The lens of personal experience is probably the lens of critical reflection that's taken the least seriously. Yet, as I hope this chapter illustrates, it's incredibly formative in the development of our teacher identity. Using it reminds us of the anxiety and terror many of our students are feeling. The next (and final) lens we explore— the lens of theory—seems, on the face of it, to be the opposite of personal experience. Theory is often thought of as analytical, bloodless, and unemotional, a statement of truths developed over time by a community of scholars. Yet, as we shall see, theory can produce strong emotional responses. It can provoke and anger us in a productively disturbing way, yet it can also warm us with the reassurance of recognition, the feeling of coming home to an analysis we feel that captures something we've long been struggling to understand.

10

Learning from Theory

The final lens through which we can view our practice is the lens of theory. Although this book argues strongly for the importance of learning from experience, this doesn't mean that formal educational literature is, by definition, irrelevant; far from it. If I believed that I would have wasted a good part of my own life writing words that meant nothing. In fact reading educational literature can help us investigate the hunches, instincts, and tacit knowledge that shape our pedagogy. It can suggest different possibilities for practice as well as help us understand better what we already do and think. In this chapter I want to examine how reading educational theory, philosophy, and research can provide new and provocative ways of seeing our actions and the meanings students take from our work.

It's a strange truth that teachers are often suspicious of theory, regarding it as the enemy of practice. Theory is seen as the province of lofty theoreticians who are disconnected from the "real" world and live in some sort of abstract conceptual realm, a Rivendell of the mind. In fact, theory is eminently practical and is something we all produce, an inevitability of sentient existence. A theory is nothing more (or less) than a set of explanatory understandings that help us make sense of some aspect of the world. To the extent that making sense of existence is a natural human activity it's accurate to say in Gramsci's (1971) terms "all men are intellectuals" (p. 9); he would surely say "all people" were he writing today.

Interpreting, predicting, explaining, and making meaning are acts we engage in whether or not we set out deliberately to do so or whether or not we use these terms to describe what we're doing.

So the idea that theory and practice exist on either side of a great and unbridgeable divide is nonsense. Making this distinction is epistemologically and practically untenable. Like it or not, we are all theorists and all practitioners. Our practice is theoretically informed by our implicit and informal theories about the processes and relationships of teaching. Our theories are grounded in the epistemological and practical tangles and contradictions we seek to explain and resolve. The educational theory that appears in books and journals might be a more codified, abstracted way of thinking about universal processes, but it's not different in kind from the understandings embedded in our own local decisions and actions.

Theory can be more or less formal, wider or deeper in scope, and expressed in a range of ways, but its basic thrust—to make sense of the world, communicate that understanding to others, and thereby enable us to take informed action—stays constant. The more deliberate and intentional an action is, the more likely it is to be theoretical. To this extent theory is inherently teleological; that is, it imbues human actions with purpose. We act in certain ways because we believe this will lead to predictable consequences. Of course, our theory can be bad or wrong—inaccurate and assimilated uncritically from authority figures. We can act on understandings that consistently lead us into harmful situations yet remain committed to our theory because we're convinced we haven't understood it or its implications properly. But always in the midst of practice, action, judgment, and decision is theory.

In an eloquent passage in *Teaching to Transgress* (1994) bell hooks testifies to the way theory saved her life. In describing her need to make sense of her own family's dynamics she writes, "I came to theory because I was hurting—the pain within me was so intense that I could not go on living. I came to theory desperate, wanting to comprehend—to grasp what was happening around and within me. Most importantly, I wanted to make the hurt go away. I saw in theory then a location for healing" (p. 59). Theorizing—generating provisional explanations that help us understand and act in the world—helps us breathe more clearly when we feel stifled by the smog of confusion. We theorize so we can understand what's happening to us and so we can take informed actions.

What Reading Theory Does for Us

This fourth lens of critically reflective practice does something that no other lens can: it provides us with a coherent and comprehensive explanation of a piece of the world. Students' eyes alert us to things we've missed or misunderstood, colleagues' perceptions offer different takes on familiar situations, and our personal experiences remind us of what counts viscerally in learning. But reading a theoretical analysis, more than any other lens, enables us to stand back and see the big picture. Studying this picture often productively disturbs the familiar interpretative and perceptual ruts we travel in as we try to understand our practice. It opens new worlds to us, stopping us short with the shock of disorientation. Sometimes it enables us to recognize ourselves, such as when we read an account that makes explicit something we've suspected. Theory also stops us getting caught in the groupthink that sometimes develops when colleagues talk through a familiar dilemma.

It Drops Bombs of Productive Dissonance

One of the best things theory does is upset your settled understanding of some part of your life you'd thought was unproblematic. I described examples of this in chapter 2 with my use of the circular seating arrangement in class and my belief that I was a fly on the wall in discussion-based classrooms. Reading Foucault's (1980) analysis of power disrupted my neatly ordered judgments that I was "giving" my power away and moving to some kind of democratic, power-free zone. His work slapped me in the face and completely destroyed the self-congratulatory smugness I was feeling about my student-centered pedagogy. Up to that point the received wisdom in my field of adult education was that I was doing exactly the right thing. I remember colleagues and students complimenting me on my teaching style and the professional literature of the times urging me to get out of the way of students' natural self-directedness.

Reading Foucault and the analyses that derived from his work stopped me right in my tracks. It was the theoretical equivalent of emerging from a sauna. One minute I was luxuriating in a warm glow of self-satisfaction regarding my humanistic empathy, the next I was plunging through the ice, dizzy from the shock of a freezing reality. Throughout my teaching life the best theory has worked that way. It brings me up short and makes my life immensely more complicated. I'm forced to reappraise some fundamental paradigmatic assumptions and to suspend my provisional interpretations as I swim around in a sort of limbo. All the while I'm doing this I'm also trying to incorporate new perspectives. In the short run this is frustrating and I often wish I'd never been exposed to this new reading of an important part of my world. But over the long haul I know that having my life complicated in this way is going to give me a better understanding of the dynamics of teaching and learning.

It Opens New Worlds

Bombs of dissonance explode familiar understandings of current situations. But theory sometimes also introduces us to new vistas that broaden our understanding and force us to reappraise old assumptions. It also helps free us from falling victims to the traps of relativism and isolationism. To quote Freire (Horton and Freire, 1990), "Reading is one of the ways I can get the theoretical illumination of practice in a certain moment. If I don't get that, do you know what can happen? We as popular educators begin to walk in a circle, without the possibility of going beyond that circle" (p. 98). By studying ideas, activities, and theories that have sprung from situations outside our zone of practice, we gain insight into those features of our work that are context-specific and those that are more generic. Embedded as we are in our cultures, histories, and contexts, it's easy for us to slip into the habit of generalizing from the particular. Reading theory can jar us in a productive way by suggesting unfamiliar interpretations of familiar events and by suggesting other ways of working.

For example, emerging research on brain science (Johnson and Taylor, 2006; Lang, 2016; Taylor and Marineau, 2016), digital storytelling (Alexander, 2011), flow (Csikszentmihalyi, 2008), and playfulness (Brown, 2010; Kane, 2004) opened me up to the importance of incorporating visual, dramatic, and musical elements into my teaching. I'd estimate that I've spent thirty-five of my forty-seven years as a teacher working in an extremely linear manner, planning out activities, trying to stick to an agenda, and communicating almost wholly through words. Because of the literature introduced to me by Alison James (James and Brookfield, 2014) of the University of the Arts in London, I am much more inclined these days to ask students to present creative representations of their understandings of ideas using poetry, digital images, streaming, graphics, and mp3 files (although I do usually ask for a narrative explanation of abstract work).

Another profoundly unsettling body of work for me is critical race theory's analysis of the enduring nature of racism and the way whites enact the ideology of white supremacy (Bonila-Silva, 2013; Taylor, Gilborn, and Ladson-Billings, 2015). For most of my life I have considered myself to be one of those "good white people" (Sullivan, 2014) who don't see color but rather take people as they present themselves. Adjunct teaching in Chicago throughout the late 1990s and early 2000s with two African American female colleagues (one an Africentric theorist, one a critical race theorist) introduced me to literature that argued that my field of adult education was racialized almost wholly in favor of white Europeans. I read books like *Critical Theory in the Interests of Black Folks*

(Outlaw, 2005), *What White Looks Like* (Yancy, 2004), and *Black Bodies, White Gazes* (Yancy, 2008) and was forced into a deeply uncomfortable reappraisal of my own supposed absence of racism.

This reading meant that I could no longer elide questions about my own learned racism and the persistence of the ideology of white supremacy in my consciousness. I realized I had, and will always have, a set of learned racist instincts, intuitions and perceptions that frame how I see the world and how I approach working with students and colleagues of color. More recently, work on racial and gender microaggressions (Sue, 2010, 2016) has helped me to understand better how I enact my racism in the smallest of daily interactions.

So, after five decades spent thinking of myself as one of the good guys who's escaped racist conditioning I've spent the last decade and a half considering the alternative: that I've very successfully learned and internalized a lot of racist ideas. I'm complicit in unthinkingly supporting structures that legitimize racism and have a history of looking the other way when my own racism has stared me in the face. Theory has profoundly shattered how I think about my own racial identity and commitments and has caused me to rethink completely how I teach about race and racism. It has opened up a whole new world of pedagogic possibilities that I explore in chapter 12.

It Helps Us Recognize Ourselves

One of the most interesting things that sometimes happens when I read theory is to experience jolts of recognition. Sometimes this is pleasing, as in "hey, that's exactly what I feel but haven't been able to express!" This happened when I read Paulo Freire's distinction between being authoritative and being authoritarian (Shor and Freire, 1987). It clarified very helpfully something I'd already been feeling but had not yet put into conscious thought: that my commitment to democratic practices did not necessarily mean that I had to deny my own authority. Another was reading Ian Baptiste's meditation on a pedagogy of ethical coercion (Baptiste, 2000) and realizing that despite my language of facilitation and invitation I was still requiring students to do certain things and backing that request up with the weight of institutional authority. A third was reading Michael Albert's exploration of decision making in participatory economics (Albert, 2004, 2006) and appreciating the principle that those most affected by a decision should have the greatest influence in determining its outcome.

In all three of these cases reading theory crystallized and confirmed something I'd been pondering almost at a preconscious level. One of the hardest points of apparent contradiction I've faced over decades of trying to work in a student-centered, participatory manner is knowing that sometimes a democratically expressed majority preference is wrong and realizing that I had to fight it. An example would be facing a predominantly white group that declared itself "done" with race and that asked me, "because we've got race now can we please move on to something else?" In such situations I'd keep insisting that we needed to work more on this issue while simultaneously feeling somewhat guilty that I wasn't staying true to my democratic commitments.

Reading Freire, Baptiste, and Albert clarified for me why I wouldn't give up an agenda in the face of student resistance. Freire made me comfortable with acknowledging that sometimes my job as a teacher requires me to exercise my authority based on my greater experience, understanding, and study of an issue. Baptiste confirmed that the directive and coercive impulses I feel are an unspoken yet necessary element of teaching. And Albert helped me understand that the people of color most affected by racism were often not the ones represented in the classroom, and that what I knew of their wishes (that whites needed to engage in a sustained dialogue regarding their own embedded, aversive racism) needed to be factored into my decision of whether or not we were "done" with race.

Sometimes, however, the moments of recognition we get from reading theory are not so pleasant. For example, reading about racial and gender microaggressions (Sue, 2010, 2016) was pretty revelatory for me. The notion that I was an antiracist, pro-feminist educator is a big part of my self-image so to encounter a body of work that specified many examples of racist and sexist behaviors that I could recognize in myself was unwelcome and disturbing. A microaggression is a small act of behavior—a comment, a gaze, a rolling of eyes, directing eye contact to one person and not another, not hearing a comment made by one person but acknowledging the same comments made by another—that's experienced by someone as diminishing their humanity and marginalizing their significance. When this act is pointed out to the perpetrator that person typically denies any exclusionary intent and other members of the dominant group start explaining it away as forgetfulness or a simple error of communication.

As soon as I started to read this literature I became aware of the multiple microaggressions I commit in my teaching. I thought about classes in which I'd "inadvertently" overlooked students of color, how I remember male students' names far more than women's, and how quickly I shut down racially based expressions of anger so as to keep things calm. I recalled classes in which students of color had described instances of racism and how white students had piled on to convince them they were "just imagining it." And I shuddered to think about my structured blindness (pun intended) around visual disability when I would project a PowerPoint slide on a screen in class and proudly say to the group, "well, because you can all see it, obviously I don't need to read it."

It Stops Us Accepting Groupthink

For teachers who lack the opportunity to belong to a reflection group and who are unable to benefit from listening to the contrasting perspectives and interpretations of colleagues, the written word may be the only source of alternative viewpoints available. By reading books and articles we can engage in a simulated conversation about practice with interested colleagues. Freire (Horton and Freire, 1990) puts it like this: "when I meet some books—I say 'meet' because some books are like persons—when I meet some books, I remake my practice theoretically. I become better able to understand the theory inside of my action" (p. 36). A conversation with a book is written, not spoken. Books that end up with comments scrawled throughout the margins, pages turned down, and peppered with yellow slips are books we have talked with, as are e-books cluttered with our inserted comments.

Even for teachers lucky enough to belong to a reflection group, reading educational literature still serves an important function of combating groupthink. Groupthink (Bond, 2014; Janis, 1982) describes the way that groups' desire for unanimity and cohesion blinds them to unsettling but provocative new ways of understanding their collective experience. Teachers in peer learning groups often display an ideological homogeneity, sharing paradigmatic, framing assumptions about purposes and methods of education that are so deeply embedded that their existence is hardly even realized let alone subjected to critical analysis. They tend to value the same philosophical ideas and organizing concepts (being student-centered, working humanistically, creating inclusion, encouraging self-directedness, etc.) disagreeing only on technical matters concerning how best to realize common aims.

In such groups the prospect of groupthink is very real. There's a mutual reinforcement of pedagogical correctness and a corresponding dismissal of inconvenient points of view as irrelevant, immoral, or ideologically unsound. To stay intellectually alive, groups may need the stimulus of unfamiliar interpretations and perspectives. Having the study of educational literature as a regular feature of a reflection group's existence reduces the likelihood of groupthink and intellectual stagnation. This is especially true if group members deliberately seek to expose each other to ideas and materials that have previously been considered off limits, radical, or contentious. Viewing common practices through the lens of an alternative theoretical critique can expose contradictions of which we were previously unaware and can help us make explicit those paradigmatic assumptions that are part of our intellectual furniture.

Narrative Theorizing

When we use the word *theory* most of us think of dense prose, abstract reasoning, unfamiliar jargon, and generalizable statements about a particular phenomenon. For example, a theory of student engagement sets out the conditions under which students are most likely to become actively interested in learning, a theory of resistance accounts for the dynamics of noncompliance observable across multiple contexts, and a theory of hegemony describes and explains how people learn to embrace and collude in their own oppression. Theory stated in these terms can be immensely helpful and revealing, providing us with the analytical tools to understand what's happening in our particular corner of the world.

Sometimes, however, this kind of theory can be hard to contextualize. The specifics of our practice are experienced as so idiosyncratic that translating general insights into particular practices becomes problematic. I might know, for example, that Foucault (1980, 1997) believes that power is an ever-present circular flow, but how does that help me understand what's going on in a particular discussion session? Or, I may be intrigued by Axel Honneth's (2015) assertion that searching for recognition is a basic human need, but how does that connect to the way I give feedback to students?

One of the most interesting ways to contextualize theory is through the use of teacher narratives. Teachers' stories (Preskill and Smith-Jacobvitz, 2000; Shadlow, 2013) draw us into another person's experience and prompt us to look for connecting points and generalizable insights. When theory is woven into narrative experience, its utility and insightfulness are far more likely to be appreciated than if a stand-alone theoretical explanation is provided. For example, understanding hegemony as the process by which people learn actively to embrace their own oppression is made far easier when linked to an individual narrative describing how a faculty member enthusiastically filled up his or her life with work commitments that culminated in a mental or physical breakdown. Alternatively, the concept of microaggressions comes more alive when attached to particular stories of their enactment.

Scholarly Personal Narrative

In recent years Robert Nash (2004) and his collaborators (Nash and Bradley, 2011; Nash and Viray, 2013, 2014) have pioneered a form of writing they describe as a scholarly personal narrative or SPN. An SPN places the writer's narrative of her experience at the heart of the writing. The writer chooses a central dynamic of some kind of change and tells a story that she feels illuminates the complex dynamic studied. The SPN becomes a sustained exploration of one's own narrative experience of a particular question or problem that has broader social significance. It's not just telling a story of an interesting episode in your life. For starters, whatever aspects of your narrative are included in an SPN must illuminate some kind of central transformative dynamic you're exploring. Also the story you tell is constantly compared to relevant theory that confirms and challenges your narrative. So the particularities of your experience are illuminated or questioned by the research and theory you explore.

For example, an SPN doctoral dissertation that I chaired was Unger's analysis of how to build reciprocal relationships across racial and class boundaries (Unger, 2014). A white suburban minister, Sandra Unger used her experience of moving to the inner city and founding a program to help black teens prepare for work. Her attempt to build relationships with her working-class African American neighbors was the "data" she drew on to write her narrative. But the unfolding narrative was constantly informed by excursions into theoretical literature on race, class, tribalism, and power. Each set of events she described was accompanied by multiple, and sometimes contradictory, theoretical interpretations of the meaning of these.

It's this frequent use of research and theoretical literature to illuminate the particularities of a narrative that is the distinguishing characteristic of an SPN. Concurrent with telling a story the writer keeps bringing in theory that amplifies and critiques it. She or he offers multiple theoretical responses to a narrative excerpt, many of which challenge the writer's own organization and telling of the story. It's important to emphasize that the theory that's woven throughout the narrative should *not* always support the narrative as it's framed. The literature should challenge the narrative thread, give markedly different perspectives on what happened from those held by the author, provide multiple and contrasting readings of experience, and be critical of times when the narrative is becoming too neatly contrived. In this regard the dissertation supervisor or (in the case of a book the editor) plays a crucial role in identifying "inconvenient" theory or research that challenges the writer's presentation of his or her narrative. The reader must also insist that the author respond to this criticism.

Because an SPN moves back and forth between individual narrative exposition and theoretical commentary, there's no separate section called "Theory, Research, or Literature Review." This constant integration of theory means that the narrative is always deepening and changing. As the writer considers different research and theory that illuminates and questions the way the narrative is unfolding, he or she continually builds that new awareness of complexity into the story. Symbiotically, as new aspects of the experiences recounted are revealed, the writer often branches into theoretical areas not identified in the initial proposal.

A good example of an SPN (though written before Nash introduced that term) is Cale's (2001) analysis of his attempt to work critically and democratically in a community college freshman composition class. Cale spent a semester teaching writing through the analysis of race, class, and gender in contemporary America. His narrative illustrates how his attempt to teach his students to resist dominant ideology became an instance of ideological reproduction. Despite giving lectures critiquing the concept of meritocracy, identifying examples of racist stereotypes, and outlining capitalism's deliberate creation of an underclass, Cale notes, "once I allowed the 'common sense' of the dominant ideology to be voiced, nothing could disarm it" (p. 16).

It didn't matter that a disproportionately large amount of time was spent in criticism of dominant ideologies of capitalism and white supremacy. As long as Cale permitted his white students (the majority in the class) to voice their own opinions regarding racism the focus was continually shifted away from white privilege and toward discussions of reverse discrimination and black "problems." Cale refreshingly and courageously admits that his efforts to work democratically by respecting all voices and encouraging the equal participation of all learners "actually helped to silence some of my students, to reinforce the dominance of the status quo, and to diminish my own ability to combat racism, sexism, and classism" (p. 17). He is brutally honest about the way the theoretical tradition he drew on (critical theory and its application via critical pedagogy) resulted in actions that negated that same theory. He concludes his study by noting that his use of "democratic" discussion achieved little effect other than to provide "opportunities for students to attack and silence oppositional thinkers, including myself" (p. 17).

Anyone who's tried to get reluctant students to engage with challenging and diverse perspectives and feels he or she has only increased those students' recalcitrance will find universal and recognizable aspects in Cale's work. He may be dealing with one class in one particular semester at one community college in Michigan, but the demoralizing discovery that his attempts to emancipate were only confirming students' conservatism and the pedagogic dynamics he clarified helped me understand a lot of what has happened in my own classrooms over forty years of trying to do the same thing.

Narratives that are theorized and generalized as they are shared offer a powerful avenue for the scholarship of teaching and learning to have a dramatic impact on educators' practice. A narrative does not need to be an uncritical celebration of heroic struggle. It can be a reflective opportunity to present the details of experiences that feel and smell authentic and to see how the interpretations of these experiences can be framed in multiple and contrasting ways. This can be done in a scholarly manner by weaving theoretical illumination into the narrative. Such theoretically informed narratives have a more enduring influence on how a teacher actually acts and thinks than theory unadorned by narrative experience or story unleavened by theory.

A Productive Theoretical Insight: Repressive Tolerance

One of the most helpful theories I have come across in my career has been Herbert Marcuse's notion of repressive tolerance (Marcuse, 1965). Marcuse's analysis of tolerance was like an intellectual bomb going off in my life. I can even picture where I was when I first read it, sitting in the lounge area of the Lanchester College of Technology library in Coventry, England. Suddenly, things that had nagged away annoyingly at me became clear. In a brief essay, Marcuse had nailed the contradictions embedded in the educational urge to hold free, open discussions that actively included the widest range of views and to withhold judgmental condemnation of ideas that differed from our own familiar beliefs.

I was so taken by Marcuse's essay that when I became a professor of adult education I would scour used bookstores for used copies that I could distribute to students. Typically a corner of my office would have thirty to forty copies of the booklet stacked up in the corner ready for me to hand out in class when the notion of repressive tolerance came up. Now it's available online for free download from the website maintained by Marcuse's grandson (www.marcuse.org).

What was it about his idea that was so compelling to me? One central idea of repressive tolerance is that an all-embracing acceptance of diverse views in curriculum and classroom discussions always ends up legitimizing an unfair status quo. Such tolerance, for Marcuse, is repressive, not liberating. Broadening the perspectives reviewed in a curriculum makes teachers think they are giving equal weight to radical ideas when in fact placing them alongside mainstream ones always dilutes their radical qualities.

How does repressive tolerance work to achieve this? Essentially it ensures the continued marginality of minority views by placing them in close, comparative association with dominant ones. When a curriculum is widened to include dissenting and radical perspectives that are considered alongside the mainstream perspective, the minority perspectives are always overshadowed by the mainstream. This happens even if the radical perspectives are scrupulously accorded equal time and space. As long as the dominant perspective is included as one of several possible options for study, its presence inevitably ensures that the minority ones will always be perceived as invalid alternatives—as "others"—never as the natural center to which students should turn.

Marcuse argues that repressive tolerance is hard to detect because it masks its repressive dimensions behind the façade of open, even-handedness. Alternative ideas are not banned or even censored. Critical texts are published and critical messages circulated. Previously subjugated knowledge and perspectives (Africentrism or queer theory, for example) are inserted into the curriculum. The defenders of the status quo can point to the existence of dissenting voices (such as Marcuse's) as evidence of the open society we inhabit and the active tolerance of a wide spectrum of ideologies. But the framing of meaning accomplished by hegemony effectively defuses criticism. Sometimes the impact of radical texts is diluted by the fact that the texts themselves are hard to get or incredibly expensive. I've often thought about this when I buy books exploring radical ideas that cost over $100.

I constantly use Marcuse's theory of repressive tolerance to make sense of the contemporary discourse of diversity, of opening up the field of higher education to diverse voices, perspectives, and traditions. An honorable and emancipatory position to take on this issue is that college curricula should draw on multiple cultural traditions and different racial perspectives. Providing an array of alternative perspectives and sensibilities seems to be a major step in moving away from a situation in which white, male, European voices dominate.

By widening curricula to include a variety of traditions we appear to be celebrating all identities, cultures, and positions. But the history of white supremacy—the way that whiteness is presented as the natural home of scholarship and guardian of scholarly legitimacy—means that the newly included voices, sensibilities, and traditions are always positioned as the exotic "others." Administrators and faculty members can soothe their consciences by believing progress is being made toward racial inclusivity and cultural equity, and they can feel they have played their small but important part in the struggle. But Marcuse argues that as long as these subjugated traditions are considered alongside the dominant ideology, repressive tolerance ensures they will always be subtly marginalized as the exotic quaint alternative to the natural center.

Conclusion

Theory and other forms of educational literature comprise the fourth critically reflective lens. For theory to have maximum impact in working teachers' lives it needs to be written clearly. I don't mean that theory has to be dumbed down or denuded of radical intent. But for it to serve as a useful reflective lens it must speak as directly as possible to recognizable concerns and situations. So, whenever I introduce a theoretical concept such as hegemony or repressive tolerance I try to link it to a concrete event or dilemma that I know teachers will recognize. Embedding theory in a narrative flow is particularly helpful, which is why I'm such an advocate of the scholarly personal narrative form. The details of the story draw you in and then the theoretical analysis turns the tables on you by presenting different interpretations of what you've just been considering.

These days one of the ways people encounter theory is through *Wikipedia*. You hear a term such as *microaggression* mentioned at a professional event and, if you want to find out about it, the first thing you do is type the term into a search engine such as Google. Often the top line in the search results is the *Wikipedia* entry on that term so, by default, *Wikipedia* has become an entry point for, and major dispenser of, theoretical knowledge. In the next chapter we consider the role that search engines, online tools, and social media play in the critically reflective process.

11

Incorporating Social Media and
Back-Channel Communication

The first edition of this book was written early in the last decade of the twentieth century. At that time online learning was pretty much nonexistent and no popular social media tools existed. In the decades since then we've seen a genuine transformation in the ways people share information and communicate with each other. In the world of higher education the digital revolution has changed how institutions organize and market their programs. Because digital natives (those who've grown up communicating naturally through social media since an early age) now comprise the chief market of higher education, programs have to be designed, delivered, and marketed to incorporate social media. The first digital natives—the millennial generation (Bonner, Marbley, and Howard-Hamilton, 2011)—are also now becoming the first generation of university and college teachers. They assume as a matter of course that course announcements, details of assignments, and updates will be distributed via Twitter, Facebook, and other social media. Many classrooms will soon be completely paperless with no need to cart assigned books to class and all course readings shared via hyperlinks posted in the online syllabus, itself accessible only via learning management systems such as Blackboard or Moodle.

These days every college teacher works in a de facto hybrid manner (Caufield, 2011) combining electronic and face-to-face communication. "Smart" classrooms change the configuration of classroom space (Baepler, Brooks, and Walker, 2014), sometimes to a coffeehouse format (Morrone, Ouimet, Siering, and Arthur, 2014). The flipped classroom (Keengwe, 2014) or just-in-time teaching (Novak, 2011; Simkins and Maier, 2010) means that classrooms become sites for problem solving rather than delivery of content. Everything is now an example of blended learning (Glazer, 2012) because social media (Joosten, 2012) and mobile devices (Quinn, 2012) offer new ways of communicating with students and accessing information. The only question remaining is the degree of blending that happens, that is, how much electronic communication is integrated into course activities.

One of the paradigmatic assumptions that teachers of my generation have typically embraced is that online learning is an inferior experience because it lacks the stimulation and vividness of classroom environments that are populated with living, breathing individuals tossing ideas back and forth. Online education is frequently caricatured as an alienating, disembodied process that is in stark contrast to the warmth, fluidity, and intellectual excitement of bodies gathered together in face-to-face classrooms. But the assumption that traditional classrooms are stimulating and congenial learning environments brimming over with interpersonal empathy and intellectual energy, and online classrooms are lonely and isolated, needs hard scrutiny. I've participated in many face-to-face classrooms as student and teacher that have been (from my perspective) lonely, isolating, uncongenial, and unbelievably boring. As a learner I've suffered in such classrooms from disrespectful, unresponsive, and uninterested teachers and from being expected to study disembodied content in a lonely and stress-inducing competition with peers.

One of the most interesting realizations I've come to is that online teaching is not necessarily qualitatively different from its face-to-face counterpart. Indeed, research documenting the conditions for teaching online (Lehman and Conceicao, 2014; Palloff and Pratt, 2011, 2013; Smith, 2009; Stavredes, 2011) emphasizes that online instructors adhere to the fundamental principles of good teaching in any environment. These teachers set clear expectations at the outset, establish the relevance of learning early on, organize content into manageable chunks, use a range of learning modalities, employ questioning skillfully, provide continual feedback to students, develop students' sense of responsibility for their own learning, and organize relevant learning tasks incrementally to move from simple to complex. They also face many of the same classroom management problems confronted by face-to-face teachers: encouraging reluctant students to contribute, stopping an articulate minority from dominating, responding to diverse learners, working with larger and larger groups, providing opportunities for students to work at different paces, and so on.

Assumptions about Social Media

In terms of social media there are many paradigmatic, prescriptive, and causal assumptions I hear from colleagues. Many of these are contradictory, standing in direct opposition to each other. The following are some examples of assumptions voiced most frequently:

- Social media has turned human relationships into simulacra.
- Social media galvanizes classrooms and fosters student engagement.
- Social media have democratized civic engagement.
- Social media have reduced authentic democratic participation to single-issue politics via petition.
- Social media allows for direct engagement with a wide variety of perspectives on important issues.
- Twitter means students can't reason in complex ways anymore.
- Twitter has destroyed students' capacity to read and absorb arguments.
- Instant access to a plethora of information teaches complexity.

- Instant access to a plethora of information robs students of the chance to develop analytical skills.
- Texting has destroyed grammar.
- Texting has dramatically reduced students' command of vocabulary.
- Texting broadens participation and equalizes power and identity politics.
- The instant accessibility of online tools and information means students don't need to participate in class anymore.
- Instagram means today's students think in images, not words.
- The ubiquity of hand-held devices means today's students are much better at multitasking.
- The ubiquity of hand-held devices means students have lost the capacity to reflect deeply on concepts.

Most of these varied assumptions are drawn from the lens of autobiographical experience and reinforced by the lens of colleagues' perceptions. As a technophobe and Luddite I initially believed that online learning represented a concerted effort to de-skill teachers by producing standardized courses that almost ran themselves. To me these courses were a cash cow that kept down labor costs and opened up new markets for revenue: the twin pillars of successful capitalism. For those reasons I avoided any involvement with online learning and colleagues with a critical theory cast of mind enthusiastically supported my skepticism.

It was the lens of research that stopped me in my tracks, particularly the oft-quoted fact that the most reliable indicator of student success in online learning is teacher presence (Lehman and Conceicao, 2010, 2014). Indeed, once I taught a full-time asynchronous online course I realized I was giving far more detailed, individual feedback than happened in my face-to-face classes. So, far from removing teachers from the equation and de-skilling their ability to foster intellectual development, teachers who work online are often asked to be more centrally involved in designing activities and demonstrating responsiveness to students than is the case in their face-to-face classrooms. And the depth and frequency of evaluation is, at least in my experience, greater in an online classroom than in its more traditional equivalent.

Assumptions we hold about social media have real import. For example, if you believe that communicating in 140-character messages has destroyed students' capacity to read and absorb arguments, then (depending on your teaching philosophy) you're likely to ban smart devices from class and insist that students undertake copious reading. If you think the enormous popularity of Instagram means that large numbers of students think visually as much as textually you're going to redesign your lecture materials to include far more graphics, cartoons, and images. If you believe that YouTube allows students to engage directly with scholars who articulate a wide range of views on a particular issue you're going to introduce students to complexity through video, not just text.

I've sat in meetings or have been part of a teaching team in which different faculty members have held very different assumptions about the academic legitimacy of social media, and this has led to real conflict. For example, these days I tend to have a mostly positive view of social media. Although I'm wary of corporate monopolies, online advertising, and government surveillance of search engines, and although I deplore the fact that I now have an online profile that tracks my passions, political inclinations, spending patterns, and so on, I'm excited by the accessibility of information and the opportunity to build alliances afforded by social media. But if I work with someone who believes that social media dumbs down curricula and inhibits critical thinking then our team teaching is going to veer wildly from extreme to extreme.

Social Media as a Lens on Practice

In terms of the critically reflective lenses outlined in this book, social media have now become important in two of the four lenses identified: students' eyes and colleagues' perceptions. Let me talk first about the lens of students' eyes. Using a tool such as TodaysMeet has helped me get a quick read of where groups are in terms of their responses to classroom activities and their levels of understanding. This means that I now worry far less about going wildly off track in class or missing students' confusion regarding their understanding of content than used to be the case. I can pose a check-in question to assess student comprehension (perhaps by asking them to provide examples of a difficult concept we're examining), and within thirty seconds I have a sense of whether or not it's being properly understood. Similarly, I'm much more confident than I used to be that if a problem exists with any aspect of learning that's happening that that difficulty will show up on the TodaysMeet feed.

Experience has convinced me that (at least in my subject area) banning hand-held devices and screens doesn't really work. They're so ubiquitous that if I took points off every time students used them I'd be deducting points so often that the modal grade would be a C, something that did not represent the range or quality of work done in the course. Even if I thought these had disappeared I'd probably find out later that students were surreptitiously using them anyway but shielding them with clothes, bags, and bodies.

These days I assume that most students will have some kind of laptop, tablet, smartphone, or Android readily available and that they'll be using these throughout the class session. My approach now is to make a virtue of necessity and incorporate the use of social media into my class as frequently as possible. So the first thing I do when I get to class is set up a TodaysMeet web page for that day's session. As described in chapter 6, I can very quickly name a room—let's say "Cell Division," "Hegemony," "The Spinal Cord," or "Victorian Art of Yosemite"—that represents the topic for that day's class. Students can enter the room using any identity they want to create for that session, which is helpful when they want to ask questions or give reactions but don't want to reveal themselves as the authors of particular comments. They text responses using pseudonyms or even random numbers as their identifiers and if they're satisfied their anonymity is assured they have little hesitation in posing difficult questions or giving critiques.

I also have a live Twitter feed open for every one of my classes where I similarly encourage students to ask questions, make comments, express confusion or enlightenment, wonder aloud, and so on. I use Poll Everywhere or Socrative to create polls in which students vote for a choice among multiple options. Posting quick anonymous responses to a well-designed poll question provides a useful read of the range of opinions students hold on an issue, and it also shows you different levels of comprehension and understanding among class members.

The lens of autobiographical experience can also be crucial to our understanding of teaching online. If I had the administrative power to mandate it, I would require all new online teachers to take a class as a learner in that format before starting to teach this way. There's no better way to learn the importance of teacher presence in online courses than to be a student who has his or her posts ignored, concerns unacknowledged, and questions unanswered.

The lens of colleagues' perceptions of online teaching is also accessible in a way that often isn't the case with face-to-face teaching. Let me explain. Before I started teaching my first fully online course I asked to see how several of my colleagues structured their own online teaching. What did an online syllabus look like? How did they encourage student-student communication as well as student-teacher communication? What discussion prompts or questions did they use? How did they provide feedback to individuals and the whole class, and what was the frequency of teacher comments? What opportunities were created for synchronous office hours, top-off tutorials, or open question-and-answer sessions? How were Voicethread, YouTube, and other streaming tools incorporated?

It was remarkably easy to visit my colleagues' online classrooms, far easier in fact than if I'd had to arrange to go to a campus building at a specific hour on a specific day to observe them in action. My colleagues would give me their log-in details and I was away!

Similarly, by giving them my details I was able to share my own online course architecture with them, get advice on the clarity of my directions, the pacing of my content, how well my evaluative criteria and rubrics fit my stated learning purposes, and so on. Once the course was up and running I could ask colleagues to look in occasionally and give me their reactions to my assignments, directions to students, and responses to posts.

In a manner I'd not anticipated I find that online teaching is in a strange way more public than my traditional face-to-face practice. My colleagues can constantly pop in and out of my online classroom and I can visit theirs. And, instead of having to describe particular classroom interactions, as would be the case with my traditional face-to-face teaching, colleagues can witness them directly. This is in stark contrast to most of my collegial conversations over the years in which I've had to describe a situation as best I could and ask colleagues to give me their perspective. Now colleagues have direct access to the situations I want advice on instead of relying on my own, inevitably distorted, versions of events.

Power and the Use of Social Media

Critical reflection concerns itself with power and hegemony, so in this section I want to consider the intersection of power dynamics and social media. Although online teaching makes education accessible to populations who otherwise would be excluded, it also makes learning more public by externalizing students and teachers' thinking processes. But this public dimension means social media is also an experience in surveillance. Students are stripped of the right to privacy in an online classroom as instructors monitor participation and require a set number of postings by a certain time. From a student's viewpoint there's no hiding at the back of the class, no getting through a semester without being noticed.

An online classroom is often compared to the Panopticon that the French cultural critic Michel Foucault (1975) wrote about as the perfect architecture of surveillance. The Panopticon is a design for a prison system in which the prisoners are under constant surveillance in a perimeter of backlit cells and able to be observed 24/7 by a single guard shrouded in darkness in a tower situated at the center of the circle. The guard can see all the prisoners in their backlit cells but the prisoners can't see the guard behind the tinted windows of the tower. Because each individual prisoner doesn't know when he or she is under observation it's better to be safe than sorry and not commit any inmate infractions.

In much the same way the instructor in an online environment is theoretically able to observe student postings and activity at any moment of the day. He or she knows not only what a student is posting but also when it's being posted. If a posting time of 11:59 PM is specified and a flurry of students log on to post at 11:58 PM that fact is very public. Every student-student comment is also accessible to the instructor unless he or she deliberately creates separate student-only chat rooms or allows students to do so. The kinds of comments that students make to each other in face-to-face small groups or in the corridor before or after class are now on public display as a matter of permanent record.

In terms of face-to-face classrooms, social media offer a unique opportunity to illuminate power dynamics between students and between teachers and students. This is particularly the case with tools such as TodaysMeet, which allow for a degree of anonymity. Students are understandably unwilling to unearth power dynamics if they're worried about the repercussions of doing so. Having a public and anonymous forum that allows people to name what they see as a violation of limits, the dominance of a few group members, or an uncritical exercise of privilege is crucial if you as a teacher are to become aware of these. Similarly, naming and critiquing a teacher's behavior involving an abuse of power is much more likely, at least initially, if an anonymous channel of communication is open.

One problem of anonymity of course is its lack of accountability. People can say anything under its cloak without having to justify their comments or provide supportive evidence for them. So one important element in using the lens of social media as a channel of communication is to establish ground rules for participation. If I have a back channel of communication set up in class I need to let students know how to use it as a tool for constructive critique. One instruction I give is that negative personal comments about another student or students that clearly identify peers by name or some other distinctive characteristic are not allowed. If students see behavior that they think is shutting other people down then I ask them to identify a dynamic that's problematic and state it that way. So, for example, instead of saying "David is talking too much—other people don't have a chance to participate," people should post something like "we need to get more people into the conversation" or "can we hear from people who haven't had a chance to contribute yet?"

I don't apply this ground rule of restating particular criticisms as a general dynamic when it comes to comments critical of me as the teacher. If I believe in the value of critical reflection then I feel I have to be willing to model the process for people, even when it costs me personally. As a teacher my power location is different from that of other students. Certainly there are inequities and asymmetries among students based on identity politics, but I as the teacher have the full weight of institutional authority behind me. When calling me out on an abuse of my power it would be nonsensical to ask people not to mention me by name but only to identify a general dynamic. Clearly, in a comment such as "the directions for the assignment are unclear" or "the promise made last week to cover topic x today is not being kept" there's only one person it could be—me!

Of course opening up an anonymous channel of communication through which students can express dissatisfaction can sometimes be discomforting. When it comes to criticizing me the only thing I ask is that students provide concrete examples of the actions that exemplify my shortcomings. So, for example, if you call me a racist, let me know the comments I've made, behaviors I've displayed, or policies I've set that demonstrate that racism. If you believe I'm abusing my power and privilege, let me know specifically how that's happening. Is it in my choice of language, the way I'm controlling a discussion, the materials we're studying, the questions I'm asking in class, or the way I'm not creating enough opportunities for questions to be raised?

Once a social media back channel is established it's necessary to ensure that any questions raised and criticisms voiced be publicly addressed. Publicly addressing a criticism of your behavior as a teacher in a way that doesn't come across as defensive or self-justifying is very difficult to do but absolutely necessary for the critically reflective process to be taken seriously. When I read a comment criticizing my actions on a social media live feed such as TodaysMeet I try to follow the same process of responding every time.

First, I thank the anonymous person for expressing the criticism, saying that even one or two apparently isolated criticisms might actually represent a deep-seated problem with my teaching or leadership. Then, if the criticism expressed is in general terms such as "Brookfield isn't being honest with us" I ask anyone in the group to provide information about events, incidents, comments, or situations that demonstrate that dishonesty. Third, I usually admit that it's upsetting to read comments that call my competence as a teacher into question but that part of being an effective teacher is to be open to radically different perspectives on, or interpretations of, my actions. Finally, I try to do some in-the-moment reflection on the assumptions I hold that might be underscoring the actions or comments that are the focus of the criticism.

The criticisms I take most seriously have to do with the abuse of power. The lens of personal experience has convinced me that the classroom, community, or organizational dynamic that people are most disturbed by is the feeling that they're powerless to change an unsatisfactory situation. To feel trapped in a classroom where you judge yourself to be subject to the whims of a capricious and arbitrary teacher is to feel unheard, unacknowledged, and ignored. This feeling is why students drop out, change advisors, or suffer through boredom purely to get a required grade. At work it's why people quit jobs or, if that's not an option, why they fall ill from stress or go on automatic pilot.

What count as typical abuses of teacher power? Overt sarcasm is one, ignoring student requests another. You might disagree with student requests but you owe it to people to state clearly the basis for your disagreement. Making humiliating and disrespectful comments to individuals is clearly an abuse as is the more covert example of never bothering to try and find out what students' concerns might be. I've had students or workshop participants post how tired they are of discussing race or how fed up they are with a focus on critical thinking. Conversely, and sometimes in the same session, I've also had students post that I'm not focusing enough on race or that I'm holding back from a truly critical analysis. Another key disconnect that bothers people is when they hear me say I'll be doing one thing and then see me apparently doing another.

When these kinds of student comments show up on a social media feed there is a real opportunity to model critical reflection in action. I can set out the assumptions guiding my actions that are being criticized, show how the alternative perspectives proposed on social media are challenging these, and then try to re-assess the accuracy and validity of these assumptions based on students' criticisms. Of course this doesn't usually happen in the neatly formulaic manner I'm describing. Sometimes I'm caught doing something just because I've always done it that way and have to own up to that. But showing the power of habit is, of course, useful in and of itself.

Back-Channel Communication and Student Decision Making

I want to end this chapter by diving deeper into a theme I mentioned briefly when discussing social media in chapter 6. One of the things I'm most intrigued by as a teacher is the challenge of decentering my power and creating more democratic learning environments, all the while of course acknowledging the apparent contradiction that doing those things requires that I exercise my power to make it happen! Unless I make a deliberate attempt to stop external power relations automatically reproducing them-selves inside my classrooms, the voices of the usual suspects in the wider world outside will come to dominate the conversations that happen within. When it comes to classroom process there's a real temptation for students to slide into a traditional "let's make the teacher make all the decisions" posture. My interest has been reversing this whenever possible so that people feel they have the chance to affect what's going on.

Creating opportunities for students to be involved in meaningful decision making can be helped enormously when teachers delib-erately engineer the inclusion of certain processes and classroom protocols. Sometimes the kinds of teaching and learning decisions that students can control are pretty inconsequential, such as when they want to call a break. At other times they can be more substantive, as when students are asked to generate curricula, identify unresolved contradictions and unanswered questions in a topic area, or suggest overlooked course resources. These kinds of decisions usually happen sequentially toward the end of a semester or program because it's difficult for students to make good choices about topics, questions, and resources or to raise challenging questions without first having developed some broad familiarity with a field.

Of course there are many instances when an external agency has predetermined very closely the content to be covered or when a department requires a particular course to focus only on teaching particular content so that students can move success-fully through a program. In these situations social media can still help with creating greater participation and inclusivity. After all, even if you're teaching accounting procedures or the work-ings of a hybrid car engine, you need to know how well students are understanding the content, what needs to be re-explained, when more examples are necessary, and what questions students have about the content. You need to know if your instructional pace needs quickening or slowing, whether more or fewer visuals are needed, and if students are making relevant connections between seemingly disparate ideas and skills. Social media can help enormously in regard to all these things because they enable students to provide immediate information to you about how they're responding to learning activities.

Democratic decision making is a conversation characterized by the deliberate inclusion of as wide a range of possible perspectives and the consideration of as much relevant information as can be engineered. *Diversity, democracy,* and *inclusion* are to some degree synonyms. When the intent is to include the widest possible range of voices and views in decision making, and to prevent a dominant few from taking over the lion's share of participation, social media back channels can be very helpful. This is true not only in college classrooms but also in organizational and community contexts. Unless you insist on creating different channels of communication to hear multiple opinions and contributions, those who are used to exercising the most power outside an environment will do the same thing, often with no resistance, within it. They will likely speak the most, expect to be listened to carefully, and be used to having significant influence on decisions.

Social media tools such as Facebook, Twitter, TodaysMeet, or Backchannel Chat greatly enhance the opportunity to circumvent the power dynamics usually evident in face-to-face classrooms and include diverse perspectives that would otherwise have been overlooked. For example, for most of my career I've been pretty conscientious in trying to get students and staff members to think through difficult issues and engage in critical thinking and practice. Some of the questions I've grown used to asking in classrooms, staff meetings, and professional development workshops are the following:

- What are we missing here?
- What important questions are not being raised?
- Whose voices are not being heard?
- What perspectives are being ignored or overlooked?
- What do we *really* need to be talking about?
- How are our declared intentions and our actual actions contradicting each other?

These questions are designed to help groups and communities be more self-aware of the power dynamics that structure their decision making and habitual communication, in other words, for them to be more critically reflective. Pretty much every group professes itself to be open to a wide range of views, to welcome all voices and perspectives, and to be concerned that no one is overlooked. But when it comes to unearthing and confronting power, groups often fall short. I've been in multiple meetings in which the group is either unaware of its habitual pattern of communication and decision making or queasy about identifying and addressing a problematic power dynamic head on. When I pose the six questions previously identified directly to group members, people are consequently wary of answering them honestly for fear of stirring up animosity and fostering resentment with colleagues.

But if an avenue of instant anonymous communication is created the process often becomes more substantial. Provided that people trust the anonymity of the tool being used they'll post responses that ordinarily they wouldn't speak aloud. So in a class or meeting I'll put one of the questions on a TodaysMeet live feed and give people time to think about it and to post their own responses. This usually produces far more revealing comments than just posing the question verbally to the group and asking for reactions. The latter is often a stilted and hesitant process as people try to decide whether the environment is safe enough for dissension to be expressed without punishment. But when a back-channel communication is brought into a live environment it can release people to speak about what's really on their minds. It also gets many more people to express their opinion in a very short period of time, with no individual contribution exerting greater dominance than any other.

Back-channel communication has also been extraordinarily effective at surfacing critical perspectives on my own practice. One of my favorite things to do is to change slightly the questions so that they focus directly on my own actions in the following manner:

- What am I missing here?
- What important questions am I not raising?

- Whose voices am I not hearing?
- What perspectives am I ignoring or overlooking?
- What do I *really* need to be talking about?
- How are my declared intentions and my actual actions contradicting each other?

I've found that people are far more likely to answer these questions honestly on an anonymous live social media feed than to speak their responses to me. So I try to pause at an appropriate time in a class, workshop, or meeting and pose one of them. But instead of asking for verbal comments I ask that people post their responses to TodaysMeet and always create an anonymous identity for themselves before they post. After allowing people time to reflect and letting them see that I'm not watching those who are texting, the screen starts to fill with very pertinent responses. I can then give my verbal reaction to these and the group can move into spoken conversation.

After I've done this a few times and people have seen me take their criticisms seriously, my hope is that they'll start to speak future criticisms directly to me rather than under a cloak of anonymity. But I can't expect this level of trust to be there at the beginning of my time with any group. Using back-channel communication I can model an open, non-defensive response to criticism that eventually may lead to people trusting that they can express their criticisms and concerns directly to me.

Conclusion

In this chapter I've argued that the explosion in online communication that has occurred since the first edition of this book appeared has broadened the way that the lenses of students' eyes, theory, and colleagues' perceptions can be brought to bear on our practice. Social media have immediacy and inclusivity built into them that enable much quicker access to information and speedier responses to critique. Theory that previously could only be read in books that may have been checked out of the library for weeks or journals that are only stocked on a campus several towns away is now immediately available. We don't have to wait for books we've ordered to show up or for borrowers to return them to the library. Neither do we have to ask colleagues in a different state to photocopy articles in journals they subscribe to but that we can't afford. So, properly used, social media are very useful enhancements to our practice of critical reflection.

In the next chapter I extend the analysis of social media to the role they play in prompting critical reflection on race and racism. In particular I look at the ways teachers can model critical conversation about race in front of students and colleagues and the crucial role of narrative self-disclosure as a critically reflective tool.

12

Applying Critical Reflection
to Teaching Race and Racism

Uncovering assumptions about race and racism is one of the hardest critically reflective projects, particularly for white teachers unused to seeing themselves as racial beings. In my own work I find it very difficult to detect the ways racism lives within me and how racist instincts and intuitions manifest themselves in what I assume are seemingly benign behaviors. I also find it incredibly hard to lead conversations designed to uncover racism. I feel it's my responsibility to do this but I know these conversations will invariably be tense, fraught, and leave people very unsettled. Pain, anger, and frustration will inevitably be expressed and most participants will conclude that we've ended up at what feels like an unsatisfactory point of nonresolution. Furthermore, people of different racial identities often feel that others in the group "just don't get it" and that authentic communication across racial differences is impossible. Over the years I've had many people tell me that the one thing they've learned from starting a discussion of race is never to initiate such a discussion again.

Why Is Critical Reflection on Race and Racism
So Difficult?

There are several reasons why applying the four lenses of critically reflective practice to issues of race and racism is so problematic. Some of these have to do with the general nature of critical reflection that requires that we consider perspectives we sometimes find alien and disturbing. Others have to do with the particularities of the topic. Race and racism are hard to talk about in any way and at any level. A whole new level of critical complexity emerges when we start to unearth and challenge assumptions about race that we've lived by and acted on for many years. This is particularly so for whites who consider themselves "good white people" (Sullivan, 2014) opposing racism.

The Problem of Perspective Taking

The attempt to try to understand the world as someone else experiences it is what Mezirow (1991) labels as the process of perspective taking. He argues that it requires empathy, the ability to bracket beliefs, and a critical curiosity exercised in the asking of revealing questions concerning someone else's experience. Getting yourself out of a familiar perspective and looking at an event or experience in a fundamentally different way is an enormously complex task. It requires you to suspend temporarily all the instincts, frames of reference, and interpretive filters that you trust to guide you as you make sense of the things you see around you.

One of the biggest problems in fostering critical conversation on race is struggling to see the world through a fundamentally different racial lens. As mentioned previously, students and colleagues of color have often told me that they see *everything* through the lens of race. To whites such as myself, many of whom think of race as something that comes up only occasionally in specific situations, this is a very hard reality to appreciate.

When perspective taking about race is concerned there's also the fact that the experiences you're striving to understand and take seriously are often ones that you find unthinkable. For most whites being told that they live in a racist world where their unearned power and privilege causes them to perpetuate an unjust system is, quite literally, inconceivable. They can't imagine that this might actually be the truth. Furthermore, this unimaginable truth is one that sometimes implicates them in maintaining a racist system, something they'd much prefer not to contemplate.

The Ideology of White Supremacy

A second difficulty is connected to the ingrained ideology of white supremacy. This ideology holds that whiteness is the natural order of things. Leaders look white, people in positions of power and authority look white, and the knowledge we take most seriously in life is produced by whites. This ideology holds that what are assumed to be the normal ways of communicating along with what counts as legitimate speech and artistic forms are all defined by whites.

White supremacy is *not* going around thinking of oneself as an Aryan super being. It's more of an ingrained, unexamined understanding that the experts and leaders we take most seriously look white. White supremacy is experienced as a momentary register of shock when a black pilot enters the cockpit of your airplane, a Pakistani female surgeon enters the OR to conduct your surgery, or the president of the United States is black. The momentary disconnect whites feel in these instances reflects a deep-seated and ingrained belief that authority, legitimacy, and leadership naturally look white.

Defining Racist and Racism

A third difficulty is the severe discomfort produced by thinking of oneself as racist or complicit in racism. Part of this has to do with how racist and racism are defined. In general parlance people call each other racists to signify that they're ignorant bigots. So when the term is introduced into a critically reflective conversation people quickly jump to assume that they're being told that they're fundamentally bad and immoral creatures who deliberately cause harm to others based only on their skin color and phenotype. No one wants to hear himself or herself described that way so analysis and conversation often explode or freeze when the term *racism* is introduced.

This is why it's crucial early on that the leader or facilitator explain that the terms *racist* and *racism* are used to describe systems and structures that teach and reproduce beliefs and behaviors designed to keep a racially exclusive system intact. By this definition a racist is someone who has learned these beliefs and behaviors while being immersed, without realizing it, in the ideology of white supremacy. Racism thus becomes a way of thinking and behaving that we learn every day without being aware that this process of informal education and socialization is happening. Once racism is understood as an all-pervasive ideology that's systemically disseminated then people find it easier to see how they're affected by it. Viewed this way it would be strange for someone *not* to have assimilated elements of racist ideology because we breathe and drink it in every day of our lives.

The Slippery Nature of Racial Microaggressions

Another difficulty is that ever since the civil rights movement brought in legal reforms banning overt discrimination, and in an era that many people describe as post-racial (largely owing to the election of a black president), identifying exactly what counts as racist behavior has become more complex. Overtly racial slurs, policies, and actions are still plenty in evidence as the Black Lives Matter movement attests. However, as critical race theory (Delgado and Stefancic, 2012; Stefancic and Delgado, 2013) points out, legal changes mean that racism these days is also expressed in covert ways. When confronted with evidence of racist ideas or practices whites will retreat to a position of aversive racism (Pearson, Dovidio, and Gaertner, 2009), strenuously denying any racist intent in their behaviors.

One of the most frequent contemporary expressions of racism is in racial microaggressions (Sue, 2010), that is, small apparently matter-of-fact behaviors that are experienced as exclusionary or diminishing by people of color. Examples would be patterns of eye contact in meetings that favor whites, making stereotyping jokes and asides that go unchallenged and are assumed to be benign, and overlooking unequal patterns of contribution in a racially mixed group. When challenged on their commission of these microaggressions whites will typically band together to convince the person of color that he or she is imagining things and that the white involved is a good person and had no idea that he or she was excluding or marginalizing someone.

I can't tell you the number of times when I've heard whites say of themselves or of colleagues that they "don't have a racist bone in their body" when a racial microaggression is pointed out. This "racist bone in their body" denial supports the mistakenly essentialist approach to defining racism. From an essentialist perspective you're either born racist or not, either a bad person full of racist bigotry or a good antiracist working for harmony. This essentialist approach completely elides the analysis of racism as a structural, systemic phenomenon, a set of institutional practices that maintains the dominance of white supremacy.

Racism comprises a set of values and beliefs that are learned and assimilated over a lifetime and that cohere into a framing perspective on the world. Racist perspectives and assumptions are paradigmatic; they structure how we look at life. When they're uncovered and challenged our world is shot to pieces and our notion of us as good, moral people crumbles (Sullivan, 2014).

Because I don't go around using the n word and making crude racial jokes I can convince myself I've escaped racial conditioning. But faced with the reality that I may be committing racial microaggressions it's much harder for me to think of racism as something that hasn't touched me. As long as I can conceive of racism as a big overt thing out there in the world outside me, I don't need to think about my small acts of racist invalidation. However, once I think of racism as an ideology that is learned and reinforced every day and that manifests itself in the micropolitics of daily interactions, it's much harder for me to pretend that it's something I've escaped.

The Inability of Whites to See Themselves as Racial Beings

Finally, critical reflection on race is difficult for whites who don't see themselves as racial beings or having any kind of racial identity. The way that the white discourse of racism and diversity is structured typically casts racism as a problem only for those on the receiving end. Because racism is thought of as something that people of color experience, the burden of confronting it is unthinkingly placed on their shoulders. But racism is just as much a problem of white Euro-Americans. After all, people like me are experts on enacting racism. Over my life I've assimilated racist frameworks, attitudes, beliefs, and behaviors very successfully. For many years I accepted unquestioningly that encountering racism was the province of people of color and that meant that I was somehow above the fray. I was not a raced being; I was white! It was *other* people who exhibited race.

If you're white and don't see yourself as having a racial identity it's very easy to think that focusing on issues of race is something that doesn't really apply to you. You can say to yourself that of course you condemn racism, that you're not racist, and that seems to be the end of the matter. To be asked, "what does it mean to be white?" is to contemplate something you've never thought about before in your life. If you've moved through life thinking that you are the norm (which is a central element in the ideology of white supremacy) and that racism is a problem of others who don't share your skin color or phenotype, then it's extremely difficult to start thinking of yourself as a racial being.

Using Narrative Disclosure to Set a Tone for Examining Race

Given the outlined difficulties it's daunting to think about how we might become more critically reflective about examining our own racism and helping others do the same. However, the lens of personal experience offers a useful starting point. Time and again when I've been working with colleagues, students, and communities of color I've heard the same message: "we don't need you to find out about *us*—we need you to find out about *you*." In other words, they'd like me and other whites to consider what it means to be white, what are the elements of a distinctly white identity, and how that identity confers unearned power and privilege.

This is why any attempt to get people talking about race and racism really needs a hefty amount of initial self-disclosure by the leader. As a participant in diversity and antiracist professional development workshops over the years this dynamic is often noticeably absent. Instead the workshop is set up to help participants learn about cultural and racial difference and to help them be more alert to the ways they fall into reproducing racist behaviors by perpetuating cultural stereotypes and holding inaccurate assumptions about different racial groups. The underlying assumption is that through education and self-reflection people can learn to work in ways free of racist undertones. In this approach antiracist and diversity education is something done to you by those who have cracked the code of cultural misunderstanding and who have come out the other side of struggling with racism to a point where they can now teach others how to think and work in non-racist ways.

What's often missing from this approach is an explicit examination of personal experience by those in charge. A narrative disclosure of how the leader or facilitators have striven to uncover their own racial assumptions and how they've tried to open themselves up to new and troubling perspectives is a necessary precondition for good conversation about race. It's absolutely crucial for white teachers engaged in this work to talk about the ways they learned racism and the way it still lives within them. I know that in my own case I'll never lose the racist instincts and intuitions I've learned; white supremacy has successfully inscribed itself way too deeply within me for that to happen. To the extent that I constantly commit microaggressions, remain blind to others' microaggressions, and still see students and colleagues of color as the exotic or threatening "other," I will always be racist. However, I can strive to be aware of these things as best I can, to watch out for them, and push back against them.

When I'm in charge of a class, workshop, training, or meetings in which uncovering racism is the declared purpose I usually begin by disclosing my own racial history. As with most whites of my generation in Britain, I grew up in a world in which whiteness, and all things white, was taken as the "natural" order of things. I adopted, without ever thinking about it, what Yancy calls a *white gaze* (2008, 2012), that is, a view of blackness that interpreted every black action and statement through a lens confirming my supposed superiority as a white person.

I've had six decades of ideological conditioning into white supremacy and, as a result, I don't expect it ever to leave me. It's very clear that, far from having no racist bone in my body, my skeletal framework has racism as its bone marrow. I learned stereotypes and bias through jokes with peers, family conversations, and media images that flourished in the vacuum of no contact with anyone other than whites like myself. I don't think I had a conversation with a black person until I was eighteen years old. This ideology of white supremacy rarely named itself as such. Overt declarations of white racial superiority were rare and, even as racist attitudes were being learned, I was engaged in apparently antiracist acts. For example, as an undergraduate I participated in demonstrations against the South African rugby team that represented the then-apartheid regime. But external behavior often masks learned instincts, and so it was with me.

External events sometimes challenged the power of this ideology. One pivotal event in adolescence helped disrupt the way white supremacy moved in me. This happened at the age of seventeen when I was being beaten up by a gang of white youths (they were "rockers"; I was a "mod") in an English town one Friday night. A black American serviceman from a nearby USAF base crossed the street and broke up the fight telling us "everybody's got to be cool now." In my memory I was on the verge of falling to the floor as the GI intervened to save me from potentially severe injury.

Being born in Bootle (Liverpool) I knew that once you were on the floor things got a lot worse because then people could kick you in the ribs, kidneys, and head. That event formed what critical race theory calls a counter-story that disrupted the white supremacist script forming in my head. The supremacist script said that black people are violent and start fights and white people are peacemakers who sometimes have to use force to reign in black instigators of violence. Here was a stunning role reversal that made a big impression on me. Whites had initiated the violence, and a black person had stopped it!

As well as talking about their own learned racism, teachers, leaders, and facilitators can begin classes, meetings, or workshops by disclosing their own recent enactments of microaggressions. When I want to introduce this concept to a group I typically begin by conducting a public analysis of my own recent racial and gender microaggressions. One example I've often used happened in an academic class on leadership in which I asked all the students in a discussion to give their preliminary take on an issue we were examining that day. After hearing from each student I summarized what I felt were the main themes and differences revealed in the discussion. On finishing my summary a white female student raised her hand and said I'd missed out hearing one member of the group, a young Asian American woman. I was momentarily flustered and apologized to the student and then invited her to speak.

During the coffee break I thought the incident over and realized it was a classic example of a microaggression. I certainly had no plans to exclude this student. I hadn't come to class thinking, "I must make certain student A doesn't have the chance to speak." So when I returned to class after the break I began the session by apologizing again and saying that what the students had just witnessed was a classic example of a racial microaggression. A representative of the dominant culture had unknowingly and unwittingly marginalized someone from a community of color.

One of the white students told me not to be so hard on myself and said I was reading far too much into a momentary lapse of forgetfulness. I explained that microaggressions are never intended. Instead, they're ingrained, seemingly instinctive behaviors that represent years of unconscious assimilation and socialization. They're ideological in the sense that they become part of our daily repertoire, behavioral minutiae that actually represent a socially ordered system of structural inequality. At this point the student I had overlooked spoke up and said that the same thing had happened to her in every class she had taken at the university. Her experience had been that of being repeatedly ignored.

Colleagues as Critical Lenses on Race

Deeply embedded paradigmatic assumptions are almost never surfaced without the involvement of others. These assumptions are constituent of our identity in that they seem to be obviously true renditions of the world. The only way they're challenged is if some external circumstance forces them to the forefront of our consciousness. One way this often happens is when another person provides a starkly different version of reality. This idea is at the core of critical race theory's emphasis on counter storytelling (Bell, 2010; Nash and Viray, 2013). For whites to hear students or colleagues of color describe their experience of racism with all the pain and anger that involves is what theorists of transformative learning (Taylor and Cranton, 2012) call a *disorienting dilemma*. This is particularly the case if the situation being described is one in which you've participated or eerily close to one you're currently experiencing.

Optimally, a multiracial team should facilitate every discussion, meeting, workshop, or class convened to uncover racism and explore how we might talk across racial differences. It should open with team members discussing their own dynamics and the way that their different racial identities have affected their patterns of communication and decision making.

What Students' Eyes Tell Us about Examining Race in the Classroom

Students of all racial identities often complain of race fatigue. White students say they're tired of always being asked to focus on what they regard as a nonissue or of being made to feel guilty when they had no direct hand in the racial oppression of the past. Students of color are tired of having to speak for their race and being expected to raise the racial consciousness of reluctant whites. In predominantly white institutions faculty of color also live with the institutional expectation that as well as teaching about their subject they will have essentially a full-time second job teaching their faculty colleagues about race.

But avoiding discussions of race is *not* an option. Given the changing demographics of students in higher education, issues of race will force their way into the classroom. The reality is that faculty members in every discipline will sooner or later have to deal with racial dynamics and tensions in their classrooms and departments. Also, talking about race is just the right thing to do. So what can we learn from students' experiences of participating in discussions of race? In particular, what do students tell us about the kinds of classroom climates, arrangements, and activities that help get them participating in racial discussions? In this section I want to build on twenty years of data collected from Critical Incident Questionnaires administered in multiple classroom, workshop, and community settings all focused on fostering discussion of race and racism. These provide a number of insights and guiding principles that constitute a starting point for a critical reflection on race.

We Need to Prep Students

It's clear that in students' eyes faculty members need to prepare for racial conversations by creating some ground rules that lay a foundation for what lies ahead. Students need to be made aware of the fact that discussions will get fraught and heated. They also need to trust that they're in the hands of a capable discussion leader (about which I'll discuss more). The idea of safe spaces and brave spaces (Arao and Clemens, 2013) is a useful one to invoke as a way of getting students to focus on what's coming. People often say they want discussion of race to be in a safe space. By this they mean that no one will be pilloried for saying the wrong thing, people won't call each other names, and everyone will treat each other respectfully.

The problem is that safe spaces can also be interpreted to be spaces in which no one is made to feel uncomfortable. In racial analyses that's going to be impossible. If discussions of perceived racism reach a point at which people can stop further analysis by saying, "I just don't see it that way so we'll have to agree to disagree" then no real progress is being made. Participants need to be ready to hold differences in tension and exercise critical curiosity on the origins of this difference and the reasons why people feel so strongly that an alternate viewpoint is wrong. This is often called a *brave space*.

A brave space classroom is one in which challenges, not attacks, are present. For example, one person saying to another "you're a racist" is an attack. By contrast, saying "I hear that comment as containing an element of white supremacist ideology in the idea that whites are the natural gatekeepers of truth" is a challenge. In brave space classrooms the perspectives, theories, and arguments people would prefer to avoid are ever present. This sometimes gets emotionally draining, a reality that also needs to be acknowledged.

A colleague of mine, Lucia Pawlowski (2016), writes in her syllabus for a course on Race, Gender, and Sexuality in Language:

> Know that there will come a point in the semester for most of you (1) when you think: "I've heard ENOUGH about oppression. I am DONE." At this point, come see me or a counselor to talk it out; (2) when you want to stop reading and doing your work for this class because

you are so emotionally exhausted from thinking about this stuff. That is to be expected; it is normal. When that happens, try to push through, and reassure yourself it's something you can overcome—and of course, let me know if I can help. The point is, this is not just an intellectual journey; it's an emotional one. You're going to have to invest your whole self in order to learn about oppression, power, and privilege.

One thing that prepares people for brave space workshops and classrooms is the presence of clear ground rules and criteria for participation. It's helpful to have clear discussion protocols that students understand are designed to stop one or two strong voices dominating. Examples of this would be the Circle of Voices exercise, the Bohmian Dialogue approach, or the Circular Response method (see Brookfield and Preskill, 2016, for descriptions of all these). All of these are introduced to participants as ways to democratize participation and create alternate conversational rhythms. Others such as Chalk Talk or TodaysMeet build on visual modes of communication and are done silently.

Modeling by Leaders Is Crucial

Students and colleagues also say that they appreciate it when leaders begin an examination of race by first modeling their own participation in any of the risk-full activities they plan for the class or workshop. Not only does this modeling provide clear examples of what brave space behaviors look like but also it earns teachers and facilitators the right to ask students and colleagues to begin this difficult work. If you show you take a task seriously enough to do it yourself in front of students you're on much stronger moral ground when it comes to asking them to conduct the same activity.

So, for example, if I'm going to ask people to recall microaggressions they've enacted I need to do this first in front of everyone by listing some of my most recent transgressions. If I believe in the importance of racial perspective taking then I need to show people that I'm willing to listen to a statement full of pain and anger directed at me. In doing this I need to demonstrate my commitment to listening carefully and exercising critical curiosity by asking questions about the experiences that informed that expression. Before asking students to discuss racial topics in groups, I and other faculty colleagues need to do a fishbowl or some other modeling of this process. We need to show students how in our own discussions we strive to understand different racially based perspectives, disagree respectfully but constructively, remain curious about dissenting views, and try not to shut people down prematurely. And if I'm going to ask students about the formative experiences that helped them develop their own racial identities, then I'm going to have to start the process off by disclosing my own.

Conversations about Race Will Not Produce Solutions

This may appear to be a very depressing reality for students and colleagues desperate to know what they can do to help fix the problems identified. There'll be a strong desire for closure at the end of a discussion. People will want to leave with a clear plan for ending racism, a desire to do something, anything.

So it's important as you enter an examination of race and racism to make it clear that racism is far too complex a phenomenon to be analyzed and understood in a semester-long course. Probably the most we can hope for is that people will leave with a deeper understanding of how racism operates in a structural and systemic way, rather than just at the level of individual prejudice and stereotyping. In syllabus statements, workshop objectives, and as we introduce meeting agendas we need to acknowledge that we shouldn't put the burden on ourselves of expecting to generate a solution to something that has confounded so many people for so long.

However, it's equally important to pay attention to considering what small next steps might be taken. Students say they need to leave the class with something other than a sense of total demoralization, a numbing radical pessimism. This is a very difficult dynamic to negotiate. After all, part of learning about racism is to understand its pervasiveness, the way it's systemically disseminated through the ideology of white supremacy and how it's embedded in institutional policies and practices that come to seem normal and natural. To end a class discussion with some next steps risks trivializing the deep-seated, historical nature of the problem.

But we also need to keep students committed to examining the topic and to answering quite legitimate questions about their future personal, professional, and civic action. One way to do this is through narrative disclosure of your own movement forward into greater understanding or small steps and localized actions you've observed, such as the following:

- A time when you identified a microaggression in yourself and made it public
- An instance when someone who'd dismissed a workshop on racism as political correctness subsequently called out institutional bias
- A situation in which a group discussion that had threatened to shut down was remedied by someone asking a specific question
- A moment when a person of color nominated a white colleague as an ally and explained what informed this judgment
- A moment when someone interrupted a racist statement and made the speaker or group aware of what was being said

Another way to provide some critically tempered hope is to highlight video streams of college and community groups engaged in concrete projects, particularly those involving multiracial groups committing to some common action. The national networks of Showing Up for Racial Justice (SURJ) and Black Youth Project 100 (BYP 100) groups would be examples.

Normalizing Racism

One of the biggest inhibitors to whites participating in racial discussions is the fear of saying the wrong thing and sounding racist. The desire to be seen as a "good white person" (Sullivan, 2014) is quite understandable but it often gets in the way of honest declarations of how racism lies at the core of many whites' identities. To use myself as an example, I've been brought up to fear blackness, particularly when it's manifested in groups of young black men. When I'm walking along the sidewalk and a group of black men approaches I start to tense up and begin the internal debate of whether crossing over to the other side of the street is racist or justified. When I see black professionals in leadership roles I instinctively assume they're there because of affirmative action and that consequently I'll receive an inferior quality of professionalism from them. I tend to think that all blacks share the same views on politics, music, or culture. And as I mentioned in chapter 8, I'm much quicker to grant extensions to black students because I assume they're not as academically talented as whites; consequently, they automatically require special help.

I believe it's crucial for me to talk publicly and in a relaxed manner about these feelings, instincts, and perceptions. Whites need to understand that racism is an ideology that's widely disseminated and learned as part of growing up. To feel these things is empirically normal. Indeed, it would be surprising if a white person grew up in a racist world *without* learning many of these attitudes and beliefs. So part of encouraging critical reflection on race is to normalize its presence.

By normalizing racism I mean getting it out into the open and talking about how racist instincts, judgments, and perceptions are widespread. I want whites to know that sensing and feeling these is not an essentialist verdict on your basic immorality, not an indication that you've failed the test of humanity; rather, it's an empirical confirmation of how successfully the ideology of white supremacy has exerted its influence. Once you think of racism as an ideology—a set of beliefs, habits, and attitudes that you grow up around and that embed themselves in you—then it becomes easier to acknowledge them. A problem arises when you infer that having these thoughts somehow marks you out as a bad person who's beyond the pale. It doesn't; having racist thoughts in a racist world is completely normal.

So beginning a discussion, workshop, or training with a white facilitator talking about the ways he or she has learned racism and how it manifests itself in his or her behavior helps whites in the group move beyond the guilt they feel about admitting to any racism. Once its normality is understood then they can start focusing on the ways white supremacy shapes behavior and frames interactions across racial differences. Of course, this isn't to approve of racism, but neither is it to condemn someone who's felt it or unwittingly enacted it as inherently evil. Racism is a set of learned behaviors and attitudes picked up in daily interactions, not a sign that someone's been born with a fatal character flaw or an absence of morality or compassion. And, because racist perceptions and practices have been learned it's important to show that they can be challenged and that new behaviors and attitudes can also be learned.

Conclusion

Fostering a critically reflective examination of race is fraught with risks. Identity politics means that if you're a teacher of color you're likely to be accused of having an agenda and of playing the race card. Conversely, if you're a white teacher then sooner or later you'll probably be called a racist. When you bring racial issues into the classroom you always risk making things worse by increasing rather than decreasing the amount of racial misunderstanding in a group. You also risk endangering your professional future by asking people to examine issues they'd often much rather avoid, possibly leading to poor student evaluations. A meta-pedagogic risk is thinking that things are on the verge of getting out of control. Because of the raw emotions associated with any discussion of race, things can change in an instant and you're often faced with situations in which you feel clueless. You constantly feel like an impostor.

This perception of being an impostor who's faking it is a common experience among those who engage in critical reflection. In chapter 13 I examine this and other risks associated with the process, such as cultural suicide and lost innocence.

13

Negotiating the Risks of Critical Reflection

One of the risks in writing a book that attempts to demystify the critically reflective process is that of making it seem too straightforward. All I need to do, a reader might conclude, is review my autobiography, research my students, talk to my peers, and read some provocative theoretical literature, and then everything will fall into place. Hey presto! At a stroke I will become a living exemplar of critical reflection, able to detect abuses of power with my incisive analysis and ready to inspire colleagues to uncover hegemonic assumptions.

But becoming critically reflective is hard work, a long incremental haul. In the struggle to do this teachers run political and professional risks and exorcise personal demons. In this chapter I want to clarify these risks and suggest some ways teachers can keep them to a minimum. There's little point in taking the critically reflective journey if along the way you're battered and bruised beyond recognition.

Anyone who engages in critical reflection is going to run a variety of risks. First, there's the personal one of damage to your self-image as a competent professional. Realizing that your teaching actions might be grounded in uncritically assimilated and unchecked assumptions that turn out to be distorted or oppressive is sometimes humiliating. Finding out that you've been blind to important power dynamics is always humbling. Then there's professional risks. Going public with stories about critical moments in your practice—especially if these highlight poor judgments and missed opportunities on your part—can damage your reputation to the point where your continued employment is in jeopardy. After all, who wants to hire people known mostly for their mistakes?

There's also the epistemological risk of having your clarity of understanding muddied. Once you start seeing your classrooms and your teaching through multiple lenses you realize that things are actually far more complicated than you imagined. Critical reflection complicates your life by showing us what you're missing and what you've overlooked. As such it challenges the innocent belief that by following some neat methodological model you can ensure unequivocal success. You start to sense that complex problems are inherently unsolvable and that the best you can hope for is to make uneasy and constantly shifting partial responses to these.

Finally, a category of political risks is involved in the critically reflective project. Asking awkward questions about the nature of power and control sometimes means calling powerful people to account for their ideas and actions. This inevitably brings the questioner face-to-face with power structures whose representatives and beneficiaries are often eager to quell dissension and discourage divergent thinking.

In colleges and universities, becoming known as a raiser of awkward questions can gain you a reputation as a troublemaking subversive who refuses to play by the rules that everyone else accepts. Speaking truth to power and calling out institutional abuses makes people uncomfortable. The hegemonic notion of the team player is one way that groups and organizations nip critical reflection in the bud. After all, team players show loyalty and contribute toward furthering group goals; team players don't keep interjecting questions about power dynamics or the unethical exercise of authority.

To keep the risks of critical reflection manageable we need to know what we're going to experience as we engage in this process. Being aware of the risks we're taking helps us negotiate them. It also increases the chances that our actions have the effects we're intending while keeping the threat to us to a minimum. In this chapter I want to explore some common risks of engaging in critical reflection and consider how to negotiate these. My working assumptions informing this analysis are fourfold: (1) it's better to keep a job than to be fired, (2) many people want to effect change even if they have very little positional authority behind them, (3) if you don't have much institutional power then you need to be politically smarter than those who are in control, and (4) I may be *in* the organization but that doesn't mean I'm always *of* it.

Impostorship

The first risk is that of impostorship: the sense that you're faking it, trying to look as though you know what you're doing even though you know you're just muddling through the day trying not to fall flat on your face. Teachers often feel like impostors, certain that unless they're very careful they'll be found out to be teaching under false pretenses. There's the sense that just round the corner is an event that will demonstrate to everyone around you that you have no idea what you're doing.

Those who feel like impostors have a destructive tendency to accept all the blame for failure in a particular situation. If things go wrong there's the automatic presumption that it's because they're not good enough and lack the basic competence to be a teacher. If things go right it's assumed to be a matter of luck.

Every day teachers devote a lot of psychic energy to hiding their impostorship and looking confident and assured, wearing the mask of professionalism (Kasper, 2013; Bahn, 2014). But there's always the suspicion that it's only a matter of time before the mask slips and there's a humiliating public unveiling waiting for us. When this event happens we imagine that our colleagues' jaws will drop in synchronization. With their collective mouths agape they will wonder out loud, "how could we possibly have been so stupid as to hire this obvious incompetent in the first place?"

Viewing our practice through any of the four lenses of critical reflection heightens considerably the chances of our feeling like impostors. Asking our students what they think of us carries with it the risk that they'll tell us what we already know but have hidden—that we're incompetent. Anyone who reacts to students' evaluations of their teaching by ascribing great significance to negative comments and discounting positive ratings is displaying impostorship. For example, if ninety-eight out of one hundred students give me terrific evaluations I usually infer that the people who praised me are operating at a lower level of critical discrimination and insight than the two who said I stank. I decide that these two have caught my pedagogical soul. They've seen through my facade and realize I don't really know what I'm doing.

For anyone who's desperately trying to avoid being found out, the last thing they want to endure is a systematic scrutiny of their practice by colleagues. There is always the fear that once their impostorship has been discovered they'll be punished. One of the most important aids to critical reflection—having one's practice observed by peers—is therefore one of the most common triggers to impostorship.

When a colleague asks if he can sit in and watch how I teach a unit I smile and say—usually through gritted teeth—"Of course, that would be wonderful!" I know I'm supposed to welcome external observation and constructive criticism, even if inside I'm terrified at what my colleague will find out. Then when the visit happens I spend the whole session trying to prove to him that I know what I'm doing. Instead of thinking primarily about what will most help the students learn I direct the bulk of my comments and eye contact to my visitor. Really I'm performing for him.

Reading theoretical literature as part of a critically reflective effort can also end up convincing us that we're not very bright or sophisticated. If we don't get a theoretical analysis immediately, we conclude that it isn't for the likes of us journeyman practitioners. Because I've written a book on the dense and complex field of the Frankfurt School critical theory (Brookfield, 2004) my students and colleagues quite legitimately assume I've cracked the code of hegemony, reproduction, objectification, and alienation. But I can't tell you the number of times I've read a paragraph, or even a sentence, in a critical theory text and had absolutely no idea what it meant. During my doctoral work and at academic conferences my engagement with theory has left me constantly intimidated, and I know I'll never lose the sense of feeling like an unqualified outsider sullying the pure realm of theory.

Feelings of impostorship accompany most attempts at pedagogic experimentation that spring from our reflection. We're bound to be taken by surprise any time we depart from comfortable ways of acting or thinking to experiment with a new way of teaching. The further we travel from our habitual practices the more we run the risk of appearing incompetent. In the midst of experimentation it's not uncommon to resolve never again to put ourselves through the experience of looking foolish in front of students and trying desperately to conceal the fact that we don't really know what we're doing. The moments of failure that inevitably accompany change and experimentation increase the sense of impostorship by emphasizing how little we can predict and control the consequences of our actions.

Dealing with Impostorship

How can this feeling of impostorship be kept under control? The key, I think, is to make the phenomenon public. Once impostorship is named as an everyday experience it loses much of its power. It becomes commonplace and quotidian rather than a shameful, malevolent secret. To hear someone you admire talking graphically and convincingly about her own regular moments of impostorship is enormously reassuring. If she feels exactly the way you do, then perhaps you're not so bad after all. In public forums and private conversations teachers who are acclaimed as successful can do a great deal to defuse the worst effects of impostorship by admitting to its reality in their lives.

Being involved in team or peer teaching also makes you less prone to being smitten by impostorship. When you teach a class with one or two colleagues you have built in reflective mirrors available to you. As you walk across campus after what you think is a bad session and you start to engage in your usual enthusiastic bout of self-flagellation, your colleagues are likely to point out the things that went well. They'll tell you about the situations you handled confidently and how impressed they were with your abilities. They'll provide you with multiple perspectives on events that you've only seen one way and suggest readings of students' actions that would never have occurred to you.

Critical reflection and informal teacher conversation groups invariably surface the theme of impostorship. Once one person has revealed feeling like this, a ripple or domino effect occurs. One after the other, the members of the group offer their own illustrations of the phenomenon. The tricky part is to get someone to admit to it in the first place. This is when experienced teachers can be particularly helpful. By admitting to their own feelings of impostorship experienced teachers can ease the way for junior colleagues to speak. So joining or forming a reflection group will be an important strategy to keep impostorship in its proper place.

Impostorship can ruin a teacher's life. Taken to extreme levels it's crippling. The worst way to live as a teacher is to believe that you're the only one who's falling far short of the perfection that you suspect is exemplified in all your other colleagues' classrooms. Few of us are strong enough to continue working if we're burdened with the sense that all around us are paragons of pedagogic virtue while we're incompetent amateurs struggling to keep intact a false mask of command. The sense of aloneness this induces is almost impossible to bear.

However, a degree of impostorship is not totally negative. Indeed, properly controlled it can be productively troubling. It stops us becoming complacent and ensures that we see our practice as being in constant flux and evolution. Teachers who remain completely free of any feelings of impostorship may well be teachers who have an unrealistically developed sense of confidence in their own perfectability. Never to feel humbled in the presence of students or colleagues can betoken an unhealthy streak of arrogance or a well-developed capacity for denial. Additionally, any teacher who steps into a faculty or staff development role needs the humility borne of an awareness of his own impostorship. If teachers pick up a whiff of presumed superiority in a staff developer, that person may as well pack up and go home.

Teachers who've never had the feeling that things are slipping beyond their control are teachers who are probably staying safely within habitual, comfortable ways of thinking and acting. Teachers who see themselves as fully formed and capable of responding appropriately to any crisis that circumstance throws their way are in stasis. So we should never lose the sense that we're impostors struggling in the dark, trying to draw meaning from contradictory and often opaque experiences. To feel this is to open up permanent possibilities for change and development in our practice.

Cultural Suicide

A danger facing teachers who move into a critically reflective mode is the risk of marginalization. Marginalization has two dimensions. The first is committing cultural suicide, that is, of enthusiastically engaging colleagues in questioning basic assumptions and uncovering hegemony while simultaneously unknowingly alienating those peers. Cultural suicide happens when your practice of critical reflection threatens colleagues and, without your realizing it, you begin to be viewed as betraying them or regarding yourself as better than them.

Teachers involved in critical process are bound to have that fact noticed by their peers. For teachers who are keeping the essential unpredictability of teaching at bay by clinging to self-fulfilling interpretations of practice, seeing a colleague engaged in purposeful reflection and experimentation can be extremely threatening. A teacher who's challenging assumptions, experimenting with different approaches, and trying to realize democratic values is an affront to those who've settled for the illusion of control and predictability.

Teachers working critically remind those who are in stasis of their own slough. They do this not so much by accusatory statements and condemnations of those who are comfortable with their lot but just by the fact of their existence. Consequently, teachers who expect their efforts to ignite a fire of enthusiasm for critical reflection and democratic experimentation will be sorely disappointed.

Teachers who are seen to be reinventing themselves and their practice can commit cultural suicide without even being aware that this is happening. As they speak about how they're questioning and reevaluating their practice or how they're doing things differently, they run a real risk that colleagues will see them as engaged in an act of betrayal. They are whistle-blowers on the culture of stasis—the collective agreement not to rock the boat by asking awkward questions or doing things differently.

One common scenario for committing cultural suicide concerns teachers who reenter their institutions after a provocative period of reflection. This reflection might have been occasioned by a professional conference, a faculty development workshop, informal conversations with colleagues, or a private period of sustained reading and introspection as might happen on a sabbatical. One common result of reflection is a newly realized conviction of the importance of getting colleagues to ask more questions about why they work in the ways that they do. Surfing on a wave of unbridled enthusiasm for critical questioning (and unaware of the possibility that others might not share this zeal) teachers report how their wave collapses in on them as colleagues seem at best bemused, and at worst angry, at being confronted with new and challenging questions.

As newly reflective teachers begin talking enthusiastically about the need to challenge taken-for-granted assumptions, they can easily and unwittingly alienate their colleagues. The hostility they face is borne primarily of incomprehension. Instead of being seen as "one of us" they are now viewed as having taken on airs and pretensions, as growing too big for their boots.

Teachers who start to distribute articles and blog postings on how college curricula mask racism, sexism, and classism can force otherwise progressive teachers into a defensive, overly reactionary posture. When teachers return from graduate classes talking about new concepts, theoretical constructs, and fifty-seven brands of hermeneutic post-modernism, they can easily be perceived as having "gone native" and turned into fully fledged participants in the tribal culture of academe. This feeling may be completely unjustified, but the sense of betrayal remains.

Avoiding Cultural Suicide

How can we minimize the risk of committing cultural suicide? When I've asked teachers to participate in role-plays of how they reenter their institutions and talk about a new insight they've had or a new question they're asking, those observing the role-play point out several things. These newly reflective teachers often speak evangelically about their raised awareness, probably using language that's unfamiliar. They are so excited to share the good news of their enlightenment with peers that they end up almost haranguing them. Very soon after introducing an insight they start to sketch out how colleagues can act on it to change what they do. The combined effect is to make colleagues feel like the victims of a reflective onslaught. Not surprisingly, they beat a retreat.

Out of these role-plays and the debriefings that follow them have emerged some simple rules for avoiding cultural suicide:

1. If you've just come back from an event (for example, a conference) that triggered some important reflection but that your colleagues didn't attend, the first thing you should do is ask them what happened to them while you were away.

2. If your time away has involved colleagues covering for you, find some way of acknowledging that and returning the favor.

3. Before talking about the event, person, or book that triggered a reflective insight, affirm your colleagues' experience and abilities. Tell them that attending the conference made you realize how much expertise your colleagues have, because any one of them could have been presenting there. If you've been reading an edited collection let them know that you feel that they had just as much to say as did the contributors to the book. This sets an important tone by affirming the experience of the people to whom you're speaking.

4. Introduce information about your reflection by saying how it helped you deal with some feature of your teaching about which you feel embarrassed or worried. Grounding critical reflection in a description of the shortcomings of your own practice doesn't threaten fragile egos to the point that people feel they have no option but to turn away from you. It heartens rather than intimidates. It prompts colleagues to look critically at their own practice in a way that's invitational and affirming rather than confrontational. If the problem you've been helped with is graphically described in concrete terms, the chances are high that your colleagues will recognize their own dilemmas in the story. Consequently, they'll be likely to come to you asking for further details about what you've learned.

5. At all costs hold back from telling colleagues what they should do. Wait till they start knocking on your door asking for information and advice.

6. Try and find a small group of peers—just one person is better than nothing—who shares your convictions about the need to work differently. Meet with that group regularly to do some informal strategizing, to talk about the meaning of reflection for how you teach, and to give each other support as you run into problems with hostile colleagues.

Lost Innocence

Epistemological risks accompany the journey into critical reflection and can be just as threatening if not immediately as dramatic as cultural and political ones. One of these risks is that we come to recognize the essential ambiguity of teaching. "The best way I can help this student is to stop giving him help," a colleague once told me. This simple observation helped me understand that there are occasions when doing something that contradicts everything you've ever believed makes perfect sense. It was just one of many small realizations regarding the contextual ambiguity of teaching. In some situations reversing yourself is entirely appropriate. The more we examine our assumptions through the four lenses of critically reflective practice the more we abandon the reassuring prospect of ever finding final solutions or eternal verities.

Because of this, teachers' stories of critical reflection are often tinged with sadness caused by letting go of the belief that neat solutions are always waiting to be found for difficult problems. This thread of sadness can be described as lost innocence, which is the gradual realization that difficult pedagogic dilemmas have no ultimate solution. It dawns on us that becoming a critically reflective teacher will always be an unformed, unfinished project, a true example of lifelong learning. We become progressively attuned to teaching's complexity, its contradictions, and its chaos, particularly when we're trying to put some purposeful experimentation into our practice. These realizations often signify the beginning of wisdom. Teachers look back to their belief that unequivocal solutions could always be found to difficult problems as a golden era of innocence.

My own existence as a teacher is one of sustained epistemological demolition as my certitudes keep crashing to the ground. This process began early, in the first week of my career, in fact. Similar to the eponymous hero of Tom Sharpe's novel *Wilt* (1976) I was teaching compulsory liberal studies to adolescents in an English college of further education. (The irony of mandating a weekly fix of liberalization did not go unnoticed by me at the time.) My students were united mostly by their contempt for my efforts. The fact that I was only a couple of years older than they, wore clothes bought in thrift stores, and had long curly locks down to my shoulders may, in retrospect, have played their part in inspiring a resistance to my entreaties that was admirable for its doggedness. On the Friday morning of my first week at the college, during a discussion of some topic I now can't remember, a brief scuffle broke out between a young white man and a young black man.

So, after four days of teaching I had to deal with a racially motivated fistfight between two young men in the middle of a discussion period that I had thought would be characterized by civility and thoughtfulness—a kind of Algonquin round table without the sarcasm. The question that flashed through my head was, "what would John Dewey do in this situation?" The authors who were most influential in my life at that time—Erich Fromm, Alan Watts, and C. Wright Mills—didn't really offer much advice on how to deal with physical manifestations of racial tension in college classrooms.

In the range of early crises that are possible in a teacher's life I realize now that this was pretty mild. At the time, however, I was aghast at the astounding difference between what I was experiencing and what I'd imagined would be the gentle reflective life of a teacher. I don't remember how I reacted but, luckily, the class didn't descend into total chaos, the fight was stopped, and I ended my first year with an awestruck reverence for those who made a career out of what I'd just endured.

Knowing that lost innocence is a necessary and predictable moment in any critically reflective episode makes it much easier to accept. So some way has to be found to name and describe this experience publicly. Here senior teachers have a special role. As with their admissions of impostorship, respected teachers' descriptions of their own lost innocence serve to reassure those new to the experience. Hearing someone you regard as an exemplar put into words the same feelings of confusion you have about a problem is wonderfully heartening. Teachers who are lucky enough to have experienced colleagues as mentors quickly learn that moments of lost innocence are spread over a whole career.

The moments of bewilderment and confusion that accompany lost innocence are also a staple item of conversation in reflection groups. People bring to these groups examples of problems caused by their inability to make a standardized curriculum or teaching approach fit their students. They talk about how disappointing it is to feel that you've found the solution to a recurring classroom problem only for the problem to rear its head in another form. They identify a difficulty they have in common (such as dealing with resistance to learning), and each person gives an account of the different ways they respond to its manifestations. So joining or forming a reflection group helps us realize that regularly experiencing a feeling of lost innocence is normal. It's a sign that we're staying awake in our practice.

Marginalization

People practicing critically reflective teaching ask questions and play around with different possibilities. Because they make their practice the subject of constant inquiry they're drawn to activism, to changing their ways of working as they try to make their classrooms more varied, experimental, and inclusive. Any attempt to do this sooner or later brings you into conflict with institutional norms. Just doing something as simple as spending too long on a unit or activity in a core course causes problems for other faculty members who need students to have covered required content. If you make any effort to change administrative structures to match pedagogic dynamics you invariably suffer the consequences.

A couple of years ago I was team teaching a course with a colleague of mine, Tom Fish. Our students were given two end-of-semester teaching evaluation forms and told to evaluate each of us individually. Because our whole dynamic as a teaching team relied on the interplay between us, particularly the modeling of critical conversational interchanges, we told the students to fill out only one form and write both our names on that form. That way they were evaluating team, not solo, teaching. But the office documenting teaching evaluations declared students' ratings and comments void, meaning we weren't able to have our teaching count toward merit pay, promotion, or tenure.

Attending to power dynamics in your classrooms always spills out into an analysis of power dynamics in staff rooms and college politics. You start to notice whose voices are heard most in department meetings and whose proposals tend to be taken seriously. You realize how few faculty members of color get tenure yet how those same faculty members are prominently featured on literature advertising college programs. The fact that custodial and cafeteria staff are overwhelmingly black and Hispanic and faculty members are overwhelmingly white becomes too glaring to ignore. The commitment to diversity and inclusion trumpeted in the college's mission statement and public pronouncements rings hollow as you observe the attrition rate for students of color. And the fact that the most powerful decision makers in the institution—the trustees—are invisible and unaccountable makes a mockery of the administration's declared wish to be as transparent as possible.

The critically reflective impetus to make your classrooms more democratic, creative, and experimental inevitably transfers itself to the wider organization. If your assumptions that colleges operate by reason, value all members equally, and work democratically start to crumble, you're going to want to do something to rectify this reality. So you start to voice criticisms at departmental and faculty meetings and suggest proposals to change how decisions are made. When you see microaggressions you point them out. If someone is exercising her authority in an arbitrary or abusive way you bring that to the community's attention.

As your change agency develops there's always the danger of political marginalization. Your suggestions will be threatening to anyone who doesn't wish his institutional routine to be disturbed.

Critiquing how the powers that be operate and calling for more democracy and transparency will always make you enemies. If you do this as a relatively junior faculty member it's easier for those who've been around a while to marginalize you and sabotage your efforts. You might not be shut down in an overt way but your proposals will be sidelined or delayed as people tell you that your issue is valid and something to be looked at in the future. Or you'll find that an enemy will quote her knowledge of departmental history to disqualify your arguments for change.

Avoiding Political Marginalization

The first rule of change agency is to know what you're dealing with. In departmental meetings, whole community e-mail conversations and senate gatherings try and work out whose voice is taken seriously and where the power really resides. You need to know what's really rewarded, what organizational symbols are revered, and how far the mission statement is taken seriously. You also need to learn something of the cultural and political history of the institution. There's nothing worse than blundering in with a well-meant, supposedly new suggestion only to find out later that a couple of years before you arrived the faculty members spent six months considering, and then rejecting, something very similar.

In this regard knowing the mission statement is crucial. I've found that whenever I wish to propose something challenging, even threatening, the more I frame this using the language of the mission statement, the further I get. Most mission and vision statements are purposefully vague. They have to be this way in order to unite people working in disparate disciplines behind a common project.

For example, most mission statements support thinking critically or embracing diversity. Faculty members with very different conceptions of the purpose of a university or college can usually agree that these are something the institution should be doing. You can justify almost any classroom activity by citing these things. You can introduce explosive content arguing that it forces students to see things from diverse viewpoints, and you can question institutional norms and practices by saying you need to model critical thinking for students. It's surprising how much you can accomplish with no one objecting to, or even noticing, potentially threatening activities you introduce as long as you describe these in familiar and approved terms.

Building alliances is also crucial to survival. Taking on an institutional culture alone usually has very predictable outcomes. Either you become demoralized and throw in the towel, resolving to put in your hours and keep your head down, or the institution picks you off as someone to dispense with. The one time I was fired I had no ally in the institution. I had built no connections to other departments, and I had never involved them in my programming. Consequently, no one had any stake in supporting me.

When we fight organizational battles it's also easy to focus all our attention on internal foes and obstacles and forget the world outside. Yet one of the most important hedges against our efforts being squashed internally is having those same efforts be noticed approvingly by eyes outside the college. If people outside the institution are talking favorably about a program inside it, then it's much harder for the institution to shut that program down.

So one of the greatest assets teachers can call on in support of their activities is that of external recognition. Nothing disturbs an institution so much as knowing that if a program is cut or closed, or its staff members fired, there'll be an outcry from alumni, institutions, associations, and individual academics outside the organization. Colleges take alumni particularly seriously. If you teach in a way that's challenging or threatening to colleagues, you need to document any recognition of your teaching that comes from an alumnus. On those very rare occasions I've received a letter of thanks from an alumnus I always ask them to copy their comments to the president and provost.

Conclusion

This chapter has explored how to manage the disruptions critical reflection causes to oneself and others. I've mostly explored critical reflection initiated by those with little institutional authority who seek to make organizational change from a position on the periphery. In this scenario leadership usually tries to prevent any disruption to the status quo. In chapter 14, the final chapter, I switch focus and consider how leaders themselves might engage in critical reflection. In particular I examine how a public modeling of the behaviors associated with critical reflection can help set a tone that encourages others to engage in the process.

14

Practicing Critically Reflective
Leadership

When you ask students about the problems they experience with faculty members, some very predictable themes emerge. Students complain that their teachers are out of touch and unavailable, that they don't keep their office hours, and that it's hard to contact them. Digital natives (students) say that too many of their professors (who are digital immigrants) don't understand or use technology and that they can't be contacted via social media. Adult college students have to arrange childcare, find public transport to and from college, and work several jobs to get by, so if their teachers are unresponsive to these conditions life becomes very difficult. Students of all ages complain about grading criteria being unclear and professors who are inflexible and punitive in their grading. I often hear students say they've done everything their instructors ask of them only to receive an inferior grade and that this constitutes an act of betrayal.

There's a remarkable congruence between how students talk about their teachers and how teachers talk about their leaders. One of the most common complaints I hear from college teachers is that the administration in their institution is shortsighted and irresponsible. I'm told that deans, provosts, and presidents are out of touch, that they don't understand the problems that faculty members face, and that they exercise power in an arbitrary and unethical manner. In performance appraisals faculty members claim they've met their goals for the year yet feel their work is not sufficiently recognized.

Strategic plans are rolled out with pomp and circumstance to be greeted with cynicism from faculty members who say they've been conceived and developed by trustees and administrators without faculty interests in mind.

When I travel outside academe to work in various community and organizational contexts I hear exactly the same observations. Senior leadership is frequently parodied as locked away in some secret enclave spinning webs and planning reforms with no input from members. As budgets contract or state and federal funding dries up, fear and anxiety increase as organizations announce a "realignment" of priorities and structures. Leaders rarely come out of this well, being perceived by rank-and-file members as motivated by self-interest and driven relentlessly by strict adherence to a financial bottom line.

A perceived abuse of power seems to be at the heart of all these situations, and this perception is something I've adapted in my own teaching of leadership. One of the courses I teach fairly regularly is on critical theory and organizational development. Essentially I'm teaching a Marxist-inspired theoretical perspective to students who work in corporate America. This is most definitely not a course on techniques for organizational intervention, capacity building, or fostering alignment of employees and organizational goals. Instead, it's a course exploring how organizations and society at large reproduce a system that benefits a small minority. It looks at the ways ideological manipulation (corporate branding, slogans, corporate songs, metaphors such as "team player") secure consent to a corporate order that keeps people marginalized.

On the face of it, this course might seem to comprise content that students from corporate America will reject out of hand as communist-inspired unpatriotic subversion. But there's a simple way round this potential rejection of critical theory. All I have to do is start the course off by asking students to describe a time when they felt they were on the receiving end of an abusive exercise of power. In response to this request the stories of perceived wrongdoing, shortsightedness, manipulation, and self-interest immediately start flowing as people document what they believe is the injustice, incompetence, and mendacity of senior leadership. Power screams through these experiences as the daily reality of organizational life.

So although this book is primarily about critical reflection in classroom contexts, the process of examining assumptions, particularly as they relate to illuminating the exercise of power and uncovering of hegemony, is something that has enormously wide application (Bradbury, Frost, Kilminster, and Zukas, 2010; Fook and Gardner, 2007, 2013; White and Fook, 2006). I believe that leadership is just as much the practice of critical reflection as is pedagogy and to that end I've taught a course on "Leadership as Critical Reflection" for the past two decades. Constantly inquiring into the assumptions underlying the way leadership is exercised is also a major theme of the book I coauthored with Stephen Preskill, *Learning as a Way of Leading* (2008). In this final chapter, then, I want to broaden the analysis of critical reflection from its location specifically in teaching and consider how it applies to the exercise of leadership.

What Is Critically Reflective Leadership?

Ask most people to name influential leaders and they will typically choose prominent individuals whose energy, charisma, fortitude, and skill mobilized a movement or organization to achieve some major change. These will likely be figurehead leaders—Nelson Mandela, Aung San Suu Kyi, Dr. Martin Luther King, Cesar Chavez, Wangari Maathai, Mahatma Gandhi—who exemplified the spirit of a movement and crystallized the desire for change in their words and actions. I admire this kind of leadership but I also admire leadership from below, behind, and among.

When I think of critically reflective leadership I think of it as enacted by people who hold formal designations as leaders but also by those with little positional authority or public profile. This latter kind of leadership is exercised by those rank-and-file members who ask important questions on discussions, set up websites to bring people together, or design protocols for meetings that create maximum participation. Leadership is just as much about getting other people to speak as it is about speaking yourself.

Critically reflective leadership implements the same core project as critically reflective teaching. It seeks to uncover assumptions of power and hegemony that inform one's leadership practice by viewing that practice through the four complementary lenses that match those of critically reflective teaching.

Followers' Eyes

Although I use the term *followers* here, this will probably not be the one that is used institutionally. By followers I mean those who report to you, those whom you supervise or evaluate, or team members in a task force or other project grouping in which you're in the role of designated chair or leader. Sometimes these groupings will be very small, such as a department of five or six full-time and adjunct faculty members or a team composed of the same number of colleagues from across an organization. In these settings people will need to feel they can give their perspective honestly without fear of retribution so it may be necessary to incorporate anonymous channels of communication.

For example, in their guide to best practices in implementing 360-degree feedback the Center for Creative Leadership (2011) observes that "several research studies have shown that anonymous raters are more likely to provide candid, objective feedback than those who are not anonymous" (p. 3). This is particularly so when we consider hierarchical power dynamics. Just as students will think twice before publicly criticizing a teacher, so report-tos, team members, and junior faculty members will be wary of giving a supervisor critical feedback in full view of their peers.

Colleagues' Perceptions

One of the pitfalls of moving into leadership positions in higher education is that of seeing one's peer group become smaller and smaller. As you rise through the ranks the possibilities for peer support and critique dwindle. I have reported directly to several university provosts in the last three decades and all have cited this problem. As major public leaders in their institution they just don't have a peer to talk to unless they go outside of their organization. Apart from regional and national meetings for others working at your level you're limited to informal meetings, as was the case with the agenda-less breakfasts one of my provosts used to hold regularly with one or two peers in the Twin Cities. This small group had a standing early Monday morning routine of meeting at the same restaurant to help each other think through the various problems they were dealing with.

Theory

The leadership literature is full of ideas that connect in some way to the notion of critical reflection. Transformational leadership (Shields, 2013), for example, emphasizes the negotiation of change in a complex and uncertain world, a process that involves a continual investigation and reappraisal of assumptions. In a similar vein, situational leadership (Hersey, 1992) emphasizes contextual adaptability, the readiness and ability to reframe assumptions and perspectives in response to new situations. This is the same openness and flexibility called for when teachers change their approach based on data emerging from the four lenses on practice.

Servant leadership (Greenleaf, 2003) requires its practitioners to seek out information regarding the ways people experience their workplace and community and then decide how best to support their growth. This is an almost exact parallel to the process of consulting the lens of students' eyes to find out best how to foster their learning. Authentic leadership (Terry, 1993; Thacker; 2016) stresses leading from within so that external actions, decisions, and judgments somehow manifest an inner commitment to principles that spring from an authentic sense of self. And, finally, learning leadership (Preskill and Brookfield, 2008) explores, among other things, the ways that practicing critical reflection is central to leadership in social movements.

Personal Experience

The most fruitful lens for uncovering assumptions of power and hegemony is probably that of personal experience. In organizations, community groups, or social movements everyone has a rich experience of working with various kinds of leaders. In my own case some of the most important insights into effective leadership have come from awful experiences with those who exercise authority over me. I've got almost five decades of personal experience with leaders under my belt and can easily recall the highlights—or should I say lowlights—of ineffectual and dysfunctional leadership. These experiences are united by some very common themes—arbitrariness, secrecy, and betrayal, all the elements of a prime-time cable drama!

Arbitrariness is typically seen when decisions seem to come out of the blue and are handed down without explanation. Time and again I've witnessed deans, provosts, principals, and presidents announce initiatives that they declare will solve myriad institutional problems without ever consulting the staff or faculty members beforehand. Strategic plans or rebranding initiatives are declared, departments or schools are reorganized, and protocols for faculty member evaluation are changed, all because an individual leader or senior leadership team sees some kind of logic for these changes. The grievously misconceived assumption here seems to be that staff and faculty members will automatically see the same logic and thereby endorse the wisdom of leaders' institutional perspectives.

Secrecy is strongly connected to arbitrariness. I've lived through multiple strategic plans and realignments in my career and the most common response to them is the widespread perception that the defining elements of these are decided in meetings that staff and faculty members are not privy to. Most of these changes are rolled out with some opportunity for consultation that is viewed by community members as counterfeit. Counterfeit consultation happens when organizations create flawed channels for communication so it looks like democratic decision making is in play but those consulted feel they have no real input.

Examples I've experienced have been proposals for organizational realignments that are announced in the summer when faculty members are off contract. Although feedback is requested no one is around to give it! I was once part of a mission development exercise in which faculty members were put into small groups and given fifteen to twenty minutes to come up with suggestions for mission language that would be forwarded to the senior administration. The inadequate time allotted for this process killed any chance of us taking this seriously. How could we give serious thought to the question of the institution's future in what was in effect an extended classroom break?

Betrayal is evident when promises are made, then broken or forgotten. It also happens when leaders say they're going to do something and then offer something different in response. Nothing destroys a leader's credibility more quickly than having her words and actions be inconsistent. I've seen leaders say they welcome open dialogue and then close people down. I've seen people say that nothing is off the table and that all perspectives will be welcomed and then make it clear that some opinions are inappropriate. One scholarly leader whose work I deeply respected surprised me by declaring that he was creating an open process for decision making and then subsequently manipulated the conversation to lead to the outcome I knew he desired.

Personal experiences such as these have been incredibly influential in shaping my own leadership style. Essentially I try to behave in the opposite way to how these leaders did in the situations described. If institutionally imposed changes are in the offing I try to give the longest possible warning of these and to explain, to the best of my ability, the rationale behind them. If a problem arises in my own team or department that needs addressing, the first thing I do is let people know about it and then arrange for open meetings in which everyone can weigh in on how we should address this. I try to allow ample time for any brainstorming or problem-solving activities and to use decision-making protocols that ensure that everyone has an equal opportunity to have his or her voice heard. Finally, I try never to make promises unless I'm 100 percent certain I can keep them. Even then I probably still don't make them because even cast-iron 100 percent certainty can be wrecked by unforeseen contingencies.

Of course all these things seem so simple and commonsensical that it's staggering to me that they even need to be stated! And yet, time and again my personal experience of being on the receiving end of leadership practices has been that these most basic insights are ignored. Even more damningly, I know I've ignored them myself! I can think of several times when I was so convinced of the clear relevance and utility of a program reorganization I'd designed that I went ahead with the first implementation steps until my staff members protested. Not surprisingly this came back to bite me as festering resentments slowly sabotaged the program I'd put into effect.

Embedding Critical Reflection in Meetings

The life of institutional leadership is the life of endless, back-to-back meetings. I'll be honest here—I *hate* meetings. I've sat through so many unnecessary meetings, mostly called purely for the sake of calling a meeting. The most frustrating thing is to show up for a meeting in which you think consequential decisions will be made only to find out that 95 percent of the time is spent reporting the progress of various task forces. I often wonder why I'm spending time listening to people summarizing what's happening in their department when they could just have well e-mailed their comments to me.

Then there's the problem already alluded to of the practice of counterfeit democracy in meetings; these are meetings in which the chair plays at listening to the input of participants in what is in effect a hoax. Everyone participates in a sort of Kafkaesque charade by expressing their opinions but everyone knows that the decision either has already been made or will be made by people who aren't genuinely interested in any input that challenges their existing analysis. Finally, there's the tendency for the usual suspects to dominate in meetings. Either a vocally expressive minority takes up the great majority of airtime or those with the longest history and most seniority naturally assume they have the most to offer and proceed to take center stage.

But department, team, or project meetings don't have to be this way. By introducing a few simple meeting protocols it's possible for leaders to make their meetings more responsive, democratic, and consequential and thus to encourage critical reflection. In the rest of this chapter I outline briefly some different activities that I've used in different organizational and community settings to make people aware of the diversity of perspectives on an issue. By creating opportunities for everyone to be heard, and requiring careful listening, I've tried to turn meetings into an arena in which individual and group assumptions can be surfaced and examined. Most particularly I use the following techniques to foreground power and hegemony, the distinctive project of critical reflection.

The Circle of Voices

The Circle of Voices is a small-group exercise (four to six members) designed to secure the early participation of all participants in a class, meeting, staff development training, workshop, or any other group event. Its purposes are to (1) make sure the widest possible range of views are heard early on, (2) prevent a premature consensus or focus emerging, (3) socialize people into the habit of actively listening to others' contributions, and (4) stop the most extroverted or domineering from having undue influence.

The process begins with the chair introducing an agenda item by reframing it as a question, issue, or problem posed to the group. Everyone is then given one to two minutes to think quietly about his or her responses to the question. The chair stresses that this phase is silent and makes sure this silence is observed. When the two minutes are up people form into groups of five and each person in the group takes a turn to present his or her initial response to the question. They are asked to keep their response to a minute— which usually means each person takes more like two. If it's a team or small department meetings that has only six to eight attendees, you don't form into groups but instead conduct the process with all the members.

As each person gives a response to the question posed, the ground rule is that there are to be no interruptions, not even supportive statements such as, "yes, I've found that's true" or "you hit the nail on the head." These are in effect five or six brief monologues. Once the initial round of individual responses is over the circle moves into the second round of conversation, which is open and relatively unstructured. There is no order that needs to be followed. People contribute whenever they wish to.

In this second round, however, a ground rule comes into play about the kind of contributions people can make. They are only allowed to talk about what another person said in the first round. This can include asking questions about someone's initial contribution, commenting on something that resonated, disagreeing with a comment, or indicating how a first-round contribution opened up a new line of thinking.

The exercise ends with the meeting summarizing any new perspectives or resolutions heard, any new questions that were raised, and presenting the group's best thinking on how to move forward with the agenda item raised.

The Critical Incident Questionnaire (CIQ)

I've already described this instrument in chapter 6 so I won't repeat that information here. Although this instrument began as a classroom assessment technique I've found it adapts remarkably well to meetings. The only difference is that as leader or meeting chair you never see the responses yourself. Instead, a different member of the department or team collects the responses for the week and summarizes them. Then he or she begins the next meeting reporting out the results to the meeting.

When the results are shared participants can see that the same meeting, moment, or event was experienced in multiple ways and that the rationale for a particular decision was interpreted very differently. This stops people universalizing their own experience and assuming everyone thinks about an issue or action the same way they do. As the results are being reported the leader or chair can comment on how the results confirm or challenge the assumptions his or her decisions were based on or how he or she ran the meeting. Leaders and facilitators can also describe the new perspectives that the CIQ results suggest to them. The CIQ provides solid, reliable information that helps you make informed decisions based on assumptions that have been confirmed as accurate and valid. Instead of relying on instincts and observations about how the department or team is responding to your leadership, you now have direct evidence on your effectiveness that comes from the participants themselves.

Responding non-defensively to criticisms here is very important. If your staff members really trust their participation is anonymous they'll say things that will sometimes hurt. I've been told I don't listen to people, am arrogant, and push things through against the will of the group. I don't like hearing these things because in my own mind I'm fair-minded and give everyone an ear. But when these criticisms are voiced regarding my leadership I try to thank people for expressing them and then invite them to suggest how I might do things differently. It's particularly important that I don't dismiss people for whom I have no respect and whom I privately dismiss as lightweight or uninformed. I'll own up and say this is *very* hard for me to do and I'm sure I usually fall short.

Clearness Committee

This is a close listening and questioning exercise, drawing on the work of Parker Palmer (2007) and the traditions of Quaker practice. It focuses on people asking questions about a situation that are deliberately open-ended and to which they don't have the answer. At its root is the belief that we can uncover answers to difficult problems with appropriate support from peers, friends, and colleagues. It's most appropriately used when a team member brings a seemingly intractable problem to a group for consideration. This person is the "holder of the problem" and starts the process off by describing a troubling issue at work.

The exercise continues with group members querying the holder of the problem using honest, open, nonjudgmental, and nonleading questions. Every question should be one in which the questioner has no idea what the answer is. Questioners are told to avoid analyzing the problem or giving advice. The intent is to help the holder of the problem become aware of the assumptions informing his or her understanding of the situation and to come to some new insights about how to respond to it.

Questioners are told to take time to think, to become comfortable with silence, and to pose questions that seem to emerge organically from the situation. Occasionally, the chair may step in to disallow questions that are not sufficiently open or nonjudgmental. The holder can choose to ignore those questions that are uncomfortable or unanswerable and to make comments and offer reflections throughout.

The full Clearness Committee exercise can take several hours, but I've used it mostly in short bursts to vary the tempo of a meeting's interaction. To repeat, this is used only when people are at their wits' end of dealing with a difficult situation. It wouldn't be used to address an agenda item needing immediate, very specific recommendations. But when a colleague asks for a difficult problem to be included on the agenda I'll often go to this activity.

Appreciative Pause

One of the most neglected behaviors in institutional and community meetings is showing appreciation for contributions that have enhanced our understanding or led to new lines of questioning or thinking. One of my favorite meeting activities—Appreciative Pause—is intended to build cohesion in a group that is dealing with an issue in which different strong opinions are in evidence. In a group that's fracturing into sides because of differing strong opinions on an issue, it's important to try to keep lines of communication open, and this exercise attempts to do that.

As you move toward the conclusion of a meeting you call for a pause of a minute or so. During this time the only comments allowed from participants are those that acknowledge how something that someone else said in the meeting (*not* the chair) has contributed to his or her understanding of the agenda item. Appreciations are often given for questions asked that suggested a whole new line of thinking, comments that clarified something that up to then was confusing, new ideas that were intriguing and had not been considered before, observations that clarified the connection between two other suggestions or contributions, and examples that helped demonstrate how a new suggestion might be implemented.

Modeling Critically Reflective Leadership

These five meeting protocols are designed to integrate the habit of critical reflection into daily organizational life. Meetings are the most quotidian of events, and those of us in leadership roles can easily spend an 8:00 AM to 5:00 PM day solely in meetings with no time left to work on actually implementing the decisions arrived at in those same meetings! But they also provide opportunities to model critical reflection. Every time a chair, department head, dean, provost, or president talks out loud the reasoning for his or her decisions and quotes the evidence informing these, that person is providing a model of critical reflection in action.

One way that administrators can send a message concerning how seriously they take critical reflection is for them to show how they themselves engage in the process. In some institutions, including my own, administrators regularly invite faculty members to appraise their work. Asking faculty members how well the administrator exemplifies critical process ensures that there's no perception of a double standard operating where teaching and administrative effectiveness is concerned. Both groups are clearly held to the same criterion of good, critically reflective practice.

Modeling critical reflection seriously means that deans, department chairs, and even provosts and presidents and principals will be explicit regarding their own efforts to check their assumptions, particularly those informing their exercise of institutional power. In college newsletters, faculty meetings, and in speeches they should re-create in public the private reasoning behind their decisions. They should pay particular attention to talking about those times when events had caused them to rethink their basic assumptions or to see things from an entirely different viewpoint. They should invite critique of their actions and, when this critique isn't forthcoming (as it won't be at first given the level of mistrust in most educational institutions), they should play the role of devil's advocate in offering alternative perspectives on their actions.

Leaders also need to take pains to ensure that their words and actions are perceived as being as consistent as possible. They can do this by soliciting regular anonymous commentary on how they're doing (the anonymity being crucial to make faculty members feel safe in being honest) and then by making this commentary public. Administrators can also do their best to build a case for critical reflection by using their autobiographies to illustrate the benefits of the process in their own lives. They can start faculty development days by talking about the role that critical reflection plays in their own practice. They can also invite faculty members and administrators from other institutions where critical reflection is valued to come and talk about its importance.

A central tenet of my own modeling of critical reflection is my belief that I have to earn the right to ask colleagues to think critically about their practice. I can't assume that they share my enthusiasm for critical reflection or my convictions about its importance. Given the risks the process involves, it's important that I be seen to run such risks first and that I never ask colleagues to do anything that I've not already done. To skip an initial modeling of the process is a grave tactical error. This is the logic that informed chapter 12's emphasis on my needing to disclose my own racist inclinations, instincts, and microaggressions before asking any of my staff members to do so.

At the core of leadership is the exercise of power. Whether you lead from behind, below, among, or in front you're using power to help movements and organizations effect change and to help individuals grow. But a public honesty about power is rare. Most of us probably prefer to think that we lead by consensus and that an absence of public criticism means we've persuaded people by the clarity of our arguments. The practice of critically reflective leadership requires us not only to critique the misuse of power we see around us but also to own up to our own abuses.

Using the lenses of critical reflection to examine your own exercise of power is hard enough without thinking about the need to model this activity in public. A strong cultural inhibitor to critical reflection is the way in which self-disclosure that reveals the discloser as something less than perfect leads to her being chastised, even punished. For critical reflection to happen there has to be a trustful atmosphere in which people know that public disclosure of private errors will not lead to their suffering negative consequences.

Too often, however, the institutional rhetoric that emphasizes the importance of "learning from our mistakes" is contradicted by the penalties that accompany admissions of failure. If owning up to fallibility does nothing more than earn you a reputation for incompetence (with all the organizational injuries that implies) then you're going to present yourself as always being in total control. Only saints or fools draw attention to their errors in cultures in which maintaining the mask of command is prized above all else.

Crucial to creating a climate that encourages the public disclosure of private errors is the modeling of this behavior by those in positions of symbolic or actual power. Unless senior and respected figures in the organization (presidents, provosts, deans, department heads, program chairs) take the lead in this kind of self-disclosure—with all the risks to their professional standing this entails—there's little chance of this happening among rank-and-file teachers. So, even if you don't have a lot of room to maneuver around institutional barriers, and programmatic or cultural constraints mean you can't effect much substantive change, you can still model a public commitment to critical reflection. In publicly clarifying the assumptions you operate under, seeking feedback from colleagues and followers on the accuracy and validity of these, and inviting, as well as practicing, critique of your own exercise of power you'll provide an example of critical reflection that will influence those around you more than you realize.

Conclusion

At the end of my second edition of this book I'm struck by a few closing thoughts. The first is the enduring relevance of the basic idea of critical reflection. Uncovering and checking assumptions by viewing our actions and classrooms through the four lenses explored in this book is at the core of any kind of informed practice. The lexicon of critical reflection is now widely used and in some cases has been incorporated into various forms of professional evaluation. To me this is often self-defeating. Mandating the documentation of critical reflection as an annual element of one's performance appraisal too easily turns into a cynical effort to check the required boxes of "here's how I've demonstrated critical reflection this year." Ironically, instead of it being an inquiry into the workings of power, it becomes an exercise of power often with no more justification than that of reflection being a "good thing."

The second thought concerns the focus on power and hegemony. Over the decades since the first edition appeared I'm even more convinced that this is the central reality of teaching and of institutional life generally. Yet these are rarely talked about: the twin elephants in the room. The bulk of teachers' complaints have their origins in what they see as the unethical use of power exerted over them, and the most problematic classroom dilemmas can often be traced back to complex power dynamics that are hard to understand. I know I'll spend the rest of my career pondering what comprises the justifiable and ethical use of power.

That brings me to my last comment. This book was deliberately titled *Becoming a Critically Reflective Teacher* back in the early 1990s because, although I'd been teaching for a quarter of a century when it first appeared, I felt as if my understanding of my practice was in a state of constant becoming. Almost another quarter of a century later I feel exactly the same. Certainly the intervening years have solidified some understandings, and I'm probably better prepared to deal with many situations that typically arise. But I've learned never to trust my own reading of a class without some external corroboration. I've learned that racial dynamics are far more pervasive and complex than I'd previously imagined and that race and gender constantly frame how different teachers are perceived. I'm still struggling to work out how best to manage team teaching, incorporate social media, and avoid power abuses. In other words, I'm still in the process of becoming a critically reflective teacher.

Bibliography

Albert, M. *Parecon: Life after Capitalism*. London: Verso, 2004.

Albert, M. *Realizing Hope: Life beyond Capitalism*. New York: ZED, 2006.

Alexander, B. *The New Digital Storytelling: Creating Narratives with New Media*. New York: Praeger, 2011.

Arao, B., and Clemens, K. "From Safe Spaces to Brave Spaces." In *The Art of Effective Facilitation: Reflections from Social Justice Educators*, ed. L. Landreman. Sterling, VA: Stylus, 2013.

Baepler, P., Brooks, D. C., and Walker, J. D., eds. *Active Learning Spaces*. New Directions for Teaching and Learning, no. 137. San Francisco: Jossey-Bass, 2014.

Bahn, K. "Faking It: Women, Academia, and the Impostor Syndrome" Chronicle of Higher Education, March 27, 2014. Retrieved October 6, 2016, from https://chroniclevitae.com/news/412-faking-it-women-academia-and-impostor-syndrome

Ball, S. J. *Foucault, Power, and Education*. New York: Routledge, 2013.

Baptiste, I. "Beyond Reason and Personal Integrity: Toward a Pedagogy of Coercive Restraint." *Canadian Journal for the Study of Adult Education* 14, no. 1 (2000): 27–50.

Baptiste, I. "Exploring the Limits of Democratic Participation: Prudent and Decisive Use of Authority in Adult Education." In *Models for Adult and Lifelong*

Learning, Vol. 3: Politicization and Democratization of Adult Education, ed. D. Nitri, 1–34. Detroit: Office of Adult and Lifelong Learning Research, Wayne State University, 2001.

Baptiste, I. and Brookfield, S. D. "Your So-Called Democracy is Hypocritical Because You Can Always Fail Us: Learning and Living Democratic Contradictions in Graduate Adult Education." In, ed. P. Armstrong. *Crossing Borders, Breaking Boundaries: Research in the Education of Adults*. London: University of London, 1997.

Basseches, M. "The Development of Dialectical Thinking as an Approach to Integration." *Integral Review*, no. 1 (2005): 47–63.

Bell, L. A. *Storytelling for Social Justice: Connecting Narrative and the Arts in Antiracist Teaching*. New York: Routledge, 2010.

Bohm, D. *On Dialogue*. London: Routledge, 1996.

Bond, M. *The Power of Others: Peer Pressure, Groupthink and How the People Around Us Shape Everything We Do*. London, UK: One World Publications, 2014.

Bonila-Silva, E. *Racism without Racists: Color-Blind Racism and the Persistence of Racial Inequality in America*. 4th ed. Lanham, MD: Rowman and Littlefield, 2013.

Bonner, F. A., Marbley, A. F., and Howard-Hamilton, M. F. *Diverse Millennial Students in College*. Sterling, VA: Stylus, 2011.

Bradbury, H., Frost, N., Kilminster, S., and Zukas, M. *Beyond Reflective Practice: New Approaches to Professional Lifelong Learning*. London: Routledge Taylor and Francis, 2010.

Britzman, D. *Practice Makes Practice: A Critical Study of Learning to Teach*. Rev. ed. Albany: State University of New York Press, 2003.

Brookfield, S. D., ed. *Learning Democracy: Eduard Lindeman on Adult Education and Social Change*. Beckenham, UK: Croom Helm, 1988.

Brookfield, S. D. *The Power of Critical Theory: Liberating Adult Learning and Teaching*. San Francisco: Jossey-Bass, 2004.

Brookfield, S. D. *Teaching for Critical Thinking: Tools and Techniques to Help Students Challenge Assumptions*. San Francisco: Jossey-Bass, 2012.

Brookfield, S. D. "Teaching Our Own Racism." *Adult Learning* 25, no. 3 (2015A): 89–95.

Brookfield, S. D. *The Skillful Teacher: On Technique, Trust, and Responsiveness in the Classroom*. San Francisco: Jossey-Bass, 2015b.

Brookfield, S. D., and Preskill, S. *Discussion as a Way of Teaching: Tools and Techniques for Democratic Classrooms*. 2nd ed. San Francisco: Jossey-Bass, 2005.

Brookfield, S. D., and Preskill, S. *The Discussion Book: 50 Great Ways to Get People Talking*. San Francisco: Jossey-Bass, 2016.

Brown, S. *Play: How It Shapes the Brain, Opens the Imagination, and Invigorates the Soul*. New York: Penguin, 2010.

Bruff, D. *Teaching with Classroom Response Systems: Creating Active Learning Environments*. San Francisco: Jossey-Bass, 2009.

Buch, K., and Barron, K. E., eds. *Discipline-Centered Learning Communities: Creating Connections among Students, Faculty, and Curricula*. New Directions for Teaching and Learning, no. 123. San Francisco: Jossey-Bass, 2012.

Buskist, W., and Groccia, J. E., eds. *Evidence-Based Teaching*. New Directions for Teaching and Learning, no. 128. San Francisco: Jossey-Bass, 2011.

Butler, S. M., and McMunn, N. D. *A Teacher's Guide to Classroom Assessment: Understanding and Using Assessment to Improve Student Learning*. San Francisco: Jossey-Bass, 2006.

Cain, S. *Quiet: The Power of Introverts in a World That Can't Stop Talking*. New York: Broadway, 2013.

Cale, G. "When Resistance Becomes Reproduction: A Critical Action Research Study." *Proceedings of the 42nd Adult Education Research Conference*. East Lansing: Michigan State University, 2001.

Caufield, J. *How to Design and Teach a Hybrid Course: Achieving Student-Centered Learning through Blended Classroom, Online, and Experiential Activities.* Sterling, VA: Stylus, 2011.

Center for Creative Leadership. *360-Degree Feedback: Best Practices to Ensure Impact.* Greensboro, NC: Center for Creative Leadership, 2011. Retrieved July 12, 2016, from http://www.ccl.org/leadership/pdf/assessments/360bestpractices.pdf

Cox, M. D., and Richlin, L., eds. *Building Faculty Learning Communities.* New Directions for Teaching and Learning, no. 97. San Francisco: Jossey-Bass, 2004.

Csikszentmihalyi, M. (2008) Flow: The Secret to Happiness. TED talk available online at http://www.ted.com/talks/mihaly_csikszentmihalyi_on_flow.htm. Last accessed June 28, 2013.

Dana, N. F., and Yendol-Hoppey, D., eds. *The Reflective Educator's Guide to Classroom Research: Learning to Teach and Teaching to Learn through Practitioner Inquiry.* Thousand Oaks, CA: Corwin, 2009.

Darder, A., Mayo, P., and Paraskeva, J., eds. *International Critical Pedagogy Reader.* New York: Routledge, 2015.

Delgado, R., and Stefancic, J. *Critical Race Theory: An Introduction.* New York: New York University Press, 2012.

Earl, L. *Assessment as Learning: Using Classroom Assessment to Maximize Student Learning.* 2nd ed. Thousand Oaks, CA: Corwin, 2012.

Eisen, M., and Tisdell, E. J., eds. *Team Teaching and Learning in Adult Education.* New Directions for Adult and Continuing Education, no. 87. San Francisco: Jossey-Bass, 2000.

Evans, N. J., Forney, D. S., Guido, F. M., Patton, L. D., and Renn, K. A. *Student Development in College: Theory, Research, and Practice.* San Francisco: Jossey-Bass, 2010.

European American Collaborative Challenging Whiteness (ECCW). "White on White: Developing Capacity to Communicate about Race with Critical Humility." In *The Handbook of Race and Adult Education: A Resource for Dialogue on*

Racism, eds. V. Sheared, J. Johnson-Bailey, S. A. J. Colin III, E. Peterson, and S. Brookfield. San Francisco: Jossey-Bass, 2010.

Felton, P., Bauman, H. L., Kheriaty, A., and Taylor, E. *Transformative Conversations: A Guide to Mentoring Communities among Colleagues in Higher Education*. San Francisco: Jossey-Bass, 2013.

Fejas, A. "The Confessing Academic and Living the Present Otherwise: Appraisal Interviews and Logbooks in Academia." *European Educational Research Journal* 15, no. 2 (2016): 1–15.

Fook, J., and Gardner, F. *Practising Critical Reflection: A Resource Handbook*. Maidenhead, UK: Open University Press, 2007.

Fook, J., and Gardner, F., eds. *Critical Reflection in Context: Applications in Health and Social Care*. London: Routledge, 2013.

Foucault, M. *Discipline and Punish: The Birth of the Prison*. New York: Vintage Books, 1975.

Foucault, M. *Power/Knowledge: Selected Interviews and Other Writings, 1972–1977*. New York: Pantheon Books, 1980.

Foucault, M. *The Politics of Truth*. Los Angeles: Semiotext(e), 1997.

Freire, P., and Bergman, R. M. *Pedagogy of the Oppressed: 30th Anniversary Edition*. New York: Bloomsbury Academic Press, 2000.

Glazer, F. S., ed. *Blended Learning: Across the Disciplines, across the Academy*. Sterling, VA: Stylus, 2012.

Gore, J. M. *The Struggle for Pedagogies: Critical and Feminist Discourses as Regimes of Truth*. New York: Routledge, 1992.

Gramsci, A. *Selections from the Prison Notebooks* (ed. Q. Hoare & G. N. Smith). London: Lawrence and Wishart, 1971.

Greenleaf, R. K. *The Servant-Leader Within: A Transformative Path*. Mahwah, NJ: Paulist Press, 2003.

Habermas, J. *Communication and the Evolution of Society*. Boston: Beacon Press, 1979.

Hersey, P. *The Situational Leader*. Escondido, CA: Center for Leadership Studies, 1992.

Higgs, J., Jones, M., Loftus, S., and Christensen, N., eds. *Clinical Reasoning in the Health Professions*. New York: Elsevier, 2008.

Honneth, A. *Freedom's Right: The Social Foundations of Democratic Life*. New York: Columbia University Press, 2015.

Hooks, B. *Teaching to Transgress: Education as the Practice of Freedom*. New York: Routledge, 1994.

Horton, M. *The Long Haul: An Autobiography*. New York: Teachers College Press, 1997.

Horton, M. *The Myles Horton Reader: Education for Social Change*, ed. D. Jacobs. Knoxville: University of Tennessee Press, 2003.

Horton, M., and Freire, P. *We Make the Road by Walking: Conversations on Education and Social Change*. Philadelphia: Temple University Press, 1990.

Illich, I. *Deschooling Society*. New York: Harper and Row, 1970.

James, A., and Brookfield, S. D. *Engaging Imagination: Helping Students Become Creative and Reflective Thinkers*. San Francisco: Jossey-Bass, 2014.

Janis, I. J. *Groupthink: Psychological Studies of Policy Decisions and Fiascoes*. Boston: Wadsworth Publishing, 1982.

Johns, C. *Becoming a Reflective Practitioner*. 2nd ed. Oxford, UK: Blackwell Publishing, 2004.

Johnson, S., and Taylor, K., eds. *The Neuroscience of Adult Learning*. New Directions for Adult and Continuing Education, no. 110. San Francisco: Jossey-Bass, 2006.

Jones, S. R., and Abes, E. S. *Identity Development of College Students: Advancing Frameworks for Multiple Dimensions of Identity*. San Francisco: Jossey-Bass, 2013.

Joosten, T. *Social Media for Educators: Strategies and Best Practices*. San Francisco: Jossey-Bass, 2012.

Kane, P. *The Play Ethic: A Manifesto for a Different Way of Living*. New York: Macmillan, 2004.

Kasper, J. "An Academic with Impostor Syndrome" Chronicle of Higher Education, April 02, 2013. Retrieved October 6, 2016, from http://www.chronicle.com/article/An-Academic-With-Impostor/138231/

Keengwe, J., ed. *Promoting Active Learning through the Flipped Classroom*. Hershey, PA: IGI Global Publishing, 2014.

Kirylo, J. D. *A Critical Pedagogy of Resistance: 34 Pedagogues We Need to Know*. Netherlands: Sense Publishers, 2013.

Knowlton, D. S., and Hagopian, K. J., eds. *From Entitlement to Engagement: Affirming Millennial Students' Egos in the Higher Education Classroom*. New Directions for Teaching and Learning, no. 135. San Francisco: Jossey-Bass, 2013.

Lang, J. M. *Small Teaching: Everyday Lessons from the Science of Learning*. San Francisco: Jossey-Bass, 2016.

Lehman, R. M., and Conceicao, S. C. O. *Creating a Sense of Presence in Online Teaching: How to Be "There" for Distance Learners*. San Francisco: Jossey-Bass, 2010.

Lehman, R. M., and Conceicao, S. C. O. *Motivating and Retaining Online Students: Research-Based Strategies That Work*. San Francisco: Jossey-Bass, 2014.

Lenning, O. T., Hill, D. M., Saunders, K. P., Solan, A., and Stokes, A. *Powerful Learning Communities: A Guide to Developing Student, Faculty, and Professional Learning Communities to Improve Student Success and Organizational Effectiveness*. Sterling, VA: Stylus, 2013.

Marcuse, H. "Repressive Tolerance." In *A Critique of Pure Tolerance*, eds. R. P. Wolff, B. Moore, and H. Marcuse. Boston: Beacon Press, 1965.

McNicol Jardine, G. *Foucault and Education Primer*. New York: Peter Lang, 2005.

Mezirow, J. *Transformative Dimensions of Adult Learning*. San Francisco: Jossey-Bass, 1991.

Morrone, A. S., Ouimet, J. A., Siering, G., and Arthur, I. T. "Coffeehouse as Classroom: Examination of a New Style of Active Learning Environment." In *Active Learning Spaces*, eds. P. Baepler, D. C. Brooks, and J. D. Walker. New Directions for Teaching and Learning, no. 137. San Francisco: Jossey-Bass, 2014.

Nash, R. J. *Liberating Scholarly Writing: The Power of Personal Narrative*. New York: Teachers College Press, 2004.

Nash, R. J., and Bradley, D. L. *Me-Search and Re-Search: A Guide for Writing Scholarly Personal Narrative Manuscripts*. Charlotte, NC: Information Age Publishing, 2011.

Nash, R., LaSha Bradley, D., and Chickering, A. *How to Talk about Hot Topics on Campus: From Polarization to Moral Conversation*. San Francisco: Jossey-Bass, 2008.

Nash, R. T., and Viray, S. *Our Stories Matter: Liberating the Voices of Marginalized Students through Scholarly Personal Writing*. New York: Peter Lang, 2013.

Nash, R. T., and Viray, S. *How Stories Heal: Writing Our Way to Meaning & Wholeness in the Academy*. New York: Peter Lang, 2014.

Novak, G, M. "Just In Time Teaching." In, W. Buskist, and J. E. Groccia (Eds.). *Evidence-Based Teaching. New Directions for Teaching and Learning, No. 128*. San Francisco: Jossey-Bass, 2011.

Ouellett, M. L., and Fraser, E. "Interracial Team Teaching in Social Work." In, K. M. Plank (Ed.). *Team Teaching: Across the Disciplines, Across the Academy*. Sterling, VA: Stylus Publishing, 2011, pp. 73–90.

Outlaw, L. T., Jr. *Critical Theory in the Interests of Black Folks*. Lanham, MD: Rowman and Littlefield, 2005.

Palloff, R. M., and Pratt, K. *The Excellent Online Instructor: Strategies for Professional Development*. San Francisco: Jossey-Bass, 2011.

Palloff, R. M., and Pratt, K. *Lessons from the Virtual Classroom: The Realities of Online Teaching*. 2nd ed. San Francisco: Jossey-Bass, 2013.

Palmer, P. J. *The Courage to Teach: Transforming the Inner Landscape of a Teacher's Life*. 10th anniv. ed. San Francisco: Jossey-Bass, 2007.

Palmer, P. J., and Zajonc, A. *The Heart of Higher Education: A Call to Renewal: Transforming the Academy through Collegial Conversations*. San Francisco: Jossey-Bass, 2010.

Pawlowski, L. Syllabus for *Race, Gender and Sexuality in Language*. St. Paul, MN: University of St. Thomas, 2016.

Pearson, A. R., Dovidio, J. F., and Gaertner, S. L. "The Nature of Contemporary Prejudice: Insights from Aversive Racism." *Social and Personality Compass* 10, no. 11 (2009): 1–25.

Peterson, E. J., ed. *Freedom Road: Adult Education of African Americans*. Melbourne, FL: Krieger, 1996.

Peterson, E. J., and Brookfield, S. D. "Race and Racism: A Critical Dialogue." *Proceedings of the 45th Adult Education Research Conference*. Halifax, Nova Scotia: Mount St. Vincent University, 2007.

Pharo, E. J., Davison, A., Warr, K., Nursey-Bray, M., Beswick, K., Wapstra, E., and Jones, C. "Can Teacher Collaboration Overcome Barriers to Interdisciplinary Learning in a Disciplinary University? A Case Study Using Climate Change." *Teaching in Higher Education* 17, no. 5 (2012): 497–507.

Plank, K. M., ed. *Team Teaching: Across the Disciplines, across the Academy*. Sterling, VA: Stylus, 2011.

Preskill, S. L. and Brookfield, S. D. *Learning as a Way of Leading: Lessons from the Struggle for Social Justice*. San Francisco: Jossey-Bass, 2008.

Preskill, S. L. and Jacobvitz, R. S. *Stories of Teaching: A Foundation for Educational Renewal*. New York: Prentice-Hall, 2000.

Quinn, C. N. *The Mobile Academy: mLearning for Higher Education*. San Francisco: Jossey-Bass, 2012.

Ramsey, J. "But Can We Trust the Lord? Using Team-Teaching to Model Trust Within and Beyond the Classroom." In *Teaching Reflectively in Theological Contexts: Promises and Contradictions*, eds. M. J. Hess and S. D. Brookfield. Malabar, FL: Krieger, 2008.

Rogers, C. R. *On Becoming a Person: A Therapist's View of Therapy*. New York: Houghton-Mifflin, 1961.

Shadlow, L. K. *What Our Stories Teach Us: A Guide to Critical Reflection for College Faculty*. San Francisco: Jossey-Bass, 2013.

Sharpe, T. *Wilt*. London: Secker and Warburg, 1976.

Shields, C. M. *Transformative Leadership in Education: Equitable Change in an Uncertain and Complex World*. New York: Routledge, 2013.

Shor, I., and Freire, P. *A Pedagogy for Liberation: Dialogues on Transforming Education*. Westport, CT: Bergin and Garvey, 1987.

Simkins, S., and Maier, M. H. (Eds.). *Just-In-Time Teaching: Across the Disciplines, Across the Academy*. Sterling, VA: Stylus Publishing, 2010.

Sipple, S., and Lightner, R., eds. *Developing Faculty Learning Communities at Two-Year Colleges: Collaborative Models to Improve Teaching and Learning*. Sterling, VA: Stylus, 2013.

Smith, H. "The Foxfire Approach to Student and Community Interaction." In *Promising Practices for Family and Community Involvement during High School*, ed. L. Shumow. Charlotte, NC: Information Age Publishing, 2009.

Stark, P. B., and Freishtat, R. "An Evaluation of Course Evaluations." *ScienceOpen*, September 26, 2014. Retrieved March 24, 2016, from https://www.stat.berkeley.edu/~stark/Preprints/evaluations14.pdf

Stavredes, T. *Effective Online Teaching: Foundations and Strategies for Student Success*. San Francisco: Jossey-Bass, 2011.

Stefancic, J., and Delgado, R., eds. *Critical Race Theory: The Cutting Edge*. 3rd ed. Philadelphia: Temple University Press, 2013.

Sue, D. R. *Microaggressions in Everyday Life: Race, Gender, and Sexual Orientation*. San Francisco: Jossey-Bass, 2010.

Sue, D. R. *Race Talk and the Conspiracy of Silence: Understanding and Facilitating Difficult Dialogues on Race*. San Francisco: Jossey-Bass, 2016.

Sullivan, S. *Good White People: The Problem with Middle-Class White Anti-Racism*. Albany: State University of New York Press, 2014.

Tatum, B. D. *Why Are All the Black Kids Sitting Together in the Cafeteria: And Other Conversations about Race*. New York: Basic Books, 2003.

Taylor, E. W., and Cranton, P., eds. *The Handbook on Transformative Learning: Theory, Research, and Practice*. San Francisco: Jossey-Bass, 2012.

Taylor, E., Gilborn, D., and Ladson-Billings, G., eds. *Foundations of Critical Race Theory in Education*. 2nd ed. New York: Routledge, 2015.

Taylor, K., and Marineau, C. *Facilitating Learning with the Adult Brain in Mind: A Conceptual and Practical Guide*. San Francisco: Jossey-Bass, 2016.

Terry, R. W. *Authentic Leadership: Courage in Action*. San Francisco: Jossey-Bass, 1993.

Thacker, K. *The Art of Authenticity: Tools to Become an Authentic Leader and Your Best Self*. Hoboken, NJ: Wiley, 2016.

Tuitt, F., Hanna, M., Martinez, L. M., Salazar, M. D. C., and Griffin, R. "Teaching in the Line of Fire: Faculty of Color in the Academy." *Thought and Action* (Fall 2009): 65–74.

Unger, S. M. *We Shouldn't Even Know Each Other: A Scholarly Personal Narrative of the Development of Deeply Reciprocal Relationships Across Differences of Race and*

Class. St. Paul, MN: Unpublished doctoral dissertation, Department of Educational Leadership, University of St. Thomas, 2014.

Watts, M. M., ed. *Finding the Why: Personalizing Learning in Higher Education*. New Directions for Teaching and Learning, no. 145. San Francisco: Jossey-Bass, 2016.

Weimer, M. E. *Learner-Centered Teaching: Five Key Changes to Practice*. San Francisco: Jossey-Bass, 2013.

White, S., Fook, J., and Gardner, F. *Critical Reflection in Health and Social Care*. Maidenhead, UK: Open University Press, 2006.

Yancy, G. *What White Looks Like: African American Philosophers on the White Question*. New York: Routledge, 2004.

Yancy, G. *Black Bodies, White Gazes: The Continuing Significance of Race*. Lanham, MD: Rowman and Littlefield, 2008.

Yancy, G. *Look, A White! Philosophical Essays on Whiteness*. Philadelphia: Temple University Press, 2012.

Yancy, G., and Guadalupe Davidson, M. *Exploring Race in Predominantly White Classrooms: Scholars of Color Reflect*. New York: Routledge, 2014.

Index